ALASKA

NOT FOR A WOMAN

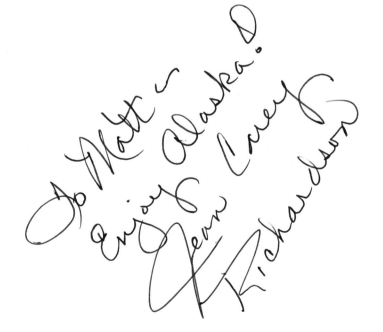

To Matt ~
Enjoy Alaska!
Jean Carey
Richardson

ALASKA
NOT FOR A WOMAN

By
MARY CAREY

Order From:

Mary's McKinley View Lodge
P.O. Box 13314
Trapper Creek, Alaska 99683
907-733-1555

or

Jean Carey Richardson
Mile 134.5 Parks Highway
Denali State Park, Alaska 99683
907-733-1555
281-217-9594

16th printing, 2013

©Copyright, 1975, by Branden Press, Inc.
Copyright assigned to Mary Carey, 1978
Library of Congress Catalog Card Number 75-16925

Printed by Everbest Printing Co., Ltd., in Guangzhou, China,
through Alaska Print Brokers, Anchorage, Alaska.

Distributed by:

Todd Communications
611 E. 12th Ave.
Anchorage, Alaska 99501-4603
(907) 274-TODD (8633) • Fax: (907) 929-5550
with other offices in Ketchikan, Juneau and Fairbanks, Alaska
sales@toddcom.com • WWW.ALASKABOOKSANDCALENDARS.COM

DEDICATION

No wayward mother could be blessed with a more wonderful or more dignified daughter than my only child, Mrs. Jean Richardson of Houston, Texas. To her I am indebted for a fine and successful son-in-law, Frank, and three brilliant and inspiring grandchildren, Linda Jane, Carol Ann, and Joe Frank Richardson.

Since "making a lady of Grandma" has been a somewhat traumatic experience for all of them, I hope this book compensates by explaining my inherent love of adventure, and my revolt against some forms of conventionality.

MARY CAREY

WHY NO FOREWORD

From the time I started writing this book, Alaska's internationally renowned bush pilot, Don Sheldon, said he wanted to give it the "big blast-off!" The reason he did not do so becomes evident in the last chapter. Therefore, the foreword remains forever—unwritten.

Although it is too late for Don Sheldon to know, he did give this book its title. Throughout my twelve years of flying Mt. McKinley with him, Don repeatedly reminded me that the things that I wanted to do in Alaska were *Not for a Woman!*

MARY CAREY

CONTENTS

ALASKA, NOT FOR A WOMAN

EXPLANATION:

Many of the stories circulating concerning my Alaskan escapades are not true. I would like to believe them myself; but find it a little difficult.

It is NOT TRUE: Absolutely not! I have never climbed Mt. McKinley, never even attempted it; but I have roared around above the summit with world renowned glacier pilot Donald E. Sheldon in search of lost mountain climbers.

It is NOT TRUE: I am not the only woman who has been on Mt. McKinley, not by any means. Others have had the guts and stamina to climb the nation's tallest peak.

It is TRUE: I am the only female who has been idiot enough to trespass on Mighty Mac's fortress in winter, where the chill factor has been known to reach 148 degrees below zero. I'll never make this mistake again.

It is NOT TRUE: I did not break my back in a fall on Mt. McKinley. I did fly there with Don Sheldon for a story while my back was still in a cast from an auto accident.

It is NOT TRUE: Although I owned my own plane, I never even received a pilot's license, much less attempted a glacier landing.

It is TRUE: In the twelve years I have flown McKinley with Sheldon we have landed on most of the glaciers for photos and stories.

It is TRUE: I did declare war on the Governor of Alaska, through the news media, to get the Anchorage-Fairbanks highway finished — AND WON!

It is NOT TRUE: I am not the only woman to homestead alone in Alaska; but in so far as I know, I am the only female to homestead alone in such an inaccessible area — between two unbridged rivers on the southern flank of Mt. McKinley.

It is TRUE: I am in love with a mountain and my greatest desire in life is to share McKinley's majesty with the world.

CHAPTER I

I WANT TO FLY MT. McKINLEY

"I want to fly Mt. McKinley with you," I said, managing to sneak within speaking distance of Alaska's notoriously shy bush pilot, Donald E. Sheldon of Talkeetna.

"Yo-u? What?" stammered the startled pilot as he jabbed more survival gear into his light plane.

"I want to fly Mt. McKinley with you, this spring, when the mountain climbers are in. I want you to land me on the glaciers with them. For stories . . ." I blurted out before losing my own courage.

"NOT FOR A WOMAN," retorted the besieged bachelor as he put distance between us by grabbing a pair of snow shoes and ducking beneath the wing of his plane where he proceeded to tie them securely to the strut. "I took a woman up there once. Took me two weeks to get my plane clean."

"But I'm not afraid. And I don't think I'd get sick. I only want an opportunity to do stories for newspapers and . . ."

"What's this newspaper bit?" he asked as he emerged from beneath the wing to do battle. "You don't mean you're a . . .?"

"I only mean someone should write your experiences. I'm here. I could try, couldn't I?"

"And what makes you think, Mary Carey, that you could write?" asked the internationally-renowned glacier pilot who was reportedly afraid of nothing, except a woman.

"I . . . I . . ."

"I know. You're a teacher. As such it is assumed that you can probably write a sentence, perhaps correctly, but this doesn't make you a writer. Besides, flying and mountain climbing, especially in the Arctic, puts one in a different world. Reporters make fools of us. Unintentionally, of course, but mistakes just the same. You have to know what you're talking about."

"That's just what I mean! If I could only fly to the nation's tallest peak and land on a glacier, then I could get photos of mountain climbers in action and . . ."

"Slow down! So you're a photographer, too. Forget it! Reporters and photographers are thicker than moose around

11

here. It's always open season on bush pilots. They don't care how they shoot you down, so long as they get a crack at you."

Evidently I looked shot down.

"Stick with your teaching," he admonished as real concern melted a bit of the glacier green from his surprisingly blue eyes. "We need teachers and I hear you're doing a mighty fine job of it. It's time for books."

It was five minutes until one, March 5, 1963. My high school students, all eight of them, had already congregated at the schoolhouse door. Clutching my mail, which I had just procured from the B & K Trading Post across the road, I evidently squeezed the packet too tightly. The feathery snow, which had been my ally in sneaking up on Don, now muted the fall of an envelope as I whirled in frustration for the thirty-yard dash to the schoolhouse door.

"Wait! I believe you'll want this," Don called. "It looks like a letter from your home town in Texas," he added in that scrutinizing manner of his which made me halfway resent his noticing everything. As I thanked him and turned to go he added:

"And come to think of it, if you were a real wide-awake writer and looking for material you would have known that Harold Paddock and his wife are here from Anchorage. They're real polar bear hunters. Their walls are loaded with trophies, even the walls in their furniture store. They've made Boone & Crockett and clobbered a world record. Now there's a story! You should have been on the ball, Kid."

"Kid" is the name Don freely applies to anyone from nine to ninety.

"Kind of you to tell me," I tried to say without sarcasm.

"There they come now. I'm flying them to the Chuckchi Sea, out over the Arctic ice. Polar bear hunting is real hairy and they might have told you about some of their hunts, but it's too late now. Time for books."

Resentment welled in my heart. I wheeled and ran to hide tears of frustration. I didn't want the Paddocks to see me. 'If I could only write, and if I were on the ball . . .'

How could I tell Don Sheldon that I was a writer, in my own estimation to say the least. I had sold quite a few magazine articles and won the national five-thousand dollar True Story

Award. And what made me think I was a photographer? I didn't dare tell him I was teaching photojournalism at Indiana University the summer my husband died. Don hated writers and photographers — and he was my target.

I knew about the Paddocks, enough to set me on fire. I had interviewed them where they were staying, at the Rainbow Lodge, the night before. I wanted to do a story on them, *but!* Seven months I had been in this isolated Alaskan village, population seventy-six, and I seemed no closer to doing stories on Sheldon than when I arrived.

Inside the classroom I was incapable of thinking of anything except — I had confided this to the Paddocks, over a few drinks — that I had chosen Talkeetna rather than another Alaskan village for teaching because I wanted to write about Don. One never worries about Sheldon entering a bar. He doesn't drink.

The Paddocks invited me along. I could have been crawling into that plane with them, but I was a teacher. Besides, if Don knew he would probably never have taken me — an unattached female — along, despite the fact that I would have been the guest of the Paddocks. I couldn't win. What if they told Don? All this time in the home town of Alaska's most renowned rescue pilot, and not so much as one photo or story.

Fortunately, book reports were scheduled right after lunch. Dorothy Marie Jones volunteered. She was my best, a constant inspiration, but I didn't hear her report.

My students, long accustomed to interruptions as pilots gradually warmed up the motors to their planes, then brought them to a high crescendo for take-off, paid little heed. Unable to be heard, Dorothy hesitated and smiled, first at me and then at the boys. All was well, at least with the boys.

I can't speak for my students, but their teacher's eyes were on the plane as Don shook its skis from the snow and gave her full throttle. Far down the runway, toward the Susitna River, the plane finally lifted from the wet, clinging snow. As the Cessna banked northward, Dorothy smiled and resumed her report. I made an honest effort to rejoin the class.

Even though the sun shone brightly, it was still cold and we had about two feet of snow on the ground. Our days were getting longer. We were having equi-daylight and dark, like

13

"outside" as we called the lower forty-nine. But unlike in the states, our days would get longer and longer until June 21, when, I was told, we would have no darkness.

This would be something to look forward to. This and the fact that there would be a total eclipse on July 20, when Talkeetna would be directly in the moon's shadow and total darkness. Our village would be visited by many scientists. Don would be flying some of them to the mountain for a better view. This I knew, but of course I wouldn't mention it to him, despite story possibilities.

In Talkeetna there were two great bi-weekly events, mail call on Tuesday and Saturday when the train made its pilgrimage along the Alaska Railroad from Anchorage to Fairbanks.

In our town there were three bars, two liquor stores, two, grocery stores and no church — at least not as such insofar as a building is concerned. The Reverend Kenneth Lobdell of the Arctic Mission held services in his quonset hut. He and his wife folded their children's cots each Sunday morning, and then unfolded a few chairs which were seldom occupied by grown-ups. Yet the children of our village loved our missionary, and Reverend Lobdell accomplished a great deal with them.

The school week dragged. Thursday afternoon it began to snow. By Friday afternoon seven or eight inches of new snow had fallen, making it difficult to reach the main road of our village, half a block away.

From our school window we watched as a local citizen bladed a temporary path from the school to the post office, then down main street, and, I assumed, to the Federal Aviation field about half a mile from our town. Several of our students lived in the federal housing quarters there.

Although there were no roads leading into our village, we did have two airstrips — the village strip, just outside our school window, and the F.A.A. strip just outside town. The federal strip was built for emergency landing for larger planes during World War II, and was still activated.

Despite the fact that we had no highway connecting us with the outside world, there were eighteen cars in our village. These were brought in on the Alaska Railroad, which was pushed through Talkeetna during World War I.

14

The name of our village, Talkeetna, I'm told, is derived from and Indian word which means "three rivers." It is aptly named, since it is located at the confluence of the Susitna, Chulitna and Talkeetna Rivers. Our town is older than Anchorage. Both the Indian and the Russian mined gold from the Cache and Peter's Creek area before white man rushed in at the turn of the century. After the gold rush subsided, Talkeetna became a hunting and fishing resort. For the past twenty years she has been a Mecca for mountain climbers.

There are four hotels in our town, two of them completely modern. They are filled throughout the summer, often empty in midwinter. The little red school house — which it is literally — serves a dual purpose. Above the classroom is the teacherage, as is often the case in Alaska. Mrs. Mildred Campbell, the grade school teacher, and I lived in this apartment.

By the time school was out Friday afternoon, the village was completely inundated by the spring deluge of snow, which kept falling. Mrs. Campbell mentioned needing groceries and I offered to go for them. Getting outside was always more appealing to me than cooking and cleaning, despite the weather.

En route I passed the Spoonholtz residence. One of their sons, Richie, had fallen beneath a snow machine some two weeks earlier, and one of his legs was so badly churned beneath the clogs that he needed skin grafts. I stopped to ask how he was getting along.

Inside the house I found the father, Clifford Spoonholtz, quite ill, almost delirious. He kept worrying about the roof of their cabin caving in. It hardly made sense to me until ten-year-old Randy, who was at his father's bedside, explained that the cabin was on their homestead about seventeen miles north of town, up the railroad track, where the snowfall was even deeper than the three-and-a-half feet we had in Talkeetna. The Spoonholtz family had moved into our village to put their three sons, Richie, Randy, and Ronnie into public school.

Since his wife, Mary Ann, was still in Anchorage at the hospital with Richie, Mr. Spoonholtz asked if it would be an imposition for me to help Randy find a man of the town who could go with him to shovel off the roof. Tomorrow, Saturday, the train would be traveling north on its pilgrimage to Fairbanks, and returning Sunday afternoon. This would furnish transportation, the only means available to the wilderness cabin, where there was no road and no airstrip. Getting there on the Alaska Railroad was no problem. The train stops anywhere along the line between Anchorage and Fairbanks, whenever and wherever a homesteader, hunter, or fisherman wants off.

"Let me go with Randy," I suggested. "I can shovel."

"Shoveling snow is hard work, besides, a woman shouldn't be out in this wilderness alone," answered the sick man.

"But I want to go! I need the exercise and I feel quite sure that Randy is capable of taking care of me," I asserted as I saw the shoulders of the ten-year-old boy square.

"Are you sure you won't be afraid? Have you ever been alone in the Alaskan wilderness? Randy does know how to take care of himself, and he's good with a gun; but you would be miles from help, in case you needed it. There's no communication. Nothing except a cold cabin. What if the roof has already caved in? You can freeze to death here, even in March. You'd better get a man."

"I'm not afraid," I tried to say convincingly, "but I will think it over. Maybe we should take sleeping bags and grub along, just in case. What do you think, Randy?"

"I know how to build a lean-to, and I've slept and camped out when it's colder than this."

"I know you can take care of me, Randy, but it's your father I'm worried about. He needs a doctor. Cliff Hudson could fly him into Anchorage — if the snow lets up."

"I'll be all right. Dr. Hume will probably fly into town tomorrow. He's overdue," explained Mr. Spoonholtz.

Although we had no physician in our village, Dr. Vincent Hume did come from Palmer on weekends, about twice a month. Most of the villagers waited for him, except in emergencies. Palmer, about eighty miles to the south of Talkeetna, is in the luxuriant Matanuska Valley. This picturesque area where the colonists settled, is the dairyland of Alaska. Here huge potatoes, turnips and cabbages grow. The world championship cabbage weighed seventy-two pounds and the largest turnip, fifty pounds. Anchorage, Alaska's largest city, lies 114 miles to the south of Talkeetna.

16

Although Talkeetna is not a completely isolated village, I felt that I was headed for the end of the world just seventeen miles to the north, the following day when the train slowed to a halt at the Spoonholtz homestead to let Randy and me off. We had been asked to come to the baggage car. Our gear was stashed around us. The conductor, Art Reekie, who knew everyone's business, and helpfully so, looked surprised when I explained our mission. He promised to stop the train on its way back the next day. I had heard he never forgets, but I didn't plan to take any chances. We would be there waiting.

As the door of the baggage car slid open the snow looked deep, quite deep. The cabin, which they said was a hundred yards off the track, looked a mile away. The low roof, which slanted toward the back, gave no hint as to whether it held under a leading mound of snow. I saw no animal in our frozen world.

"Jump down and we'll hand your gear to you," the conductor suggested as the train shuddered to a standstill.

I did, and landed waist deep in snow. I was afraid it might come over Randy's head, but he was tunneling out and reaching for gear before I could extract either of my imprisoned legs.

Randy, well schooled in wilderness living, held the 30.06 above his head to keep it dry as he broke trail. Together we floundered toward the cabin. The hip-deep snow kept sucking my knee-high boots off my feet, then I was forced to dive in chest-deep to search for them with numbed hands. Yet we were lucky. Much to our relief the roof had not caved in, but it sagged so heavily that I was afraid for either of us to stay inside. I grabbed a shovel.

"I'll build a fire in the stove and join you as soon as I can drag the rest of our gear to the cabin," Randy volunteered.

Afraid to put another ounce toward the center of the sagging roof, which sloped gently to the rear rather than having a real Alaskan pitch, I nibbled at the outer edge with my shovel. Randy finally joined me and cut a swath through the sagging center portion. The snow was over waist deep to him. We shoveled and shoveled. Snow continued falling, but our spades were faster.

"We've got to get it off," I urged as Randy mentioned being quite hungry. "If we get most of it off before dark it will probably be safe to sleep under. We can catch the rest tomorrow, before the train comes back through."

17

Again we shoveled and shoveled. It seemed hopeless. We were tired, wet, and cold. The white twilight grew opaque.

"If we can only clear the rest of the bedroom portion," I urged as I saw strength, but not courage, ebbing from the slip of a boy. Determination won the battle.

"I'm glad I thought to put that bucket of snow on the stove when I built the fire," Randy said as he sank on his bunk.

Thankful for his wilderness know-how, at least, I tried my hand at making hot chocolate from powdered milk. I made instant coffee from the steaming kettle rather than wait for some, which I saw on the shelf, to perk. The sandwiches which I had brought along tasted good. After eating some candy we turned to the home library — a couple of well-stocked shelves, which was more than I had expected. True to his training, Randy selected the Bible, but fell asleep before he ever turned a page.

I tried reading some of Robert W. Service's poems. They seemed apropos, but I had to keep pumping the lantern for enough light to read by. It didn't work as well for me as it did for Randy.

CHAPTER II

BUSH PILOT DON SHELDON IS DOWN

This was the quietest world I had ever known. The snow still fell, but there was no wind. The deep, white blanket muted every sound. The light kept growing dimmer and the room colder. Why pump the lantern again? I would just turn on the small transistor radio beside me, listen to the news, and let the light die away.

"We interrupt this broadcast," came instantaneous words, "to report that Alaska's internationally renowned bush and glacier pilot, Don Sheldon of Talkeetna, is reportedly forced down somewhere in the foothills of the Alaska Range. Sheldon called in several hours ago saying he was low on fuel and forced to attempt a landing under white-out conditions in an uncharted area. This is an unconfirmed report. Stay tuned for further developments."

I froze, but not from cold. I twirled the dial. No luck. Back to the original position. Randy slept.

The lantern flickered and I jumped up to give it a good pumping. I chunked a couple of sticks of wood into the stove, but it didn't work so well for me, either.

I wrapped a blanket about myself, Indian style, sat back down and twirled the dial. All stations were giving the same report, but no additional news. Again I tried to read.

I was afraid, but not of being alone in the wilderness with a ten-year-old boy. Eagerly I twisted the dial, almost continuously. After midnight there was only one station which I could get. Periodically came reports of "no further news on Sheldon." The cold intensified. The woodpile diminished too rapidly. I crawled back into my bunk, still fully clothed, except for shoes.

I thought of the spectacular rescues for which Sheldon was noted. The hunter was now the hunted. This seemed strange. Was he hurt? Did he crack up? If so, would he freeze to death? Not Sheldon! Not if he were able to reach for his survival gear. He respected the Arctic. He was always prepared.

Toward daylight I dozed, then was roused by a news report from the transistor, which I had left on all night. Search parties were being organized, but white-out conditions still prevailed.

19

I stoked the fire and set a bucket of snow on the stove to melt. I chucked some more wood into the reluctant embers, huffed until the flicker became a fla:ne, and crawled back into my bunk.

No new reports by coffee time. I put some oatmeal on to cook, then shook Randy. I told him the news and he came to life as if hit by an electric current.

"I remember Don bringing in our Christmas tree last winter and he flies lots of people, when they're hurt, without ever getting any money for it," Randy recalled.

"And doesn't he look funny, jumping the rope with Mrs. Campbell's first graders," I tried to laugh, assuring Randy that the station agent at McGrath felt Don had made a forced landing but was probably O.K.

"We'll get to work" I suggested, "and listen for radio reports later. We've got to finish before the train comes through at noon."

"I believe it will clear today," Randy forecasted hopefully as we climbed to the roof. "Not too much snow fell during the night."

For this I was thankful. How could so small a cabin have such a vast expanse of roof? The upper layers of snow were light and not so hard to handle, but toward the bottom they were compressed and quite heavy. By mid-morning, however, victory was within shoveling distance, so we climbed down for a coffee and cocoa break.

Randy ran for the radio. A reporter was doing a commentary on Don.

"Veteran bush pilot Donald E. Sheldon, who recently received the Exceptional Service Award, the highest peacetime award given to civilians by the Air Force, is now down somewhere in the foothills of the Alaska Range. According to the station agent at McGrath, whom Sheldon contacted via HF-radio yesterday while on a return trip from a polar bear hunt in the Arctic, weather closed in and Sheldon was forced to land in white-out conditions. The agent says he believes Sheldon made a successful landing and that he is not injured, even though there has been radio silence ever since.

"Sheldon, who has been flying in Alaska since 1942, has distinguished himself many times in rescue missions throughout the area. In 1954 he landed one of his light planes on a mountain side near a downed Air Force C-47 and brought out three surviving crew members.

"Later he identified a plane which crashed into Mt. Illiamna. Flying low through treacherous air currents, he made six passes over the ill-fated plane before he was able to ascertain there were no survivors. This C-54 had been the object of a search which started when the plane was reported missing three days before Christmas in 1958. Sheldon spotted the plane on awesome Mt. Illiamna, a 10,116 foot live volcanic crater in Southwestern Alaska. Venturing close enough to the crater to identify the aircraft involved great risk to the pilot because of turbulent air currents which commonly sweep around the mountains.

"As Major General C. F. Necrason, Commander of the Alaskan Air Command, later presented Sheldon the Air Corps highest civilian award, the entire 10th Air Rescue Division passed in review . . ."

The sun breaking through the overcast lightened our hearts a little as Randy and I crawled back upon the cabin roof for a last round with the shovels. How I hoped it was clearing in the McGrath area.

An hour before noon we had finished reducing the fluffy, continental expanse of snow to bedrock. There would be time to wash up a bit, eat the remaining sandwiches and listen to the news before flagging down the train for the return trip.

Stepping right up to the tracks, Randy waved his arms as he had seen it done so many times by his father to stop the train.

"That whistle means the engineer has seen me," Randy explained with the finesse of a conqueror as he stepped back from the rails.

My one thought was that in Talkeetna there might be news of Don. There was, a little. An unconfirmed report that he did make a radio contact saying he was O.K., but out of gas.

I called the local F.A.A. station. No dice. They were not allowed to put out reports. I went to Sheldon's office where Mrs. Lena Morrison, the widow of Sheldon's former flying partner, Stub Morrison — who was killed in a plane crash several years earlier — sat beside a H.F. radio with Mrs. Richard Jones, secretary for the Morrison-Sheldon Flying Service. To distinguish between mother and daughter while speaking of them, Mrs.

Jones was usually called "Big Dorothy" and her teen-age daughter "Little Dorothy." They invited me to stay. We listened and listened. Nothing from Don.

Earlier it had been reported that the McGrath station picked him up — then something happened. Unlike the bush pilot of early flying days in Alaska, Sheldon was well equipped. His plane had long range high frequency for radio communication with the outside world, yet there was radio silence.

My roommate, who mothered me despite my maturity, telephoned and asked if I planned to sleep before tomorrow, which was a school day. Lena and Big Dorothy both promised to call if they heard any further developments . . .

Snow, heavy snow still fell on Monday morning. I brought the transistor radio downstairs into the schoolroom. My students, all eight of them, were as interested as I, but no news. Weeks seemed to have passed before noon. I sent Little Dorothy to Sheldon's office to ask her mother if she had heard anything over short wave. Nothing except what was being put out over radio. An all-out effort was being made to locate the pilot who had always managed to be the hunter rather than the hunted on previous missions.

Newspapers were coming out with stories of Don's hair-raising rescues on Mt. McKinley. One was in 1960. A story published in the June 6 issue of *Life* termed it "Magnificent Rescue on McKinley". According to the article, it was the most massive mountain rescue in U.S. history. More than eighty mountain climbers from Stateside rescue council and most of the Alaska rescue group were flown in by Air Force helicopters — and, of course, Don Sheldon. The rescue became an elemental struggle of brave men against the unpredictable treachery of a mountain.

Two parties of mountain climbers were in difficulty. One was organized by a wealthy cattleman, John Day from Oregon, and the other by a woman, Helga Bading, an experienced mountaneers from Anchorage. For the first time in history two groups of climbers reached the summit of Mt. McKinley at the same time.

On the way down four men of the Day party, slipped and plummeted eight hundred feet down a slope in a tangled mass of ice axes and legs. One of the climbers, Jim Whittaker, recalled clawing at the ice with his ax, but he said, "Our speed was so great it was like a freight train rushing by two inches from your face."

John Day's left leg was broken. Lu Whittaker was badly shaken, and Pete Schoening was so dazed that he didn't know what had happened until two days after the accident. They landed on a ledge. The temperature was 30° below zero.

Members of the Bading party heard their cries but were having trouble enough of their own. Helga Bading, second woman to attempt the summit of Mt. McKinley, was suffering from dehydration and high-altitude sickness.

Had it not been for a radio set which the Bading party had along, help would not have reached the party for days, probably weeks. As it was, because of severe weather, it took three days of maneuvers and careful planning to execute the rescues.

As often happens on rescue missions involving such great risk, tragedy struck. Two of the rescue team were killed. A private pilot from Anchorage, William Stevenson, and Army T/Sergeant Robert Elliott crashed on the jagged rocks at the 17,200 foot level as they made a pass, in the thin atmosphere, too close to the injured climbers.

During my research of the mountain climbs, the prologue to Helen Bading's rescue attracted my attention because of its uniqueness. It started in Boston when Dr. Bradford Washburn, Director of the Boston Museum of Science — whose wife was the first woman to climb Mt. McKinley — called from Boston to Talkeetna and talked with Don. Together they had flown the mountain for many years. Having mapped Mt. McKinley and climbed it more times than any other man at this date, Dr. Washburn reconstructed the scene of the accident, via telephone, with Don's help.

On May 20, 1960, over the wires from Boston to the wilderness village of Talkeetna, the position of the climbers was pinpointed. There was an unamed snow basin (of course Don knew which one) close to where Mrs. Bading clung to life. If it was close enough, then possibly a landing might be worked out. Dr. Washburn believed the basin might be big enough — if Don landed uphill and the wind was with him for take-off. But conditions would have to be right, exactly right.

Fortunately, weather conditions were good and Sheldon was roaring off the runway before the operator could tally the cost of the long distance call. Following the Kahiltna Glacier to the 14,000 foot level, he raced at full throttle and shot up and over the jagged, granite spires of Kahiltna Peaks. Below him lay a small basin. He let the plane down, ever so slightly, like one putting his feet into ice-cold water to test it. Expected cross-currents did not suck him into the vertical rim; but it was a long way down to the bottom.

Another look. Up, up and over! Again he dipped his wings into the basin, a little deeper. No dice! There was no way out. There had to be! The instruments screamed to a stall as he saw a gap in the rim ahead. Levelling off, the prop grabbed just enough atmosphere to pull him through. But he knew! He would try her again.

On a third trial run, Don found the gap with fewer preliminaries. But what if the cross-winds caught him in the basin? He would become, as Don always termed it, a permanent fixture. A fourth run, lower yet. This time he all but touched and little storms of snow whirled behind the tail of his Super Cub as he sailed by. He could do it, he thought. Up and over. On the sixth run he cut the engine and fluttered down, effecting a successful landing at 14,500 feet, the highest a plane has ever landed on Mt. McKinley.

Mrs. Bading was carried to the plane by fellow climbers. Later, in speaking of the rescue she said: "We were flying right at an ice face . . . I thought, 'This is the end!' but there was a tiny opening and Sheldon slipped through it. We dodged peaks everywhere. It was like riding a truck without brakes down a mountain ledge."

Back in our classroom on Monday, we listened to recaps of previous news throughout the day. Don had made a successful landing and had contacted station agent Bob Huff in McGrath, giving what he believed to be his location.

While Sheldon was down, telephones in Talkeetna jangled constantly. Reporters, without a doubt, would be thicker than moose when the weather cleared enough for a plane to fly.

Tuesday morning the sun did break through, just before noon; but most of the reporters took no chances with the weather. Don's position had been pinpointed by a sonic-grid pattern. Don reported himself O.K. and advised his would-be rescuers to wait until the weather cleared. The train ran, snow or no snow, and she was loaded with reporters and photographers.

All afternoon newspeople and the naturally curious milled about the town, talking with persons who knew Don and picking up fragments of information here and there. I must admit, I was jealous.

Just before school was out, I saw reporters grabbing cameras and rushing toward the Talkeetna Air Service office. A scoop was breaking outside my window and I was tied in a schoolroom. I was dead!

Suddenly there was a rush from the office to the air strip. This was it! Sheldon was coming in! It was four o'clock. I really didn't care whether school was dismissed or not. It hardly registered.

As the room emptied I stumbled upstairs and took my camera out of hibernation and put a yellow filter on it to cut down the sun's glare on the snow. False motion, I knew, and useless — but a longtime habit. I was cleaning the lenses when Mrs. Campbell rushed up the stairs and yelled, "Come on!"

"Is he here?" I asked dully.

"No, silly, don't you listen to what's going on? He's coming in on the F.A.A. strip. Come on before we miss our ride."

We joined the multitude. Reporters with cameras ventured further and further out on the field, vying for position. It was almost five-thirty before Sheldon was reported nearing Talkeetna.

How could a plane be so slow? Soon there would be too little light to get a good shot, even if one could get within range. Why hadn't I grabbed my strobe light? Since there were so many reporters around, maybe Don wouldn't notice me at all. It was worth a try. I was looking for a ride back to the schoolhouse to pick up my flash unit when a yell went up. His plane was spotted in the distance, across the Susitna River. He would be in before I could reach the schoolhouse. I took off the yellow filter and opened up the stops on my camera as much as I dared. Maybe there was light enough, I thought as I saw his plane bank between the bluff down river and the runway approach. Then — What happened?

The plane was just behind the trees, of course, it had to be. No, it was too low. Would he crash? On the edge of the runway? My roommate and I looked at each other, realization breaking on our faces. We both knew what had happened.

It was always difficult to tell which strip a plane was coming in on, since practically the same approach was used when coming in from the west and south — skirt the bluff and skim in over the Susitna.

Now Don was past the bluff, over the river — but where? He wouldn't! He couldn't! Yes, he would — and he did.

A murmur, then suddenly those familiar with the approach knew what had happened. Sheldon was coming in on the village strip. Photographers raced for their cars, but it did them no good. The nearest one reportedly got only close enough to see a lank figure gallop across from a Cessna 180, which was pulled up between the schoolhouse and the hangar, then disappear into the office of Talkeetna Air Service.

To the best of my knowledge, no one has seen Sheldon when he was not clean shaven and his teeth brushed as sparkling white as ptarmagin feathers in winter. His heavy crop of sandy-dark hair was always newly combed. His angular six feet of raw bone was nothing but hide and muscle, always parka-clad, probably over double layers of thermal underwear. His hip bones served as hangers for his loose trousers, and shoulder bones for his shirts. His Ichabod arms swung gorilla-like from his gaunt frame, constantly working. He was never gaited for walking, and always went at an Andean lope.

Impatiently the reporters waited, and waited.

Finally Don sent word to them. "I have no comment to make at this time, except to thank everyone who helped with the search. I'll think it over while I sleep for a week. But no dice on a story right now. I appreciate your coming, but we'll just have to make it later."

There was no doubt about Don needing the rest.

In a way, I was glad it had happened this way. My thoughts completely ran away with any reasoning power that I might have had. What if I could get this interview? I must be crazy. I was the last person he would trust. I was completely miserable. I was obsessed. There must be a way.

Two days I sweated it out. Not a sign of Don Sheldon. On the morning of the third day I saw him lope from the office to the hangar, early. Although I was at my desk in the schoolroom, my eyes never left the hangar, not completely. Just before noon I saw him lope back to the office. Then I saw Mrs. Jones leave the office for lunch. This would leave Don there alone. Suddenly I just had to ask Mrs. Jones, (of course I didn't see her leave), who was president of our P.T.A., a question.

The office was in front of the schoolhouse and the hangar across the street, so the poor guy had little chance of my not knowing his whereabouts. I had not the faintest idea of what I would say to him or ask him, but I had to give it a try.

I knocked at the office door. After a short hesitancy, Sheldon answered the knock himself.

"I saw it was you," he grinned. "Is there something wrong at the schoolhouse?"

"I just had a question I wanted to ask Mrs. Jones," I put up a weak front.

"Sit down," he gestured with a swing of his arm like a long loop. "Tell me about it. How about a glass of milk? Good for you. Just push my scribbling aside," came his constant chit-chat as he went to the refrigerator and poured milk for me before I could answer. "And how about a bowl of cereal?"

"Thanks, it does sound good," I answered, grateful for a moment's reprieve and knowing how much it pleased Don for anyone to share his "good for you" goodies such as milk and goat cheese and ice cream. I was remembering what had happened to an advertising agent who wanted him to endorse a beer ad: Don all but kicked him out.

CHAPTER III

GET SHELDON'S STORY!

"My scribbling is sort of sad," Don apologized as he turned to the refrigerator and came back with his arms loaded, "but I sort of promised the newspapers . . ."

"Wonderful," I encouraged. "Is this your own story of the time you were down?"

"Yeah. The newspapers write too much about me. But since they've put themselves out so — well, maybe this way it won't get all garbled. I didn't want to do it; but this is the first time they've used a sonic grid pattern to locate someone lost and down in a white-out. It might save someone's life."

"You've done a lot of work on it, several pages."

"Yeah, but I don't know if they can read my scribbling."

"Could I type it for you?" I asked before I actually realized I had spoken. He hesitated. Maybe I had scared him out of it.

"Would you?" came his studied answer as he read my face. "I'll bring it over to you after school, if you're not too busy."

I made it a point to get the kids out in a hurry. I dashed up the stairs for my typewriter, cleared my desk, pushed it near a plug-in socket, inserted a sheet of paper and was ready to turn on the juice.

"Yoohoo!" Don called from the schoolhouse door as he dislodged the snow from his mukluks, gave a whistle, which I later found out was his calling trademark, and entered without further announcement.

"I know you can't make this out," he was saying as he closed the door tightly against the breath of the arctic, "maybe it will be better if I sort of dictate?"

"My typewriter is ready. Shoot!'

"You mean you can rattle that thing as fast as I ramble?"

"I'll try."

"Then you must be pretty good," he surmised as he began his story:

" As you know — but not for print —" he pointed out, "those Paddocks had a helluva time. I got them to Point Hope, no sweat. Then we see this large, trophy type bear, yellow against the snow, just loping along. We're out over the broken ice on the Chuckchi Sea, where conditions are unfavorable for landing my Cessna. Yeah, I guess we had better print this so the folks will know what I was doing up in the Arctic. You remember the Paddocks? Nothing but the best and only a trophy would do. But when I spotted him we couldn't land. Guess you saw in the newspapers how they got lost after I transferred them to the other pilots. Too bad. But that was a beautiful bear and they needed a lighter plane. I was already halfway back to Talkeetna when it came over my radio about them being down somewhere on the Chuckchi Sea, so I turned around, of course."

I rattled the typewriter keys.

"Oh, no," he said quickly, "this is just a fill-in for you and not a part of the story."

As I pulled the paper from my typewriter carriage and inserted another, Don kept talking, but still not for publication.

"I didn't find them, you see, someone else did. I knew about where they would be; but fortunately some one located them just before I landed back in Point Hope, where I stopped to refuel. But to get on with our story . . .

"Since the Paddocks were rescued and all was well, 39-Tango (identification of Sheldon's Cessna 180) departed.

"A three-front angry weather system boiled in from the southwest of Bristol Bay; but with any luck at all I could make Kotzebue-Talkeetna nonstop."

At least Sheldon seemed to be back to newspaper talk so I began clicking the keys, thankful for the prologue which filled me in on unknown factors.

"About 150 miles southeast of Kotzebue, weather enroute described as rapidly deteriorating, encouraged an alternate stop at Moses Point 90 degrees and 125 miles to the west of original course. Accomplished!"

Sheldon seldom took time to put in such time-consumers as understood subjects, verbs, or personal pronouns. To him they must have seemed unimportant and unnecessary as commas and periods, which tended to slow down his train of thought. Yet at the same time, he's never too hurried to give credit to those who help him in any way, and he never forgets a kindness. Before my first story was finished I found that he always stresses these points, whether it be an individual, the Army, the Air Corps, Rescue Team, or whatever or whomever.

"A blizzard shrieked in," he narrated "and howled for three nights and two days, during which time I enjoyed the congenial atmosphere of the home of Mr. and Mrs. Chuck Shenkel, local Federal Aviation Agency operator.

"Upon apparent general weather improvement 39-Tango (far be it from Sheldon to say, 'I took off in my plane which is identified as 39-Tango') departed southeast for McGrath, the early day aviation hub of western interior Alaska, (and he never fails to give a plug for a colorful village, either) as well as a most lucrative fur district studded with fabulous mercury, gold and platinum mines.

"At a point one hundred miles northwest of McGrath, unstable air turbulence and ominous head winds encouraged a refueling stop slightly south off course at the old village of Flat, at which time F.A.A. flight plan was closed via H.F. (high frequency) radio 3411.5 with Bob Huff, Northern Consolidated station manager at McGrath.

"H.F." was an unfamiliar term to me but I didn't want to stop his train of thoughts, and didn't until he pulled "V.H.F." later. Like most females, I had little knowledge of technical terms. Besides, I was a newcomer, "Chechako" as Alaskans call a tenderfoot, and had never ridden in a small plane prior to coming to Alaska.

Failing to bother with such cumbersome continuity as "takeoff after refueling and heading for Talkeetna," which he had already pointed out earlier, Sheldon began reliving the rugged portion of his flight, his hands constantly gyrating.

"A curious, shuddering type turbulence is encountered. A series of solid bottom bumps — the horizon in all quadrants is instantly obscured by a dense, endless sea of snowflakes as big as fifty dollar bills. 39 Tango peels off in a 180 degree turn . . . NO DICE!

"Air speed's got the hiccups . . . directional gyro is swapping lies with the compass. Whoops! Watch that whiteout! Miss that rock pile! Smooth that turn! Now, full bore! Climb that mountain!

"Easy, boy! Can this be the one-way pay off? After twenty years of near misses and questionable successes laced across the land from south of the border to the far north coasts, hundreds of high altitude glacier landings, wolf hunts and polar bear expeditions, lucky in rescue mission recovery, and now within an ace of being a statistic myself.

"Shut up. Cut the chit-chat! Shocking revelation! Just discovered that the sometime-exceeded red-line dive recoveries are not responsible for my near black-out condition. Simply not breathing . . . retract tongue, half bit off."

Throughout this tense discourse as Don reconstructed the scene, his eyes read the instruments, gauged the weather, and his hands constantly manipulated the gadgets. As he retracted his tongue I heard my room mate, Mrs. Mildred Campbell, come home from the grade school and go up the back stairs to our own living quarters above my one-room high school. Don and I were so engrossed that it hardly registered with either of us.

"By the clock," he continued, "one hour and three minutes so far in this rat race and still in one piece. THERE SHE IS! A whited-out ridge. One fast look and I park this holy terror. NO GOOD! Rocks as big as houses! Anyway, the whole works floated off in the white-out," he explained as he reached for the two way and pressed the button, speaking into the mike which seemed as real to him as it was while he held it in his hand during the turbulent flight.

"McGrath, McGrath, 39-Tango advises precautionary landing, about 1,500 feet in the bald Von Frank ridges, about fifty miles northeast.

"Friendly voice of Bob Huff, N.C.L. McGrath comes back instantly: 'Copy, Roger! Roger! Please advise.'

"Fast glance out the side window, more ice build-up on the windshield, leading edges of wings look like baseball bats. In luck! Some slipped off! Temperature 34°.

"By the clock . . . twelve minutes later. More ridges float around . . .

" 'N.C.L. McGrath, calling 39-Tango. Are you down? What happened? REPLY!'

"Can't see well enough to crack this thing up gracefully, low on gas . . .

"Zero-zero . . . swirling garbage . . . sand-trapped by the weather, the great deceiver, forced into a delicate compromise. Sizzle among these scattered rock piles . . . close enough to see them . . . just far enough away to miss them. Best friends are lost this way. Some leverage, in comparable position with a belligerent prisoner in a violent argument with the executioner. "There went a possibility! Don't lose it! PARK ON IT!"

"Now the spruce tips . . . SWOOSH! . . . and she's down! Rode her to a Mexican stand-still! This crooked old uphill looks like La Guardia.

" 'N.C.L. McGrath, McGrath, 39-Tango, uneventful landing.' "

I doubt if anyone tells a tale more enthusiastically, gets more wound up, or puts in more detail and pantomime than Don Sheldon — always laughing, usually at himself.

This was not what I had expected, not at all. I was more than pleased when he became so engrossed in his subject. I had to have this story, my very first one about Don Sheldon. But how? This was his story. I was only the typewriter!

After the forced landing in the white-out the first thing Don did was try to estimate his position. His plane suffered no damage. Strapping on the ever-present snow shoes he climbed to the top of a two thousand-foot rise which he thought to be a foothill of Mt. McKinley; but he was wrong. At the time he thought the white-out condition blanketed Mighty Mack. When the big ones are obscured the lesser peaks begin to look more and more alike. Don lost his perspective and made a wrong estimate of his downed position.

He returned to his plane, blocked up the skis to keep them from freezing to the wet snow, and began tramping out a runway. In Don's words:

"Beat down three thousand feet of possible runway . . . pile about an acre of swamp spruce in convenient signal fire location, split open shiny, empty gas can for reflector. Through for the day, roll in big eiderdown sleeping robe."

"And I think it is time you two take a coffee break," came Mrs. Campbell's commanding voice from the overhead apartment. "I have spiced tea for Don."

This Don couldn't resist. Although she was white-haired, my roommate was most observant. Often we ate out at the Rainbow Lodge or the Talkeetna Roadhouse, where there was always plenty of good home cooking. Don had a sweet tooth, this was apparent, and he preferred milk to tea and tea to coffee. Yet, at fifty-six cents per quart, we did not use a great deal of fresh milk.

Don made a sizeable dent in the freshly-baked oatmeal cookies and really went for the spiced tea, which was a great favorite with Mrs. Campbell. I went along with the tea angle when it was made, but coffee was my standby.

Noticing that it was already past 10:00 o'clock; Don said we had best knock it off for the night, but wondered if I could make any sense of what he had said, since he had repeated some portions so many times, adding a word here and subtracting a phrase when he thought it slowed the story down.

"I'll admit that I can hardly wait for my favorite pilot to get rescued," said Mrs. Campbell, "but tomorrow is a school day. I won't need to read the story. Every word comes through our foot warmer, loud and clear."

Don took a look at the heat register beneath our dining table.

"Say now, that's pretty neat."

I could have told him that we kept the table over the register for more purposes than one. Standing directly under it, from downstairs one could see upstairs. The table placed in this strategic position prevented our forgetting and standing over it.

"Our view of Mt. McKinley from this double window is perfect," I commented to change the viewpoint.

"She never gets enough of looking at that mountain," commented Mrs. Campbell, "but I must say I love it too, especially in winter when it is a pastel pink."

"I guess you have the best view of the mountain of anyone around here," Don remarked glancing at the shade-drawn windows as if he could see through both them and the darkness.

"And don't forget, young man, that our view of your office and hangar is completely unobstructed — as if you would," she added on second though. "We never see you except on the fifty-yard dash from the house to the hangar. Why don't you stop by whenever you have a minute. We always have tea and Mary doesn't go much for my cookies — watching her figure, you know — so they usually get stale."

"I better go now," Don said a little uneasily. Suddenly he seemed to realize that he was in an apartment with two widows, even though Mrs. Campbell was quite old enough to be his mother and I was nine years his senior. "I hope you can make this rambling out," he again apologized as he got to his feet.

"Time for bed," Mrs. Campbell remarked as the front door to the schoolhouse clicked shut.

"Not tonight," I replied calmly to her commanding tone, wondering what her reaction would be. "Furthermore," I added as she hesitated, "it may take me most of the night. Maybe I can just hang a curtain to block out part of the light and noise from my typewriter."

"Never mind. I understand."

Dashing down the stairway, I returned with my typewriter. Staying downstairs and writing would have been more or less like working in the window of a department store, since there were no blinds.

It was daylight before my typewriter stopped clicking. I worked and reworked every page, trying to orient the reader without changing Don's wording. Then, as now, I must confess that without the aid of his eyes and explicit hands, trying to reconstruct one of Don's yarns gives me the feeling of a stage without props.

Of course Mildred — as I call Mrs. Campbell now, but didn't dare to until after we had roomed together for over a year — reamed me out good for sitting up all night; but somehow it seemed a commendation rather than a reprimand. Her tongue could be sharp — very.

How often she called to me to "shut up" and let her get some sleep when I took what she called one of my "blubbering spells". I couldn't even cry under my breath, but she somehow seemed to know.

How many times I swore to myself that if I ever got away from this sharp-tongued, stone-hearted little old woman who looked and smelled like lilac but was arsenic to the core, I'd never commit myself to living with such a roommate again. At the time I kept thinking surely there must be some sympathy in her heart for one who had lost a husband and mother and father recently. In fact, I had lost six members of my family, one by one, in the three years prior to my husband's heart attack. Then, when he dropped dead at the age of forty-six, while in seemingly good health, it was almost too much.

The school day was a century long, and I found myself dozing during book reports. The last parka-clad teenager had hardly cleared the door when I heard Don's "Yoohoo" and whistle as he scraped and tapped the snow from his mukluks.

"Neat!" he exclaimed with a low whistle as I handed him the first part of the story while I dashed up the stairs for my typewriter.

"Couldn't you give a fellow a chance to be a gentleman?" he asked as he reached for the typewriter when I reappeared.

I obliged and held up the cord of the lifeless typewriter, which he had deposited ever so carefully upon my desk.

"Following day," he grinned as he plugged it in, "freezing drizzle and snow continue, overcast to sixteen thousand feet. Solid instruments."

"Does this mean that rescue planes were flying above you on instruments?" I asked, trying to follow.

"You're cookin', Kid," he encouraged without telling me whether I should or should not inform the reader. Again he picked up the story, without the use of a personal pronoun, of course.

"Advised by McGrath to listen for Col. Rodgers and his Jet Drivers (he calls himself a 'plane driver') sonic booming a grid pattern, cross checking A.D.F. Coast Guard fixes."

I didn't know what sort of "fixes" these were, but didn't dare interrupt again, nor wished to appear too ignorant concerning aeronautical terms.

"Third day out. Far to the west through the thick overcast an intensifying shriek developed into a roaring KARBOOM. Local time 1:21 P.M., direction west to east, eight or ten knots south from present position, duration three minutes, ten seconds. Sky condition obscured in all quadrants.

" 'N.C.L. McGrath,' " he again called, picking up an imaginary mike, " '39-Tango . . . —sizzle . . . crackle . . . — CHAOS! Smells like an electrical fire. Both V.H.W. 121.5 and H.F. 3411.5 do a fadeaway. Insult to injury. Idling engine quits cold. Out of fuel! Ran engine to maintain battery output while operating H.F. radio.

"Hungry country! At present rate of exchange possibility of browsing the brush like a moose for coming season.

"Tear out headliner! Revelation. V.H.F. antenna partially shorted out, probable feed back short to H.F. set. Switch off

V.H.F. H.F. checks out loud and clear. V.H.F. shot. Build tripod . . . hoist tail six feet in air, engine purrs merrily for two minutes thirty seconds. Back in business. Message delivered.

He slowed down a little, probably thinking he was carrying me a little too fast; but I was beginning to understand his curtailed sentences now. Perhaps most journalists, including myself, could say more, use less space on the printed page, and conserve the reader's time if nonessentials were deleted.

"Three hours later, distant drone of large multi-engine aircraft, east. Visibility less than one-half mile, heavy snow. Short pause . . . smooth voice of Commander Huff, Kodiak Naval Air Rescue Center:

" 'Have your position. How's the weather down there? Have supply air drop for you, plan let down and low pass.' "

" 'NEGATIVE! NEGATIVE! Have complete 60-below gear and more than five days rations aboard. In bottom of deep bowl. Pull up before you clobber ragged mountains. Come back with more suitable weather.' "

Only a slight pause separates this day from the next in Sheldon's narration.

"Seven forty-five A.M., clearing conditions, three feet of new snow. Small aircraft circling area. Dump gallon of methanol on closest signal brush pile. Flames leap forty feet into air. No dice! White cloud made by methanol smoke fades into white clouds above. Learned lesson."

The third day of the search most everyone knew better than Don himself. He could not keep radio contact because he was all but out of gas. He doubted that he would have enough left to run the motor the next day for sonic boom hitches. If he couldn't answer??

As radio silence prevailed, all Alaska seemed to have joined the search.

"Fourth day," Don continued, "distant drone of multi-engine aircraft about five miles northwest. Took dead aim with gas can reflector in bright morning sunlight and blasted away until he faded in the distance.

"Business picking up! Here comes another one! Aimed about 60° south. Maybe I can shoot this one down with 3411.5 H.F."

I wasn't sure what Don was talking about but kept my mouth shut and the keys rattling. At least I got a partial answer in the next paragraph.

"Sure enough, 3411.5 came back with the amused voice of Colonel Reed: 'Stand by for gas drop.'

"Along about this time three light planes arrived on the scene and three of my old friends: Sam Parent, Bud O'Donnel and Bob Lyman set down to lend a hand.

"Scenic wonders of Alaska are in a class by themselves . . ."

"For heaven's sake!" yelled Mrs. Campbell down through the register as Don changed the subject. "Did you get rescued? Come on up and have a cup of tea and a bite to eat. Must we work right through mealtime again without food?"

We took our story upstairs. Don half read and half ate.

"Now put it down and eat your dinner," commanded Mildred Campbell in a tone respected by grownup and child. Don took his time, even sipped a second cup of tea. The telephone rang. Mrs. Morrison, his business partner, said the *Anchorage Times* was calling, about the story.

"Call back and tell them I'll bring it in tomorrow," Don replied. "Tell them I'll have it in before noon. I have a ten o'clock flight into town."

My heart sank. Tomorrow noon! The story would be in and I would be out in the cold. It was a first person story and my name would not even appear on it. I was desperate! All Alaska would read this story, and it would likely go on the wires.

Another call came for Don.

"Gee, I hate to run, and after such fine food, but if you'll excuse me I'll fly this homesteader across the river before it gets completely dark and be back shortly. Mind if I take this copy along?" he asked of me.

"Not at all, and I'll work from my carbon. Maybe I can have the part you have just told me ready when you come back, but it's the longest sentence I ever read."

As Don left I dashed for the typewriter. No time to think of how badly I wanted the story. I worked as one obsessed, forgetting I had had no sleep the previous night.

Don was amazed that I had so much in hand when he returned.

"I don't see how you did it, Kid," he chided, "I worked three days on this and you did more in one night. Did you sleep? You really can write. Did you study journalism?"

"Did you?" I countered, noticing the many journalistic phrases which he had used. "On with the story!"

"Oh, yeah, now where were we? As I was saying, and I think we ought to get this in:

"Scenic wonders of Alaska are in a class by themselves, likewise a conspiracy of Alaska's elements, terrain, and distance are a formidable hazard to all manner of surface travel, from poling boats, dog teams, to air craft. Many are those who have stood short to these sand traps."

A short hesitation, then, "PERIOD! NEW PARAGRAPH!"

"And your rescue?" I encouraged.

"That's the most important thing. You see, it might save a life, and it's the first time such a fix has been made during whiteout conditions to effect a rescue here."

We worked and worked. We went through this part of the story many times, yet I would have run through it a hundred times, *sans* complaint, even though the story wasn't mine. It was past midnight when we got down to the "thank you" portion, and Don wanted to thank half Alaska.

"Do you think you can finish it, Kid? It'll be too hard on you. You didn't sleep last night. What can I do for you? Pay you for your time, maybe? No, I'll tell you, Kid, you've done this story, why not just put your name on it? You could change the 'I's,' couldn't you?"

"And ruin your story? Never! But I'll tell you what I would like to do. Could I possibly put, 'by Don Sheldon as told to Mary Carey?'"

"Sure, Kid. Only thing is, I sort of promised the *Anchorage Times* the story would be in tomorrow. If you have it finished by 10.00 A.M. I'll take it into Anchorage. You can mail it to Fairbanks or wherever you please."

"Mail?" I said with dismay. "But I write for the Fairbanks paper."

"You what?"

Then I confessed that I had written Dave Galloway, editor of the *Fairbanks Daily News-Miner*, asking if he could use stories on Don and on mountain climbers, if I could get them. He not

38

only wanted these, but he had asked me to do a weekly column, "Talkeetna Topics." I had done my first one the previous week, about the new high school and about rumors of a bid to be let to bring a spur road into Talkeetna from the proposed new Anchorage-Fairbanks route, which was under construction and passable to within thirty-six miles of Talkeetna.

I knew I was scooped because the train did not leave Talkeetna until noon, Saturday. None of the newspapers — neither the Anchorage nor the Fairbanks — had a Sunday edition in 1963. If I could — if I only could! But that would be cheating. I couldn't let Don see what I was thinking, he was too good at reading minds.

"That's fine," I replied, "but we'd better get finished with the story if either of us gets it off tomorrow."

On and on we worked, past midnight when Mildred finally yelled through the register that the whole town would be talking if a bush pilot was seen in the school after midnight with a widow. She did not have to remind us that anyone passing could see right through the windows, and that a goodly portion of the Talkeetna populace drank past midnight and could see us there working. In our town the "working" part would go unnoticed; but the "bachelor-widow" and "past midnight" would spread like Alaskan fireweed. This was, and still is, Talkeetna.

"I won't be leaving until ten o'clock," Don reminded, "so why don't you get some sleep and finish the story in the morning."

As Don left I dashed up the stairway with my typewriter. Again I parked it on the kitchen table and reached for the curtain.

"Not again tonight!" came Mrs. Campbell's distressed comment. Yet she said no more as I carefully tacked up the blanket to try to curtain a little of the noise and shut the light from her eyes. Although our apartment was partially partitioned, as a sort of dining-room kitchen, bedroom and living room affair, none of the partitions could be wholly blocked off from the other, save the bathroom. A bathroom in our village was a luxury and we were most thankful for same.

I wrote and wrote. As I wrote I became obsessed with an idea. Tomorrow was Saturday. No more papers until Monday. Don was not leaving Talkeetna before 10:00 A.M. It would take him approximately fifty-five minutes to reach Anchorage by air. This meant he could not get his story to the *Anchorage Daily Times* and to the *Anchorage Daily News* until shortly after eleven. Now if I could telephone my story to Fairbanks? The *Fairbanks News-Miner* could scoop the other Alaskan papers! But would they accept a collect call for such a lengthy story? Ours was a school telephone and we could not charge such a call to it. Would the *News-Miner* want or consider the story a scoop? Six days had passed since Don's rescue. It could hardly be called up to the minute. Would they consider the story this important?

There was only one way I could win. Have the story finished and ready to call in as soon as their office opened, if they would accept such a collect call. If they did, then only they would have time to get it in Saturday's edition. Even though Don flew the story into Anchorage, they would hardly have time to read it, much less edit and get it set into type before their noon deadline. Being a freelance writer, I had queried all three of these papers concerning stories on Sheldon and mountain climbers, if I could get them. All were interested, and all were afternoon papers with a 12:30 deadline. Only the *Fairbanks Daily News-Miner* had suggested a news column. Later, after the *Anchorage Daily News* did start publishing a Sunday paper, I did a column for it, too, as well as a column, "Talkeetna Ticky-Tac" for the Palmer *Frontiersman*.

But as of this date, Friday, March 15, 1963, I was unknown in ·Alaska, newspaperwise.

My roommate no doubt thought I had lost my feeble mind when I grabbed eight typewritten pages the next morning and called the editor of the *Fairbanks News-Miner* collect.

"That's a book, not a story," she commented sarcastically as I waited for the call to go through. Dave Galloway was not yet in the office, but they expected him any minute. Would I talk with anyone else in the newsroom? I told the operator I would wait, knowing no one on the staff would be authorized to accept such a call from me, collect.

"And does Don know you are making this call?" she plagued. "Did he give you permission?"

"He said I could send my story to the *News-Miner* today," I asserted, "on the train. But I didn't mention the telephone. I don't see why he should mind my giving this newspaper an even break," came my white lie which only I knew was quite black. The phone rang and I was spared further quizzing.

I explained to Mr. Galloway that I had a first person story by Don Sheldon as told to me, that it was quite lengthy and that Don would be flying it into Anchorage later in the morning, that he had promised it to all the newspapers.

"And do you think we could get a scoop?" he asked. "What time will he be leaving Talkeetna?"

"At 10:00 A.M. for Anchorage," I replied very confident that as sharp an editor as Galloway would be computing the time element involved, not only for the Saturday papers; but that the Anchorage papers, if he figured as I was figuring, could not get the story into print before Monday.

"Let me get some paper into my typewriter," Dave replied as he accepted the call.

Triumphantly I read, word for word, saying Sheldon had authorized my making it an "As told to Mary Carey" byline. This was my first, my very first scoop since coming to Alaska, and it was a story which all the newspapers would carry.

Somehow Don must have gotten word that I was calling the Fairbanks paper. I had been on the phone for twenty minutes. In Talkeetna this was enough time for news to circle the village — even phone calls. We had no direct telephone connection, nor phone lines, leading into our town. Calls did go out, however, with the aid of the Alaska Railroad Communications or the Federal Aviation Agency, usually via the railroad communication set up for that purpose.

There was no mistaking that "Yoohoo!" and whistle of Don Sheldon. I heard him hit the stairway taking the steps two at a time when Mrs. Campbell answered:

"Come on up!"

My heart sank.

"Hold everything!" Don called.

"Just a minute, Don Sheldon is here," I said to Dave Galloway as I cupped my hand over the mouthpiece.

"I heard you were calling the story in and I . . ."

That was it, scuttled! He knew my game and wouldn't let me get it to my newspaper first. He strode toward the telephone, carbon copy of the story in hand, looking at it seriously.

41

"I just found a word in here I think we should change," he said as my heart started beating again.

Fortunately it was in the later part of the story. Dave Galloway asked to congratulate Don and invited him to stand by as we finished the story via telephone.

Confidently I read the remainder of the story, nanding Don a carbon to check the closing paragraphs, which he had not seen.

"I want to extend my regards to the powers behind the grid jets," I read, "on gauges with fuel problems of their own. Coast Guard landing with one engine out and gear-up warning lights on. Colonel Reed and the precision gas drop; Bob Huff, N.C.L. McGrath; Don Hunter, N.C.L. Marshall; Farwell Lake Lodge; Sam Parent, Crooked Creek; Bud O'Donnell, Sleetmute; Bob Lyman, Red Devil."

Don thought surely the newspaper was paying far too much for the call; but Dave Galloway assured Don he could thank all those who played a major role in his rescue, so we continued.

Captains of overheading Alaska Airline Mainliner and N.C.L. Prop Jet; all those who cleared by 3411.5 frequency and A.D.F. countdown by F.D.C.; Coast Guard; Dew Line; F.A.A.; and those who lighted a candle or said it's good enough for him; especially to Colonel Rodgers who roared around on the gauges and pioneered a way to tie A.D.F. fixes to a sonic hitching post."

Mrs. Campbell poured some coffee; but Don said he didn't have time. He complimented my work and seemed quite happy with his copies for the Anchorage papers.

"I'll get them to all the newspapers on the same day," he surmised. "That way it will be fair."

I kept my mouth shut, real tight.

As Don left I fell on the bed and faintly remember Mrs. Campbell grumbling something about making coffee that wasn't even tasted. It was wasted, there is no doubt about that, because I slept, and slept.

I almost slept Saturday through, but thought Sunday would last forever. The story did not get into the Anchorage papers on Saturday. They hadn't gotten it in time and I breathed a little easier. I had no idea whether it got into the Fairbanks paper, and I would not know until Monday morning. The train wouldn't be back through from Fairbanks until 5:05 Sunday afternoon, and the mail would not be put up until Monday morning. No one in Talkeetna would know, not even Don.

I was relieved when I saw Don's plane take off before the mail was put up Monday morning. I just couldn't wait until noon recess to know, so I sent one of my students over to pick up my mail.

There it was! BIG! BIG! BIG! The Fairbanks paper had scooped the Anchorage papers. A nine-column banner headline streamed all the way across the top of the page, "BUSH PILOT TELLS HOW DOWNED POSITION WAS PIN-POINTED BY SONIC BOOM." The byline read, "By Don Sheldon, as told to Mary Carey, *News-Miner* Correspondent." I was in!

I don't know how Don felt about his story coming out in the Fairbanks paper on Saturday, March 16, and the same story not appearing in the Anchorage papers until Monday. I have a pretty good idea how the editors felt, however, because I know editors. Don never said a word about it, and if I know Don, he never will.

CHAPTER IV

MY IMPOSSIBLE ROOMMATE

Talkeetna slept. I wept, or smouldered with desire to fly Mt. McKinley. More and more I gazed out our upstairs window at the cold splendor which had become an obsession.

"Mooning at that mountain again," my roommate would use as a whet stone to sharpen her barbs.

"You love it too," I fought back.

"Of course I do; but I'm not so sure it's the mountain you love. Mary Carey, you must be nuts to think you'll ever fly that mountain."

I hated her for her cruel insinuation. It had been a year since my husband died and that mountain was the only thing which inspired me enough to make me want to write again. My keyboard seemed to have died with my heart, but the mountain could give it life.

"It's not the man, it's the mountain."

"Forget it! You know that bachelor is never going to fly you there. In the first place you're a woman and people would talk. In the second place, you're a reporter and he hates both."

Females! Why couldn't they think like men? I despised her. In fact, by the strangest coincidence, she started bugging me even before I reached Alaska.

I first saw her in Watson Lake, in Canada, where so many signs are planted alongside the road. The Houston Writer's Club had made one for me to place there. A Volkswagen pulled up, and what one might have thought a sweet, white haired lady watched as I erected the marker and took a self photo, via delayed timing on Rolleiflex. Yet vaguely I felt she thought I was taking the photo to bolster my ego. Maybe I was. I forgot her, but not for long.

The next day I could have sworn it was she who passed me speeding like a long-haired rabbit in a prairie fire. 'I hope she makes it to her grandchildren,' I said under my breath, thinking surely she would stop in the next town. She did, but she passed me again.

Would you believe that on the third day this sweet bit of arsenic passed me again, and this time on a curve! "Persons her age shouldn't be allowed to drive," I thought, "and they should have strict law enforcement along this highway — if you could call this graveled pretzel such."

The further we drove the greater seemed her joy in passing me. This wounded my pride as a driver. I'll admit I was afraid because most of my driving had been done on Texas plains and I was probably overly cautious in mountains. But she didn't have to make things worse by waving each time she zipped by.

My fervent prayer was that, if she were possibly going as far as Tok Junction, she would head for Fairbanks. I was tired of her flying rocks and her cocky attitude. A real kibitzer, she.

Driving alone to Alaska was one of the greater adventures of my life. The newspapers in Houston, Galveston, Dallas, and Cisco, Texas had all published feature articles about my making the drive alone, and I was to keep a travelogue. Some of my nearest friends and kin feared for my life and swore I could never make it. Here I was, steeled against starving, freezing, going over a cliff, and what have you, and she was making a fool of me. I had enough grub in my car to last a month, and so many spare tires and parts I couldn't see back of the driver's seat. Although I had installed overload springs, my little red and white station wagon was as full as a tortoise shell, and almost as graceful and speedy.

If you're planning a trip to Alaska in a reasonably dependable car, forget the junk. If your car isn't dependable, forget the trip. I didn't have a single flat tire en route. Neither did I have any trouble whatsoever, nor did I touch the ton of food, most of which spoiled. I did not have to sleep in the car but one night, and this was my own fault. I could have called ahead or stopped earlier, but that midnight sun just keeps one driving and driving. I had plenty of blankets, so I can't even say I got cold.

I didn't see that white-haired plague again, but she had deflated my ego. I can still see that little blue bug scoot along the gravel taking those curves faster than I dared drive. You don't get away from a plague. Her dust was still choking me.

Since there were no roads leading into Talkeetna, where I was to become "the faculty" of a one-room high school, I stored my car in Anchorage and took the train, the only transportation available except a small plane. Such a mode of transportation was about as far from my way of thinking at that time as stepping into a space ship.

For over fiive thousand miles my hands had been on a steering wheel and my eyes on the road. I was going to enjoy this 113-mile trip from Anchorage to Talkeetna on the train. After dashing to a grocery store and buying up enough coffee, eggs, ham, bacon and junk to make me look like a fool, I headed for the bush, the end of the world, where there was no road in or out.

I was carrying so much baggage that the freight agent in Anchorage knew I was another "Damn Chechako," (newcomer) but he helped me with repacking and re-organizing. My lonely little ticket fell far short of the poundage allotment, although they never seem to bother to weigh your baggage on the Alaska Railroad, unless you bring white elephants.

Finally, inside the train I was ready and set for adventure in a wild, new world — interior Alaska. I dug for my guide book. In this setting I could read ahead and watch every mile post. I would be as well oriented on this wilderness village as possible before I reached it.

Talkeetna was on the map before Anchorage was born. The Indians and Russians mined gold near Talkeetna before white man made his mad dash at the turn of the century. During her gold mining days, and while the railroad was being pushed through during World War I, Talkeetna was a roaring Alaska boom town. Now she was practically nothing, population 76.

I was so engrossed in my reading that I didn't look up until the train started moving, or something moving or entering from the other end of the car caught my eye — an apparition or something. Merciful heaven! It couldn't be!

Quickly I buried my head in my guide book. If I ignored it maybe . . . —

"Excuse me; but aren't you the lady I passed on the highway?" came the understatement of a lifetime as the apparition closed in.

She just stod there smiling, like a puppy wagging its tail and waiting for you to invite it into your lap. The seat beside me was vacant. What else?

"Where are you going?" she asked as I again buried my head in my book to indicate my preference.

46

"Talkeetna."

"Now isn't that delightful! I'm going to Talkeetna, too."

"Grandchildren?"

"Mercy, no! I'm going there to teach!"

"Teach?"

"Yes, I'm the new grade school teacher. I've never been there, I'm from Sparks, Nevada and the whole thing is completely fascinating. I'll meet my roommate when I get there."

"Roommate!" I echoed in a sort of dazed tone.

"Yes, she's to be the new high school teacher. This is the first year they've ever had a high school in Talkeetna," she babbled as I faced the firing squad.

As school began I resigned myself to the inevitable and was doing pretty well, I thought. I loved my students. They gave me life and challenge. My roommate was just a part of it. I had said I would accept a roommate when I applied for the job. There was only one apartment, of course, so there just wasn't any question about it.

Mrs. Campbell liked to cook and clean. I dreamed and moaned of my misery. I was especially miserable on the eve of my wedding anniversary, the first one in eighteen years I would have to spend alone — and alone they would be forever.

"What you need is to get out," Mrs. Campbell said. "You need to mix with folks, and to have a drink, maybe, and dance. You don't die just because someone you love dies. The world goes on. I'm taking you out tomorrow night . . . to the den of iniquity."

This was our name for the Fairview Inn, where the drinking and dancing was quite as robust as during gold rush days, in my way of thinking. There was always music and profanity and men stealing glances from the uncurtained windows as Mrs. Campbell and I went for our mail or to the grocery store. I never went anywhere alone, nor anywhere at all unless it was a school function.

Curiosity is one thing which most women can't overcome, and I guess I'm no different. The old saloon was particularly appealing to me, or would have been as a historical spot to write about, if I were still writing. Yet I had been in Alaska five months and there was still a wall between me and my typewriter.

The dinner was good Alaskan cooking served family style. Much to my surprise there were several familiar faces inside the Fairview, and it didn't look so much like a den of iniquity as I had thought.

"Come on, we're going to have a drink," Mrs. Campbell said as the music sounded more inviting. "I like an after dinner drink, and I want to see inside this bar. They can't fire us, at least they could hardly run us off before the end of the school year since the spring term has already started."

I did have an after dinner drink, and another. The people were all so friendly. They welcomed us. They didn't look down their noses at us because we were teachers in a bar. They seemed happy we had finally come to the party.

I should have known better, but one of the men on our school board, Jim Haisley, asked me to dance. His wife, Irene, insisted that I do so. In Alaska all teachers dance. Otherwise, they're considered snobbish having no desire to associate with the village folk. This was a revelation to me, so I danced.

Common sense told me not to accept that third drink; but Frank Monnekies, proprietor of the inn, had just come in and seemed so happy we were there. He had done so much for the school that we couldn't refuse. I would just sort of let it set while I danced. I had always loved to dance. I was having a ball, the first good time I had had in Alaska, until someone played a record that my husband and I used to dance by. The record that I used to dance to with Dick Carey, I was now dancing to with a stranger, and on our wedding anniversary.

I started blubbering and Mrs. Campbell took me home.

"The very idea," she cut me down the next day. "Can't you keep your bawling to yourself? Other people have had sorrow. You could at least maintain your dignity as a teacher."

Although I knew she was right, I didn't love her any the more.

"You're young," Mrs. Campbell often said, in an envious tone, I thought, "at least young in comparison to me — and not too ugly, not too bad at all. The men still look at you, I see."

The very thought of ever loving another man made me want to fight. She didn't have to desiccate my beautiful mountain, either, by reminding me of the fact that I was a female and Don

48

Sheldon a male. I hated her. I would be glad when school was out. I would finish my contract, but I would teach elsewhere the next year. I would never live with her again.

Resigned to my fate, I tried to make myself believe that she was just a sour old lady, although she did seem to have some very sterling qualities and one couldn't help but admire her guts. I wondered about her husband, if he had died. Somehow she never mentioned her husband, but always her four children and her grandchildren.

Despite my disgrace at the bar, school and civic projects and events were coming up and a teacher in Alaska is supposed to be a civic leader. Vaguely I remembered plans being made for the March of Dimes, rather elaborate ones for so small a village.

When Mrs. Frank (Minnie) Swanda is coordinator, she does things up right. Minnie is Big Dorothy's mother — and Little Dorothy's grandmother, of course.

While living in Anchorage, Minnie served a term as president of the Anchorage Business Woman's Club. She was sent to Europe to represent Alaska and stood before the heads of state in Paris, pointing out opportunity unlimited for women in Alaska, even as a territory.

Frank Swanda was one of Alaska's first registered guides. His stories, like those of his wife, would no doubt have been given recognition many times, if there had been anyone in this section of the Alaskan wilderness to write about them. Frank was the first to attempt to shoot the rapids of Devil's Canyon up the Susitna River, about a hundred miles northeast of Talkeetna. He did not make it through. No one has. All three of the boats, which carried the geophysical party he was guiding, capsized. Without Frank's quick thinking, perhaps all seven men would have drowned — or starved to death during the six days they spent without rations or shelter. Frank peeled dry birch bark from trees and started a fire. He improvised a fishhook from a paper clip one of the men had in his pocket and caught grayling with a fly made from colorful threads pulled from their clothing. Don Sheldon, as he would, featured in this rescue, landing a float plane on the river in Devil's Canyon — after a helicopter crashed and killed two persons during the attempted rescue.

49

But back to our March of Dimes. Minnie planned three gala events: a bingo game at the Talkeetna Roadhouse, owned by Mr. and Mrs. Carol Close; a spaghetti dinner at the Fairview Inn with Frank Monnekies and George Hotle as hosts; and a dance and floor show at the newly opened Rainbow Lodge which had been put in by Lena Morrison, her sister Fern Cabral from Hawaii, and Don Sheldon. This gave two completely modern hotels in our town. Both the Rainbow Lodge and the Talkeetna Motel featured a glassed-in view of Mt. McKinley — and a bath with every room. Would our sleepy village waken from her lethargy and become a resort town?

No doubt things were booming charity-wise.

"For Heaven's sake," Mrs. Campbell chided, "can't you stop mooning at that mountain long enough to get into the swing of things. Aren't you interested in 'sweet charity'? Are you going to this bingo game of your own accord or do I have to drag you?"

I did go to the bingo game, to the spaghetti dinner and to the dance — and loved it. Not so much for charity's sake; but because I was enjoying them. Like Minnie advertised, "GO TO THEM ALL AND HAVE A BALL." And like Lena said, "Any excuse for a party in Talkeetna is just what we were looking for, the more the better."

Certainly I found exciting copy for "Talkeetna Topics" and a great deal to brag about since our little village raised more per capita than any other town in the nation. How proud we were. But Talkeetna always had a heart, a big one, even though there was continual feuding from bar to bar.

"When Spring Holiday comes and we go into Anchorage for Teacher's Convention, let's have Don fly us in," Mrs. Campbell suggested one morning as we both sat long past breakfast, lost in the pink and blue McKinley mood of early morning splendor. In summer she is clothed in white ermine, but in winter her pinks and blues are as soft as silent hope. "While we are there," she suggested, "you might find a book on Mt. McKinley and mountain climbing — or even some material on Don Sheldon."

Did she mean it? Could she possibly be on my side? In Anchorage I did load up with everything which I could find on pilots and flying in Alaska. There was no book, as such, on Mt.

McKinley at that time; but I did find one on mountaineering in general and a treasure in *Glacier Pilot*, which told of Bob Reeve, now owner of Reeve Aleutian Airways, making the first glacier landings in Alaska.

When Sheldon raised an eyebrow at the number of packages chucked into the plane from the Book Cache, I stated I was going to give my ninth graders a unit on Alaskan History, and did. My motives were a bit selfish; yet we all learned a lot about the 49th state, and the boys really went for the stories I brought back about early days of flying in Alaska.

"Did you hear who's in town?" Mrs. Campbell asked one afternoon as she breezed in from school. "Dr. Bradford Washburn."

"Dr. Bradford Washburn," I repeated as if hit by a sonic boom. "You can't mean *the* Dr. Bradford Washburn, Director of the Boston Museum of Science, the one I wrote about in Don's story. The one who told Don where to land on McKinley?"

"None other," she replied in a matter of fact tone.

"What's he doing here?"

"That comes under your heading, doesn't it? You're the reporter. Don just happened to mention it to me as I walked past the hangar. Said they were going to be flying Mt. McKinley.

"Do you know where he is?"

"Don said he's staying at the Rainbow Lodge."

I couldn't get there fast enough. Doing a news column gave me an opportunity to ask what's in the offing, to say the least.

CHAPTER V

DR. BRADFORD WASHBURN

"Where's Dr. Washburn?" I asked of Lena as I entered the Rainbow and cornered her in the kitchen. I want to meet him. Do you think he will talk with me?"

"Not so fast," Lena cautioned. "I haven't answered the first question yet. Now why do you want to see Dr. Washburn?"

"For an interview. Sounds like a good story possibility. He's news within himself. I'm a reporter, don't you remember?"

"How could I forget." she answered sarcastically, no doubt thinking of the many times I had mentioned wanting to fly Mt. McKinley with Don, her partner in the Morrison-Sheldon Air Service.

"But this is news," I repeated emphatically. "The director of the Boston Museum is here."

"So what?" she countered with a little more sarcasm. "He comes here every year. What's news about that?"

"Where is he?" I asked defiantly. "I came here to talk with him. I want to see him."

"Then take a look," Lena said with a shrug of her shoulders. "He's right out there cutting trees that block my view of the mountains."

"Would it be out of order, or do you think he would mind if I . . ."

"Try and see for yourself if you don't mind getting hip deep in snow, chasing a man, that is. My dinner's going to burn. He and Don are going to have dinner right here within an hour. Couldn't it wait? Who are you to think this man will take time off for gabbing. He's busy. He's doing something for me."

My silence was pretty loud as I whirled for the door.

"There's some snow shoes stuck in the bank outside the door, if you think you can wear them. News stories are getting more important all the time."

Fortunately Dr. Washburn was quite easy to talk with. Without a doubt he is one of the friendliest, most helpful, and unpretentious persons whom I have ever interviewed. Although he was probably a little past mountain climbing age, he looked in perfect physical condition and there was no doubt in my mind that he would have no trouble keeping up with the best of them. "I've climbed the mountain more times than anyone else," he said in all modesty, "but this is not why I'm here this time. I'm completing a picture book, it should be off the press this fall." Naturally I wanted to know all about it for a story. Since he and Don worked together so much it was impossible to mention one without the other somehow cropping in. This was fine, in so far as I was concerned. In fact, I even worked it into the lead for a story published in the *Anchorage Daily Times*, April 1, 1963. I quote:

"Mountain climbing will be tough this year," commented Dr. H. Bradford Washburn, Jr., director the Museum of Sciences of Boston, as he finished a week of photographic reconnaissance flights with Don Sheldon for a picture book which he is compiling on Mt. McKinley.

"'In spots she's nothing but enormous sheets of blue-white ice. It must have rained hard up to the 15,000 foot level last fall,' said the foremost authority on the mountain.

"Only once before, in 1953, has Washburn, who has been climbing and photographing the McKinley range for thirty years seen such a phenomenon. Rain at such an altitude is rare. The men comprising this year's bumper crop of scientific and mountain climbing expeditions will face sheer rock ridges wreathed in ice. The Wickersham Wall, 14,000 foot north face of McKinley, is the world's longest continuous wall of ice and snow.

"This time Dr. Washburn did not come to climb; but perhaps no man has a more intimate knowledge of the unpredictable treachery of the peak. He has climbed the mountain no less than three times, on several types of expeditions, and by various approaches.

"For years he had been photographing McKinley, sometimes for mapping and scientific study; but this time strictly for his book of photos which will be the first large-scale picture book on McKinley.

"The book, which will contain about 125 shots of the McKinley Range, will be published by the Harvard University Press. The photo plates, however, will be made in Europe. The scientist, who has worked with the Swiss in developing a new type of contour map, says that they take more time with their work and are more precise and "meticulous" than we. This he credits to the fact that in America we always seem in a hurry. The book will be a large format, probably 12" x 14". Except for photo captions, there will be no text.

"Mt. McKinley, thanks to Washburn and the Swiss map makers, is the best mapped high country in the world. Done in seven colors and scaled 1¼ inches to the mile, the map, besides being a thing of beauty, is an indispensable atlas to scientists, geologists, and mountain climbers.

"Yet it is more than this. In 1960, during the most massive mountain rescue operations in U.S. history . . ."

Here I related the story of Washburn calling Don and pinpointing the yet un-named basin where Don made the highest fixed-wing aircraft landing on Mt. McKinley. Continuing with my story — already Bill Tobin had made me a correspondent for the *Anchorage Daily Times* — I wrote about Mrs. Washburn, since I had mentioned Mrs. Helga Bading and her rescue. Quote:

"And speaking of women climbers, Dr. Washburn's wife, Barbara, was the first woman to climb McKinley, and others have followed. Whether or not another girl has gone the north peak, Barbara was the first to climb both the north and the south.

"For picture taking Washburn is using a 1927 Fairchild. He carries a massive, seventy-five foot roll of film upon which he can make 8" x 10" photos — 110 of them. The old Fairchild K-6, which is no longer in production, is Washburn's favored camera for scenic shots in black and white. Despite its enormous size, he has flown over the mountain with it on numerous expeditions since 1936. A good many color shots will go into the book. For those he uses a 35 mm camera . . ." Endquote.

The story was even longer, telling of Washburn's infra red experiments for Eastman Kodak, and of observations made to measure cosmic radiation high up on McKinley. Uncle Sam made use of his lofty experiments in the Office of Naval Research's cosmic ray studies.

Don liked the story I did on Washburn and told me so. The trap I had set worked. He wanted to talk of the difficulties which would be faced by the bumper crop of mountain climbers, the first of which were due within two weeks.

Don told me that one of the things which made climbing McKinley more dangerous than other mountains was the fact that it was never avalanche free. In other parts of the world peaks freeze solidly at night, but in the arctic the sun never goes down during the climbing season. Avalanche conditions are encountered around the clock. The blinding glare of the sun is relentless as it can be; and in Don's own words, "only in the Arctic is the sun cruel enough to cook a man's tonsils as he gasps for oxygen."

In speaking of the unusual hazards faced in the Alaska range, Sheldon mentioned such climbers as world famed Alpine specialists Heinrich Herrer, the great Riccardo Cassin, and many other renowned climbers who have breezed through "class 6" climbs only to fall victim to the radical high altitude and chill factor in the Alaska group.

"And the first climbers this year are going to try the East Face, aren't they?" I asked hopefully.

"You bet, Kid, and she's never been climbed. Four previous expeditions on this approach have met with complete failure."

"May I quote you?"

That "Why didn't I run?" look told me Don realized he had fallen into a trap.

"Reporters make some mighty gory mistakes, which are innocent enough insofar as the reporter is concerned; but nevertheless these mistakes make a fool of the subject. You can't write about something you don't know, Kid."

Seemed to me I'd heard these words before.

"Anyone can ride in a plane, lots of people drive them; but very few people know Mt. McKinley, not even the men who have climbed her. You've got to know how she reacts. She's like a woman, always in a different mood and twice as treacherous."

"But if I ever got to the mountain . . ."

"NOT FOR A WOMAN," he reminded, then relented a bit. "But since you're so wound up in this story, go ahead. I'll give you the lists and dates of the twelve groups I have scheduled. Biggest year yet — but keep off the flying end!"

"Could I quote you, just what you've said about the mountain?"

"Should have known better, but if you won't go off on some tangent . . . !"

Of course Mrs. Campbell complained of my working all night, but I knew her better now. I even liked her, and at times we confided in each other.

I told her of my father and mother. How seven members of my family had died within three years.

"That's why I left for Alaska," I confessed. "Our family physician diagnosed my heart trouble without the aid of a stethoscope." "You don't need sympathy from your friends," he advised, "what you need is to get out. Get far enough away that you will see nothing nor anyone who reminds you of what has happened."

"It may not have occurred to you that other people have trouble, too," Mrs. Campbell reminded. "My daughter was killed in a car wreck on her wedding day."

I couldn't think of anything to say which could help. What if something should happen to my one and only daughter? "I didn't understand," I finally managed in way of apology.

"Now don't go feeling sorry for me, I'll have no part of it. I hated to be so rough on you, but I had to be."

Then she apologized, saying that the only way she felt she could bring me out of feeling sorry for myself was to incur my wrath. How well her psychology worked. No one is any dearer to me than Mildred Campbell. But that doesn't mean she isn't arsenic under lilac. She can pull some "little old white-headed lady" antics so smoothly that the best of them fall, including Don and myself, despite the fact that we have laughed at and loved her shenanigans ever since.

This was the day she agreed to my calling her "Mildred," but not in front of other persons, and no one else was to do so. A teacher should retain her dignity at all times, she reminded as I remembered the bar incident.

"And did I hear one of my pupils call you Mary Carey? If I had been sure I would have boxed his ears."

"Never mind," I said. "No doubt that's what his folks call me. Half the people in town address me that way. Seems logical to me, and not too disrespectful since I use "Mary Carey" on my newspaper columns and stories. I don't mind, so long as my students address me as 'Mrs. Carey.' "

"Well, I should think so."

That's the way things were rocking when the first group of mountain climbers hit Talkeetna. They came on the train, as many do, with all their gear. From Talkeetna Don flies them to the mountain. I saw Don's pick-up truck at the railroad station. The train came in on schedule, 12:30 noon. How I wanted to get a picture. Surely it would be time for books before they ever got together at the hangar. I just had to get photos and learn their names and a little about them. But by the time they got their gear to the hangar I had already begun my first lesson of the afternoon.

How long would they be at the hangar? Would Don fly them to the mountain one at a time? My eyes were across the narrow runway as much as on my books. I saw the student's eyes stray, too. Although mountain climbers came every year, they were always new and interesting.

We had physical education period at 2:00 P.M. Snow was still on the ground, but that made little difference to my group. We played soccer, and the snow cushioned the fall. I usually played with them. At first, when I was knocked down the boys would stop, apologize and help me up. I ended that right away. "I'm just one of the team on the playing field," I coached. "Please don't apologize or stop to help me up when you bowl me over. It slows the game."

As few of us as there were, all players were needed. Since there were six boys and only two girls in the class, the girls contented themselves with boys' sports. Clothes were no problem since the girls wore stretch pants rather than dresses, which is more practical in Alaska, and much warmer.

Living in the schoolhouse made it easy for me to wear a dress. Each day I would make the next day's written assignment and give the students a short study period just before physical education. Near the close of the study period I would slip up the stairs and into slacks. On this day I failed to do so. As the hands of the clock neared two, one of my girls, Susan Devore, a precious and helpful student, whispered and asked me if I had forgotten to change.

It was then I confessed that I was not going to play with them that day, but was going to try to get pictures of he mountain climbers. As yet, I had still never gotten a single shot at Sheldon, nor at climbers.

When Don Sheldon saw me coming toward the hangar with camera and note pad he asked why I wasn't with my "knuckle heads." When I told him what I wanted he said I should go back to my students. There would be enough time for this sort of thing after school was out.

The next hour was long and fraught with misgivings. The activity outside our window helped some. I never realized how much preparation there was to be made before flying anyone to the mountain. Stacks and stacks of gear had to be sorted and re-packed for air drops. Only a small amount of survival gear could be taken with each man for the glacier landing. Yet each one had to carry in a sleeping bag, rations and emergency gear for himself. One could never tell how long he might be alone on a glacier. Don might land one climber there and it be perfectly clear; but before he could get back with another one the mountain might be all clobbered in and stay that way for a week.

I became desperate when I saw Don tying snow shoes to the strut of the plane and the hands of the clock had not reached four. Gear was packed inside, and it looked as if the first climber would be gone before school was out. He was crawling into the plane when Don said something, pointing to a spruce tree. Don loped over to the tree, broke off a short bough, and indicated the climber should do likewise. I made it just as the climber was again crawling into the plane and Don was handing him the boughs.

"What are they for?" I asked.

"To mark touch-down," Don replied. "In a white world you cannot gauge touch-down."

It made no sense at all to me, but I asked Don if he would hold still with the last of the boughs as he handed them inside the plane to the climber. He accomodated, reluctantly, and they were off.

From the rest of the climbers I found out the name of the first climber Don had ferried in, Warren Blesser. He was stationed at Ft. Wainwright, out of Fairbanks.

The remaining mountaineers explained that Don had said the spruce boughs were to be thrown from the plane to make a dark spot on the snow, which he could see and use to help gauge touch-down. A series of these spruce boughs marked a landing field on a glacier in the vast whiteness, where it is sometimes impossible to tell where snow and sky meet.

"If the spruce just disappears," one of them quoted Sheldon, "No dice! Crevasse!"

Don airlifted all the climbers to the glacier with little difficulty and again all was quiet in Talkeetna.

Soon more climbers would be coming in. The first expedition had been on the mountain three weeks and was pinned down by weather. I had gotten that picture I made of Warren Blesser and the spruce boughs into the paper, as well of one of Don with the Alaskan-Teton group, as they called themselves.

Can you feature trying to get a picture into a newspaper while it is still news, yet having to send the film away by train to have it developed, wait for it to come back by train — and the train running only twice weekly? I did have a problem, but I got my stories out as soon as they happened, even though Mildred always fumed at my late hours, somewhat good naturedly now. Strange I hadn't noticed it before, but she was quite witty. Could I have mistaken her dry sense of wit for sarcasm? The village folk loved her.

For three weeks I worried Don for news, each time he flew in from the mountain. His glacier flights were not hard to distinguish because when he flew to the mountain he took off in his yellow Super Cub with ski-wheels. He has planes for every occasion, including a pontoon plane. The snow was gone from the village strip, but by lowering his retractable skis during flight, he could land on snow, then raise them before returning to the graveled strip.

Then, after he came in from one particular flight he seemed worried and gave in to my questioning.

"The expedition now on the mountain is fighting case-hardened ice and snow to their eyeballs," he explained, and I knew he was talking for publication. "This group of Teton guides has climbed little over 7,000 feet in three weeks, since I landed them on the 5,800 foot level," Don fretted. "Yet, considering the weather, their progress is encouraging.

My progress was encouraging, too. The story appeared May 20 in Anchorage and Fairbanks papers, and it was picked up on the wires.

I tried to help Don in every way I could with the climbers. He had many air drops to make. Soon my roommate and I were making cookies and buying fresh fruit to be put into boxes for air drops to the climbers. I was writing to girl friends and mothers for the climbers.

"If I could ever help you with an air drop I would be glad to," I reminded Don as I passed by the hangar. "Is there anything the boys especially like?"

"Ice cream," came his reply. "Nothing as good as ice cream for sun-scorched tonsils. You're doing some mighty fine writing, Kid, but the mountain is no place for you. Might have to walk back."

"But I'm a grandmother," I refuted. "I've already lived a good life. If I can't keep living — then I'm not alive anyway."

"Don't tell your secrets, Kid. You don't qualify as a grandmother and no one would believe you anyway, so keep it quiet. One thing is certain, though, no one doubts that Mary Carey is alive!"

"Sush with the mush!" I flung back as his eyes twinkled. "I just can't write a story unless I live it. I can't describe that mountain."

The Don Liska and Dick Barrymore groups came in. A Canadian group led by Hans Gmoser was expected in on May 26. A twelve-man expedition led by Dick McGowan of Seattle was scheduled for the last day of May. Thank heaven, school would be out. There were more stories than I could write, but I was no closer to the mountain.

Mildred and I became expert at packing boxes for air drops. She made cookies and we bought fruit and vegetables; but she said that ice cream, at $2.50 per gallon, was just too expensive for her Scotch blood — with so many on the mountain and each climber able to eat a gallon as an appetizer. All groceries had to be wrapped well. Mail was tied quite securely and tucked into the center of the box after it had been cached in a plastic bag and tied with a string so that if the box were to burst open when it was dropped the mail wouldn't get wet, lost or scattered. We were working together and enjoying it.

"The Sheldon 'shuttle' from Talkeetna to Mt. McKinley is now on a 24-hour schedule," I wrote, telling of mountain climbing activity through news column and story.

Only one week of school left now, and it was a good thing because I never slighted teaching so much in my life. Everything was going at such a feverish rate that the students hardly seemed to notice, or else they were too engrossed in their own activity.

Two days before school was out Don appeared at the school-house door just as we turned out for lunch.

"Hurry," he called from the doorway. "We've gotta get movin.' Can you get a substitute this afternoon? Don't just stand there. You want to go to the mountain, don't you? Grab your fluffies and cameras." (Don always called eider down and such things as Arctic wear "fluffy.")

I sent a lanky, six-foot ninth grader, Ronald Robeson, whose mother had said she would substitute for me on a minute's notice, scrambling home. Vera Robeson, a homesteading widow from Texas was as good as her word.

Mrs. Robeson arrived a breath ahead of Don. I pointed at my lesson plans on my desk as I saw him drive up and heard him call:

CHAPTER VI

I FLY MT. McKINLEY

"Hurry! Hop in the truck, got to keep movin'," sounded the familiar phrase. "We're leaving from the F.A.A. field," he explained as we drove past the hangar and headed for the larger strip, just outside town.

Trying to keep "fluffy stuff," three cameras — color, black and white, and movie — plus film together, I hit the runway before Don could open the pick-up door for me at the strip. I headed for 39-Tango, paying no attention to any other plane. As usual, there were six or eight planes parked around. Suddenly I realized 39-Tango was already inhabited — a Colonel with a lot of brass.

"You ride in that plane," Don pointed. "Colonel Bennett goes with me. Ft. Wainright wanting to check on their boy, Warren Blesser. Might be a first in it. The East Face is still unscaled, insofar as we know."

I tried not to show my disappointment, and indeed I was not disappointed because I was headed for the mountain.

"You ride with Stu Ramstad. Stu's a good pilot," Don explained. "We have eighteen air drops to make, so you'll have plenty of action. Shoot away! I see you've brought your movie camera, too."

A quick intro to Stu and we were on our way. Suddenly I was remembering what Don said about eighteen air drops and that it took him two weeks to clean his plane after he took another woman to the mountain. Tricked! I should have known it. But it didn't matter now. I was headed for Mt. McKinley!

The granduer of what we saw as we flew up glaciers and through walled canyons was something I could never describe. No one could. It was a different world. Don led the way, and just the minute I was sure he would crash into a solid rock wall of the Great Gorge, he disappeared at a right angle. We made the same sharp turn and emerged into a huge basin. Lengthwise it extended farther than I could see into the whiteness. Crosswise it was a broad, frozen river, inching its way through unrelenting walls of granite throughout the centuries.

"I've been in here several times to help Don with air drops," explained my pilot as we bored on and on through the whitest world I have ever seen. "I've helped him through peak mountain climbing and hunting seasons for several years."

"I trust you, all the way," I said. "It's just that I've never seen anything like this and it leaves me sort of speechless."

"Look! Look below us. There they are! The climbers! Don is right over their camp."

I though we were already low enough to grab a snowball, but Don's plane was below us and no bigger than a dragon fly. Those yellow and orange handkerchiefs, were they tents?

SWOOSH! Up we climbed a razor-edge while I was still looking backward, trying to figure out whether those specks beside the tents were men.

Suddenly my camera was too heavy to lift. I felt as if I would sink through the tail of the plane. My body was made of mercury. We couldn't climb any more! We would crash into this razor rim! We were stalling!

But we were not. We just levelled off and I almost caught my breath when . . . ZOOM! Down we bored. Only my seat belt held me down, otherwise I would have floated free, and my head would have hit a little harder against the top of the cockpit than it did.

"There's a good shot," Stu pointed as we levelled off again. "Don's going in low, right over their camp."

"What's the matter with you guys?" Don chided over the intercom. "Thought you were coming in close enough for a picture. Bring her in a little closer, Stu, if you have the feel of this basin."

If this was just the beginning — I thought, but there was no time for thinking. As Stu gave her full bore we again climbed that razor edge, and it seemed as close as before. The only difference was that I thought, since we had made it once, maybe we could make it again without stalling or crashing. As we levelled off I tried to get ready with my cameras but I had not caught them in my view finder until we were again down that elevator shaft.

Around and around, time after time. My stomach churned and my heart pounded and my breath failed to come. Thank heaven, Stu was most helpful and always yelled: "There they are!" and pointed, just before we zoomed over them. I really couldn't have sworn whether we were upside down or right side up.

"Did you see that?" Don chuckled over the intercom, "If that guy hadn't done a nose dive that can of alcohol would have hit him on the head. How's that for dive bombing? Is Mary getting enough pictures? Can she see the air drops beneath my plane? Whoops! Trouble! Box caught on the fuselage. Ribbon's holding her. Cut the ribbon, Colonel, cut it!"

"Wow! The Colonel didn't chuck that one far enough away from the plane," Stu observed. "There she goes! That one's lost; but it could have caused real trouble. We'll have to do better ourselves," he said as he readied his first drop.

Again we were up and over. The next time I saw a box shoot from Don's plane as from a cannon. The colonel must have given it all the push he had.

I was so engrossed and overwhelmed by the icy wind rushing into the plane as Stu lowered the window to make a drop, that I forgot to click my shutter.

"You're on target," Don complimented Stu, "but did Mary get a good shot of that drop?" he asked as if nothing had gone wrong.

I said I didn't think I had, in the understatement of a lifetime. Don knew I hadn't.

"If you'll come down a little closer," Don coaxed, "she can get a better shot. There's still a lot of room between you and the snow. But watch! This stuff's tricky."

He never made one reference to his own close call as we shot up the rolly-coaster and down again, even closer; but I did feel I got a satisfactory shot. I had to!

"Did you get her?" came Don's voice into the cockpit again.

"Sure thing!" I replied loudly enough for the mike to pick me up from the back seat. I certainly hoped my voice sounded convincing enough this time. Each time around I was sure we would crash as closer and closer we came to those yawning, blue-green chasms beneath us on the floor of the glacier. Nearer touch-down they looked bigger and deeper, and as dangerous as the granite walls above.

"One more drop and we go check on the Blesser group," Don explained. "Are you ready for the other side of the mountain? Follow me to the East Face!"

After the next drop we did not head up the rim, but up the glacier. On and on, winding in and out, dodging from one glacier to another. How many I can't remember. We headed down what seemed to be dead ends and through mile-high canyon walls. When we finally got to the north side we flew alongside an endless wall of ice and snow.

"That's the Wickersham Wall," Don explained from his plane, "longest continuous ice-wall in the world."

We flew high over the Peters glacier, then toward the East Face, dodging spires and peaks, crossing again from one glacier to another.

Then I saw what I supposed to be the three steps of the East Face. All of them vertical walls, each higher than the other.

"Can't get close enough to see," Don commented as I felt he was within wing-tip distance of the wall. "Down draft on this side. Makes permanent fixtures of guys who fly in too close. Getting low on gas. Best give her up for today. One more look and we head for home."

But we didn't find them on the next look, so back through the canyons we curled. Rounding the East Buttress and dodging a spire, we burst through a slot into space again. Beautiful space ringed with jagged peaks like in the most fantastic science fiction.

"It's the Amphitheater of the Ruth Glacier," Don oriented, speaking to the Colonel, yet with the intercom open, as if he were talking to me, too. "You could throw the State of Rhode Island in it. We leave through the Great Gorge."

I was looking hard because I had studied Dr. Bradford's map well. As I tried to make sure of my bearings, Don broke in again,

"Ask Mary if she sees that rotten hunk of granite to the left? That's what the German expedition is going to try to climb. A two-mile high hunk of vertical granite shaped like a tooth. That's the Moose's Tooth and nobody's ever climbed her."

Later I found out that it always looked darker than the rest of the range because its walls are so steep that snow and ice cannot cling to them. At the time it never occurred to me that I would be landing on a ledge at a camp near the base of it.

By air the Moose's Tooth is about thirty minutes from Talkeetna, the Ruth and Kahiltna Glaciers, upon which Don often lands with mountain climbers, thirty-four and forty minutes respectively.

By the time we reached the F.A.A. strip my stomach had almost stopped churning, and I was breathing more or less normally. As soon as we landed and I could jump from the plane I yelled "WHOOPEE! FUN!" loudly enough for Don to hear me at the other plane, whose prop was already still. The Colonel, who was crawling out, looked as pale as I felt.

Don looked at me searchingly. "You mean you really liked it?"

"Loved it!" I said truthfully. "Loved every minute of it," I said without reservation; yet if I had been completely truthful, I could have said my knees were a little trembly. But at least there was no plane to clean up.

Don opened the door to the pick-up and invited the Colonel and me to hop in.

Not knowing that Don is one Alaskan who never touches a drink, the Colonel offered to "set 'em up."

Saying "later" — as he usually passed such invitations off, Don dropped the Colonel at the Rainbow Lodge and drove me to the schoolhouse.

"You'll do, Kid," he said in the way of about the most appreciated compliment I've ever had from Don, "but if you're going roaring around that mountain you had better get some mukluks and fluffies."

Did he mean it? Was I really in? Did this mean he would fly me to the mountain himself?

"I'll have the story ready in the morning," I promised, "and the photos as soon as I can get them back. Maybe I'll just send one roll of film to each newspaper office. They promised to develop it if I get a real good story."

One more day of school. Who needed sleep? Mechanically I graded papers and averaged grades; but my thoughts were with the climbers on the mountain, especially the Alaskan-Teton group, which Don always called the Blesser Expedition. Had they made it over the sheer East Face? Twice Don flew up to check and said he failed to see them, but more than likely they were just pinned down by weather.

Saturday morning, when Don came out of his own back yard and saw Mildred and me sitting upstairs at our breakfast table, he stopped below our window long enough to ask how the mountain looked from our view. Never could the weather have been more beautiful. I knew he had flown to the mountain the day before, but he didn't say a word about it. He no doubt was trying not to disturb my last day of school. I was trying hard not to push my luck.

After grinding his toe into the gravel for a faltering minute, as if trying to make up his mind, he looked squarely at the upstairs window and said to me, "Sharpen your eyeballs, Kid, and put on your fluffies."

"You mean we're going? Did you find them? Did they make it to the top? Can I get a picture?"

"Holy Mackerel, Kid, relax. We've got to find them before you get a picture."

"She'll be lucky if she finds her head," Mildred cut in. "See to your cameras. I'll tie up this box, it's finished except for the cookies I baked yesterday and the newspaper. You did say you wanted to send the last story you wrote about them, didn't you?"

In true Sheldon fashion, Don never mentioned sending me on my first flight to the mountain with Ramstad. He may or may not have done it to see if I would get sick, or he might have tried to give me enough of the mountain in one big dose. One thing is true, we've never made so many air drops on one run since.

I don't know what Don was thinking as we started this first flight together. He was probably scared, telling himself he was a fool. I tried to leave him in peace. He didn't say a word until we came near the foothills.

"See all those tracks down there in the snow? Bear pulled down a moose. They're mean when they come out of hibernation. Look what a struggle! Tore up ten acres of snow. We could track him if we tried, but the snow is up to your eyeballs here."

"What a battle for survival," was about all I could think. "There are tracks everywhere."

"But you see who won. Bear don't pull down moose except in the high country and at this time of the year, when there's no other food. See his tracks leading off in that direction, all the way around the base of that hill. He's a monster!"

After about five minutes of silence Don spoke again.

"This is the Great Gorge of the Ruth Glacier. Remember the Moose's Tooth? The Germans will be here next week to try to climb her. That's the Rooster's Comb to the left, and Mt. Barrille to the right."

67

I appreciated his being explicit.

"See straight ahead of us there? We're sailing out into the Ruth Amphitheater — west fork to left, east fork to right, McKinley dead ahead; but you can't see her for the peaks between. I've been told you could toss Grand Canyon into this Amphitheater as an appetizer, chew it up with the Moose's Tooth, swallow it through the gullet of the Great Gorge and spew it out and lose it in the great Alaskan wilderness."

Don has a unique way of telling anything. I know now that all his stories and comments should have been recorded; but he would never have gone for that.

Our plane seemed lost in the vastness of the Ruth Amphitheater, but Sheldon held his course and we headed through another canyon.

"Today we find them," Don said optimistically as we again neared the East Face. Around and around and around we churned. Closer and closer and closer we came to that immense, foreboding wall. How could anyone climb it? It looked utterly impossible.

"They've made it!" Don yelled gleefully. "See there, they've dug their pickaxes into the ice, right there. Right up over the tip of the wall! Maybe you'll get their picture."

But they weren't there. Only signs that they had been there. We couldn't spot them anywhere. The boulders were bigger than houses and the shadows around them dark and deep. Since no one had scaled the East Face previously, Don did not know which direction they would take. Maybe they were beneath an overhanging cornice, or tunnelling through a chimney. Everywhere there was case-hardened ice and rock, jagged rock and plenty of it.

We didn't seem to have searched too long when Don pointed and remarked:

"We'd better get out of here, fast!"

Clouds were boiling in below us and shutting off the mountain in places. As we sailed toward our previously smooth riding canyon the plane took the hiccups. Suddenly the bottom fell from beneath us and my head would have gone through the cockpit if my seat belt had not been fastened.

"Did you see that?" Don asked. "We were dropping at the rate of over fifteen hundred feet per minute."

I had no trouble believing him, although I could not see the instruments from the back seat of the Super Cub. It felt more like water than a hunk of air that we landed on. I have experienced a similar feeling when surfing in a speeding boat, climbing a wave and then dropping over the crest and splatting down — hard.

We were both pretty sick at not finding the climbers. Sunday she was all clobbered in again. On Monday Don said we would make another try. The weather was compatible, but the climbers had just disappeared from the face of the mountain. Don was jubilant when we finally located their tent: just one day's climb, he thought, from the top of the mountain. But they were not there.

Around and around we sailed. No climbers. They had to be there, but they weren't.

Back home again I telephoned my story to Editor Dave Galloway; and the *Fairbanks News-Miner* gave us a full front page banner headline. It read "DRAMA UNFOLDING ON MT. McKINLEY". In a smaller head, "SEARCHERS FAIL TO SPOT MEN NEAR TOP." Then came my story, which was published May 25, 1963:

"Somewhere above 17,000 feet, six men are near the top of Mt. McKinley; but a two-hour and twelve-minute search by this reporter and veteran glacier pilot Don Sheldon yesterday failed to reveal their location.

"Weather permitting, another reconnaissance will be made tomorrow in an attempt to determine whether they have made it to the top, or if they are in any type of trouble.

"These men, all climbing instructors, have been on the mountain thirty-one days. It was determined yesterday, although not officially confirmed, that these climbers are the first to scale the East Buttress. It is believed that they may also have reached the summit of Mt. McKinley, since Sheldon spotted their tents above the third and most difficult sheer face.

"The first mountaineers to conquer the East Buttress are: Pete Lev, Boulder, Colorado; Fred Wright, Burbank, California; Rod Newcomb, Jackson, Wyoming; Warren Blesser, Ft. Wainwright, Alaska; Jed Williamson, College Alaska; and Al Read of Denver . . ."

Before I was off the telephone I asked Dave Galloway a question, which I hated to — but one which never surprises an editor when a reporter goes after a story hard enough and long enough. Sometimes a newspaper gives a bonus for an exceptionally hard-fought story; but I didn't want anything for myself. I was thinking of the gas Sheldon had been out on this search, and the time. No one pays Sheldon for this. If we got a good story, would the *News-Miner* pick up the tab? Dave's answer made me quite happy.

I don't think I could have lived until the next day if it had not been for the stories that flew from my typewriter.

"We'll go higher tomorrow," Don promised. "The climbers are bound to be near the summit. We'll go as light as possible. Only one camera and one roll of film. No extra gear and no food. Sharpen your eyeballs and get some sleep."

I was thankful school was out. Two days of flying the mountain with a third coming up! My stories were given banner spreads. The eyes of the world were with us. We had to find them!

Over and over Don's words kept coming to me, "We'll go higher tomorrow."

I couldn't sleep. I knew the flight into thinner atmosphere would be more hazardous than the others. If I dozed, the plane began falling. Yawning crevasses opened beneath us. Again we were falling fifteen hundred feet per minute.

I crawled out of bed and wrote this little note to my daughter, Mrs. Frank Richardson of Houston, Texas:

May 24, 1963
Talkeetna, Alaska

To My Darling Daughter, Jeannie,

Tomorrow I am going to try something no woman has ever done before, fly over the top of Mt. McKinley in a small plane with Don Sheldon, looking for lost *mountain climbers.*

If anything should happen, remember that I am doing what I want to do and must do as a writer. Life without adventure is not life to me. I know I'll come back to write the story but in case we should have a little trouble, take good care of my darling grandbabies

70

and Frank, he's the most wonderful son-in-law one could ever have.

God could never have given me a more precious daughter. I thank Him for all the wonderful things He has done for me and for letting me do what I love most, live the stories I write.

With all my love,
Mother Mary

Tomorrow did come, and both Don and the weather were "Go!" I was ready and watching as he finished preparations. I had assumed he would go in his Super Club with ski-wheels. Reluctantly he pulled more gear, including the survival kit from 39-Tango, his Cessna 180 on wheels. I had never seen him take his sleeping bag from a plane in which he was preparing to make a trip. He checked to make sure I had no extra weight and teased me about going on a diet.

Don started the motor to let it warm up.

"Have you noticed we're on wheels?" he asked. "Skis hold you down. We have one bottle of oxygen between us. Are you sure you want to go? There's no second chance in case anything goes wrong. You still have time to think it over. Be sure before you crawl into the plane."

For a fleeting moment I remembered the note to my daughter, then said:

"This is the greatest! Are we ready? Let's get moving!"

Don wasted no time.

"How high can we go?" I asked as we sailed over the Susitna River and headed for McKinley. "Over 17,000? Above their tents?"

"The ceiling on this baby is nineteen thousand — absolute twenty thousand; but Mighty Mack is still higher. I don't know . . ."

Again his eyes were on the mountain. He had been studying it even before we took off.

"See that umbrella over the peak?" he asked. "That cloud that looks like a tilted umbrella," he explained.

I saw but didn't understand. It didn't look mean to me, not like the boiling clouds that had dropped us from eleven thousand to nine thousand feet in one-fourth of a minute the day before.

71

"Looks like a rising thermal," he said. "If we can just ride her up! We may be able to catch the tail end of it!"

Ride a cloud? Ride on that little umbrella angling up and over the mountain?

I looked at the phenomena so hard that I swore it disappeared right before my eyes as we came nearer.

"Can't tell," Don encouraged. "We're too close to see her now, but we'll know pretty soon," he yelled back at me over the roar of the plane's engine as we burst from the canyon of the Great Gorge into the Ruth Amphitheater.

"What a tunnel," I remarked, looking back at the jagged Rooster's Comb on the left, and the Moose's Tooth, towering two miles almost straight up, to the right.

"And what a theater," Don added. "I doubt that there's another this large, nor half so spectacular in the world. Too bad there are so few spectators," he lamented as we sailed into space.

Suddenly our plane, which seemed to fill the canyon with thundering defiance of wing-tip imprisonment, flew like a bird set free from a cage. Up! Up! and up we soared, higher than surrounding peaks, now, heading straight for the mighty one.

Floating over a rim I looked down into the deepest basin I have ever seen. An avalanche crashed to the bottom, churning as in a mixing bowl for the world.

"That's Thayer Basin," Don began his commentary, "elevation 12,000 feet at the base and 17,500 at the rim. There's an airliner down there, permanent fixture with seventeen persons aboard. Bored into the rocks. Could see the tail for a while, but she's covered now."

I wondered how many thousands of feet of snow were filled in at the bottom of this basin, deeper than Grand Canyon from rim to base. I wondered, if throughout the centuries it would fill. It was hard for me to realize, even though I had studied Dr. Bradford Washburn's unusually fine map for hours and hours during the long winter nights, that Mt. McKinley, turned upside down, would be over four times as deep as Grand Canyon, her own canyons and walls and spires in like dimension. Rising from near sea level, Mt. McKinley towers higher from her base than any other mountain in the world.

Don's voice brought me out of my reverie.

"Look! See that! Look at the altimeter!" He pointed excitedly at the gauges. "We've hit it! We'll sail around and come back for another lift."

I could hardly grasp the meaning of what was taking place. Were we really being lifted? Were we riding that cloud? On the second pass there was no doubt about it, even in my mind.

"Keep your eyeballs peeled," Don reminded as we hit the 17,500 foot level near where we had spotted their tent on a previous flight. Up and over the rim of Thayer Basin again, but no sign of the climbers.

"They must be higher," Don surmised as we again circled. Up again, past eighteen thousand, and around the rim of the South peak. Don skirted her wide on the lee side. Again we hit the rising air and gained elevation.

"Watch Denali Pass, between the North and South Peak, and keep your end of the oxygen tube in your mouth. But don't inhale too much or you'll get giggly."

I was wondering why Don came so close in on the east side of the mountain and gave so much berth to the west face, so I asked him.

"Got to watch her every minute. What lifts you up on one side of the mountain will slap you down on the other. These down drafts can make permanent fixtures of you, fast."

Again we hit the rising thermal. Up she inched, past eighteen thousand feet. Eighteen twenty-eight, eighteen fifty . . . up . . . up . . . nineteen thousand.

"Ceiling," Don yelled. "Keep your eyeballs peeled. We'll make another run at her."

Another wide circle then up to twenty thousand.

"Absolute!" cried Don gleefully; "but she's still rising. We'll ride her to a Mexican standstill."

"WHOOPEE! 20,300!" Don let out a big yell. "Watch for the climbers. Next time around we'll sail right over the summit!"

Contrary to my previous opinion, there was nothing but bald ice and snow on the summit. The sun hit it so brightly that it sent spangles skyward, like the top of the world sending out light beams.

As we circled for the last climb I saw a lot of huge granite boulders sticking up in Denali Pass, but no climbers.

"The wind might have them huddled under a boulder" Don reminded, "or it might have blown them right off the face of the peak!"

Almost every time he opened his mouth to comment, the oxygen tube fell from between his lips. Finally, he kept it clinched between his teeth as he talked. I had to keep reaching for my tube, too. We had left the masks behind because of their weight. The single tube coming from the bottle of gas was a long "Y," a slip-tube affair from which each of us sucked the clean tasting oxygen.

One camera was all the weight I had been allowed, and only one roll of film. I chose black and white, naturally, for the newspapers. I grabbed the camera as we reached the summit.

"No! No! Look now and shoot later, when we find them!" Again and again we roared over the summit.

I don't need to know what eternity iş like, I saw it.

"That's Cook Inlet," Don explained as we circled above the south side of the peak, where we did not expect to find climbers. "It's over 150 miles from here . . . and you can see right over into Canada. See that peak," he pointed as we again reached the east side, "that's Mt. Logan, the one on the far horizon. It's in Canada."

Suddenly we were laughing and singing. I started on a crazy little ditty, "On Top of Spaghetti, All Covered with Cheese," a parody someone had written to "On Top of Old Smokey," which was quite popular at that time.

Don tried to join me, or say something, and the tube fell from his mouth. I fumbled underneath the front seat for it, where it seemed to have lodged. Don looked toward the back, trying to help me.

Suddenly I realized Don's lips were as thin as paper and he looked blue. Although I felt quite exhilarated, when I saw his face I realized we had gotten too much oxygen, or not enough.

"Your face is blue," I said in alarm.

"And yours is green! We'd better go down for a breath of air.

At fourteen thousand feet we sort of regained our senses.

"If you're game, Kid, maybe we should look her over once more, near the top of the wall. The wind might have kept them pinned down and they couldn't crawl out of their hole in time for us to see them. By now the Yetis have heard us and will be out. We have a little oxygen left. What say?"

"Go!"

Again we were sailing out over Thayer Basin, heading for the top.

"Holy Mackerel!" Don ejaculated. "Look!" Snowshoes! Right there. On the second ridge above their tent. They're above eighteen thousand!"

Again we tried to hit the rising thermal, but it just wasn't there. We saw tracks, but no climbers. We made her up a little past nineteen thousand, and she all but stalled when Don tried for more altitude. We never made it over the top again that day. I doubt very seriously that we'll ever make it again.

Circling at 17,500 we took a good look at their camp. Could they possibly have made it to the top and be on their way down?

"I see their trail!" I yelled just as Don spotted the climbers. Jubilantly we sailed past, but caught a glimpse of only three men.

"We'll take a second look. They must have been pinned down all this time. Did you see any of the others?"

For a moment Don fretted, then concluded:

"No, they're the best. We'll turn around and take another look. You can see they've been doing a lot of stomping around. Maybe they're relaying."

His assumption was correct. This time we saw five of the men, but we knew all was well because they pointed toward the summit.

"Jeez, they're still climbing." Don marveled. "This group just doesn't give up. They'll make her, all the way!"

We made another pass and saw all six men. I snapped a shot just as they waved and was jubilant because I had a pic for the newspapers — mountain climbers in action, taken from a plane. *If my shot was good, it would be the first such news picture made of climbers on Mt. McKinley. I had my story, headlines.*

"But we can do better," Don promised as if reading my mind. "We'll catch them at the top, tomorrow. I'll need to make a mail drop to the Zogg-Liska group on the West Buttress. What if both groups reach the summit at the same time, from east and west buttresses? What a picture! We'll have a field day!"

But the next day it was raining in Talkeetna, and the next and the next, as it sometimes does, especially in spring. Visibility wasn't far beyond the end of your nose. It rained all week.

When, after ten days, it finally cleared there were two more groups of mountain climbers in Talkeetna waiting to be air-lifted to the glaciers. We had no way of knowing whether the Alaskan-Teton and Liska-Zogg groups had reached the summit.

CHAPTER VII

GLACIER RESCUE

"Load up with goodies and ice cream," Don Sheldon advised on the following morning as I was over at the hangar getting stories and pics of the newly arrived climbers — twelve in the Dick McGowan group and four in the Canadian.

I ran to the B & K Trading post, and here I guess I may as well confess that I did run, literally. That's how I got my Talkeetna moniker, "Running Mary". There were three Marys in our village, Red Mary, Black Mary . . . and because I ran so much, I became "Runing Mary." Jim Beaver, one of the biggest pranksters in Alaska, gave me that name, and it stuck.

Jim's pranks were many — but only one anecdote at the moment. At one time he had a bar in McGrath, during her golden days, or perhaps I should say copper, because one of the richest mines in Alaska was there. Gold was only a by-product.

Sometimes, on Sunday, when the narrow gauge was not in use, visitors were taken sight seeing on the historic and picturesque little coal burner. Maybe Jim had read too many westerns, or was overly imbibed, which for him was not an uncommon state.

When the narrow-gauge slowed for a bend, of which there were many, Jim Beaver crawled aboard, complete with mask and hog's leg, ordering the startled passengers to "Stick 'em up!" He had them all come forward, one at a time, and make a neat pile of billfolds, watches and other valuables. Watching some of the females in the background trying to conceal this or that of real or sentimental value gave Jim Beaver that shoulder-shaking laugh so bad that he had to jerk off his mask. Then he rolled in laughter and the drinks were on the house, of course.

Why someone hasn't killed this practical joker is more than I can figure out. Wanted to myself, not too long after we came to Talkeetna. In winter we always wear boots and carry our shoes along for special occasions. After the March of Dimes dance at the Rainbow Lodge, I changed back to boots and forgot my shoes. When I heard about them Jim Beaver was betting drinks that he had my shoes under his bed. He did. At the time I couldn't see a thing funny about this and other pranks, which he was always pulling; but now I love this character, too.

As I was saying earlier, before I interrupted myself to tell of Jim Beaver, I ran to the B & K Trading post to get goodies for the mountain climbers.

I bought carrots, celery, apples, oranges and even rutabaga turnips. Tomatoes and bananas just wouldn't stand the drop, nor my pocketbook the price. I bought a head of lettuce for ninety cents. The apples and oranges were twenty-five cents each. With six in the Blesser group and seven in the Zogg-Liska bunch it soon added up. Then came the ice cream; but that was some of the best money I've ever spent.

None of the new mountain climbers particularly enjoyed seeing me take off with Don and all of them still waiting on the ground. But Don wasn't sure of the weather — nor that we could even reach the climbers. The Alaskan-Teton group had been on the mountain forty days, and we knew they needed food.

However heavy the load this time didn't matter. A few miles north of Talkeetna we did get a bit above the overcast and could see the top of both the north and the south peak. Never was McKinley more beautiful.

Up and over Thayer Basin to look for the climbers. Don knew they had probably made the peak already, both groups; but we had to be sure. The tents of the Alaskan-Teton group were no longer at the 17,500 level, nor were they at the next lower camping level, 14,000 feet, so out we sailed over the glacier.

Don gave a whistle and pointed excitedly. "They've already made it and are down the glacier. See what they have stamped out!"

"PICK-UP" was tramped out in huge letters in the snow.

"They've made it!" I yelled as I grabbed for my camera. Before I could get them into focus they had vanished. How Don keeps that mountain straight I'll never know. I'm still turned around and sometimes upside down when flying it, even though I should be somewhat of a veteran.

Before I could even get my bearings we were zooming down over them again. This time we came quite low and they gave the victory signal. Don let out a war whoop. I must have let

78

out some sort of screech that let them know a female was aboard, because one guy in red underwear, who was probably soaking up a little sun, headed for a tent on the double.

We circled again and Don looked over the area for a possible landing. No dice! They were still too high on the glacier.

"Quick," he said, "scribble a note. Tell them I'll be back and pick them up at the eight thousand foot level, on the park boundary.

I scribbled like mad and stuck the note through all my tightly-tied strings into the box I had ready to drop as we circled.

"Bombs away!" Don shouted as we came in quite low again. I did better than I thought.

"Bull's eye, almost. See that guy headed for it. Now that other box, way out, and we'll head for the Zogg-Liska group. Looks like she's boiling in again from the south."

As he opened the window and gave the signal I chunked the second box as far out as I could, remembering what could happen if they did not clear the plane. Don said I was a fine bombardier, and I was quite proud of my new position.

High over the Kahiltna Peaks and down the West Buttress we flew, but saw no sign of the other group — not at first, anyway. Maybe we were too low on the glacier. Could they have made it to the summit, too? Back up the buttress we headed. Around another bend and Don spotted them. He always spotted climbers before I did. I kept hoping that just once I would spy them first, but I never did.

"They haven't made it to the top yet," Don observed. "No tracks going up."

Why hadn't I been sharp enough to make this small observation?

"We'll have to hurry," Don said. "Clouds boiling in."

Around we sailed over the Kahiltna Glacier. As Don instructed, I heaved out the box with their mail, being careful the "ribbon tail" did not catch inside the plane. I worked the next box into position from behind my seat as Don circled.

"Looks like we're too late," Don lamented, "the clouds beat us to the draw."

"They're gone!" I said, not being able to believe clouds could come in so fast.

"No use to make the drop. You've got to see your target — and we've got to get out of here!

We were in a cauldron of boiling steam, racing it from canyon to canyon, hoping it hadn't spilled in before us on the next turn. We were headed for Talkeetna; but if we got cut off I had no idea what Don could do.

"She's pretty soupy," he said, "but not real bad. You watch for rocks on the right side and I'll watch my side. Sing out if one pokes its head out of a cloud at us."

I'll swear Don smelled his way through those mile-high canyon walls. He follows a trail like a blood hound. Not once did we come close to becoming a permanent fixture — that I could see, anyhow.

Back in Talkeetna I became totally engrossed with the story. Eagerly I told of the forty-day saga of the six-man team of climbing instructors who had apparently reached the summit of Mt. McKinley via the previously unscaled East Face. Of their waiting to be airlifted by Don.

Carefully I reconstructed the story from the day they were ferried in on April 19. How it was determined by photographic reconnaissance that these climbers had become first on a new route, of the unsuccessful flights and of the May 29th flight when we spotted "PICK-UP" stamped out in the snow.

Meanwhile Don managed to pluck three of the six climbers off the glacier. Then weather closed in; but I was too busy with interview stories to worry much — not for a while, anyway. Rapidly I wrote:

"Three of the six climbers who scaled Mt. McKinley by the east buttress this month, a route never previously traversed, are resting in Talkeetna today and waiting for bush pilot Don Sheldon to fly their companions off the mountain.

"Sheldon returned Jed Williamson of College, Alaska; Al Read of Lakewood, Colorado; and Rod Newcomb of Jackson, Wyoming to Talkeetna Wednesday.

"Still on the mountain and waiting for the weather to clear so Sheldon can fly in to pick them up are Pete Lev of Boulder, Colorado; Warren Blesser of Ft. Wainwright, Alaska; and Fred Wright of Burbank, California.

"The returned men report that three of their group, Williamson, Newcomb, and Blesser attained the summit ridge by Denali

Gap but because of high winds and white-out conditions, they were turned back a mere fifty yards from the summit.

"Two days later, after the wind and clouds had dispersed, another attempt was made. This time the job was completed. Read, Lev and Newcomb reached the summit.

"The men reported there had been no serious mis-adventures especially from frost-bitten extremities; and with one exception they suffered little from higher altitudes. Naturally, breathing was more difficult, but their appetites were not affected radically. In fact, Lev became hungrier as the camps became higher.

" 'I just can't believe this is the same place,' Read said with amazement when he alighted from the plane in Talkeetna. 'When I left there was five feet of snow on the ground. Now it's summer and everything is green.'

" 'Just let me stand here and breathe it in,' remarked Newcomb. Trees! Real trees!' "

At the conclusion of my story I wrote: "Perhaps McKinley does have a 'Yeti,' or an 'Abominable Snowman,' but this reporter could have sworn it was just a man in long, red underwear sailing for a tent, when he heard a female screeching congratulations from a plane Wednesday."

Like everyone else who does not know Mt. McKinley, I assumed this would be the end of the drama. While waiting for the story which would tell of Don going in the following day to pick up the other three climbers to materialize, I was still interviewing the first successful mountain climbers whom I had ever known. Their observations and experiences were as exciting to me as they seemed to be to my readers.

The high winds were responsible for the extra time it took them to reach the summit. Once they were pinned down for ten days; but they all insisted the climb was worth it.

"It's one of the most beautiful routes to the summit," reported Williamson. "The solar radiation is fantastic."

While Don waited for the weather to clear so he could bring out the other three climbers and check on the Zogg-Liska group, I was compiling background material on the new groups who had come to conquer a mountain, but stayed in Talkeetna and waited for the weather to clear.

The nine-member climbing party led by Dick McGowan of Washington proved unusual. Perhaps it was the first guided

81

tour up the mountain. I found no record of any previous climb on McKinley where climbers were invited to pay a fee and join the climb, in this case, the Rainier Guide Service. In fact, Mc-Gowan seems to hold the franchise.

Among the interesting and unusual climbers in this group were two father and son teams. Both fathers were doctors: Dr. Wayne Smith, M.D., of Chehalis, Washington; and Dr. Ted Lathrop, M.D., of Oregon City, Oregon. Dr. Smith's son, Craig, was only fifteen years old. He could be the youngest person, if the climb was successful, to reach the summit of McKinley. Dr. Lathrop's son, Jim, was twenty. Although young, both boys had considerable climbing experience.

Speaking of fifteen-year-old Craig, Tom Nash of the Rocky Mountain Guide Service commented, "He has been officially tested for this trip. At Camp Muir he underwent an intensive, high-mountaineering program. He worked on route-finding techniques over glaciers and even did rope leading. He isn't climbing because his father is along, he is climbing because he is qualified."

Craig had already chalked up two victories at Mt. Rainier, the nation's fourth tallest peak; and father and son were eager to share the rope on McKinley.

A most unusual climber with this group was Miss Freda Walbrecht, a female attorney from Los Angeles, who would not confide her age, but without a doubt would be the oldest female to reach the summit, if their climb successful. I would have guessed her to be in her forties. But age would evidently be no factor against her. She seemed quite capable of taking whatever "Denali" — the great one, as the natives called McKinley — had to offer.

Among Miss Walbrecht's successes were Fujiyama in Japan, and Ixicahautel and Popocatepetl in Old Mexico. An old hand at adventure in Alaska, Freda has run the rapids on the Chitna, Copper and Kenai Rivers. Twice she has shot through the Grand Canyon riding the churning, muddy waters of the Colorado in a rubber neoprene raft.

Now Miss Walbrecht faces the most severe test, the crumbling white snow of the arctic where the sun is never kind enough to give the eyes a respite from its day and night glare. Here there is never an avalanche free period, as in other mountains of the world, where the sun hides its face and a crust forms over the snow at night, giving the climber a chance to relax or climb without constant danger of being buried alive.

The thing which amazed me most about this female mountain climber, who looked as if she might be the quietest and most sedate person at a Phi Beta gathering; was her humble manner. No one would ever know that all the fourteen-thousand foot peaks of the Pacific coast have been but stepping-stones for the McKinley climb.

I asked her what she would do when she had climbed the nation's highest, and there were no more mountains to conquer.

"No one conquers a mountain," said Miss Walbrecht quietly.

Other climbers in the McGowan group were Dick Walstrom, Edmonds, Washington; Tom Nash, Salem, Oregon; and Wendell Stillwell of Lancaster, California.

On June 4, 5, and 6 the rains still came. Talketna became a milling mass of misfits. The Adams Carter group and the Anchorage Mountaineers had joined the mob of climbers milling about Talketna. A Harvard Mountaineering Expedition led by Henry Abroms was reported en route. This group had hoped to be the first to scale the Wickersham Wall; but the Gmoser ski team was already on the way up via this route.

Among the climbers, pilots, and other air craft personnel stuck in Talketna were two helicopter crews. One was a group of surveyors from the State Land bureau, and the other construction engineers who were laying the groundwork for the bridge to cross the Susitna River on the new Anchorage-Fairbanks highway — a direly needed project which was lagging behind, and upon which five times the purchase price of Alaska was already spent.

It rained for ten days.

On June 7, 1963, fiftieth anniversary of the first successful climb of Mt. McKinley, the three climbers of the Alaskan-Teton group and the Zogg-Liska seven were still on the mountain.

CHAPTER VIII

HELL ON THE MOUNTAIN

This fiftieth anniversary story was picked up on the wires:
"Three mountain climbers trapped at the eight thousand foot
elevation on the Ruth Glacier by seven feet of fresh snow, and
a lone bush pilot waging a continuing battle against the elemental wilds of Mt. McKinley, marks the fiftieth anniversary of
the first successful assault made by the Stuck-Karstons Expedition June 7, 1913.

"The climbers, three of a six-man team, and first to scale
McKinley by the treacherous East Buttress, who have now been
on the mountain fifty-two days are Warren Blesser, Fred Wright
and Pete Lev.

"The lone pilot, termed 'proprietor of the mountain' in the
May issue of *Reader's Digest* and the *Alaska Sportsman*, has had
this proprietorship contested daily since May 29, when, after
lifting three of these climbers off the mountain, one at a time,
weather closed in . . ."

Then I told of the three rescued climbers. How, finally,
after over a week's wait, and an overdue induction notice from
Uncle Sam, the waiting trio gave up the vigil, trusting their ill-
fated companions to Sheldon's skill.

One of the boys on the mountain, however, would have a
nice surprise when he finally did get back to Talkeetna. Pete
Lev's father, Lester Lev, an attorney from Fullerton, California,
had flown to Alaska to congratulate his son on the successful
climb, but needed a longer arm — about seventy miles longer.

During this period Sheldon did manage an air drop on June
4, but could not land. A strong tail wind might have caused him
to overshoot the tramped-out runway in the snow, thus causing
the plane to plunge into a huge, nearby crevasse.

Dropping the men a note, Sheldon asked that they stamp
out a new runway leading past one side of the crevasse. When
he finally found a hole in the weather, three runways had been
stamped out. Two new ones led past the crevasse on either side,
yet landing conditions were not favorable.

"Getting these climbers off the mountain and others on is an extremely precarious operation," I wrote. "The only way Sheldon can operate at all, in such soft, wet snow, is to undercoat his plane's skis with axle grease, about one inch thick. Although he has tried all kinds of ski waxes, none adhere to the bottom of his metal skis as well as plain old axle grease.

"On every trip now, he faces the possibility of either getting stuck in the snow or being weathered in. But it is honed that these weather conditions cannot last much longer."

The fiftieth anniversary of the first successful climb finds at least fifty persons either on the mountain, trying to get to it, or trying to get away from it.

If Archdeacon Stuck were to observe the great commotion raised by the thirteen expeditions fluttering to and from the perilous peaks, the impact would at least raise one of his saintly eyebrows." . . . End quote.

Since telling of these expeditions would fill a book within themselves, we will be forced to skip most of them, which grew in number for the following eleven years, and take time to rescue only those we have on the mountain thus far.

After the clouds finally lifted, Don went into a Talkeetna-McKinley orbit, making twenty-three round trips without rest.

The remaining members of the Teton-Alaskan expedition had been without food for three days. They amused me by telling of the turnips and carrots which I had dropped to them the day before the more fortunate half of their group was airlifted from the glacier, ten days prior to their long-awaited departure. They threw away the peelings from their oranges, carrots, turnips and a few outside lettuce leaves at their upper camp, before we wrote them the note asking them to move three thousand feet lower and tramp out another runway. During the ten-day wait they went back up to the old campsite, dug the peelings from the snow and ate them.

The Zogg-Liska group, most of whom were engineers from Boeing Aircraft of Seattle, had waited so long for Sheldon to pick them up that they erected what is probably the first and only outhouse on the glacier. (This statement was true at the time. In 1966 Sheldon built a glassed-in observatory on the Ruth Glacier, complete with wooden outhouse. Later we will tell of the grand opening party in the sky, in preparation for Alaska's

Centennial of Purchase celebration in 1967.) Although devoid of the half moon and plumbing, the "Chick Sales" built by the engineers from Seattle, with a wall against the north wind, was reported quite a success.

By flying through the night (remember it is daylight all night in Arctic Alaska during June), Sheldon managed to pick up six of the Zogg-Liska climbers. On June 8, only one man, Hans Zogg, remained on the glacier, but he, too, was in Talkeetna the following day.

The Seattle climbers who scaled the West Buttress are: Don Liska, Harold Williams, Don Mech, Hans Zogg, Stan Jensen, Cal Magnuson and Arnold Bloomer.

With eleven men off the mountain Sheldon started shuttling the new guard in. First came the Rocky Mountain Guide Service group, then the Adams Carter scientific expedition and the Canadian team. The four-man Canadian group, all experienced climbers, really seemed to come from as many countries as there were men. Karl Winter was from Bavaria; Pol Neises from Denmark; Vince Bauer from Munich, Germany; and Jim Craig from Vancouver, British Columbia.

A lone member of the Adams Carter group, Jeff Duenwals of Edwall, Washington, wanted to be deposited in the huge Amphitheatre of the Ruth Glacier, where he hoped to join Margaret Young and Jim Richardson of Palo Alto, California in an attempt at the yet unscaled Moose's Tooth, a twelve-thousand foot granite spire which had repelled all previous aspirants.

On June 21 Dick McGowan was back in Talkeetna. He gave a harried report of the fury of the mountain which had halted their climb.

The following are extracts taken from my interview with McGowan, which were published in several newspapers on June 20 and 21st. Quote:

"In a five-day white out, while 16,200 feet up on the West Buttress of Mt. McKinley, our tents were ripped to shreds. We resorted to caves dug in the snow and lived on half rations," reported Dick McGowan, leader of the nine-member Rainier Guide Service Expedition, who was flown into Talkeetna Wednesday afternoon by bush pilot Don Sheldon.

" 'Our snowshoes we·e lost in an avalanche,' McGowan further reported, 'at the ele·en-thousand foot level, where we normally leave them; but this time it was snowing up to the eighteen thousand feet, and hard. Eight or ten feet of snow fell during the five day storm.'

"But the storm on McKinley is not over. Turning around and racing back to the mountain to pick up more members of the expedition, Sheldon found it socked in. So the party still waits to be airlifted.

"McGowan said his own legs and hips were sore and bruised from fighting a path through the snow; but it was the welfare of the eight members of his group still on the mountain which worried him. 'With scant rations and sinking chest deep in the bottomless snow, we beat our way back down from 16,200 to 10,200 in two days. Another guide, Dick Walstrom, and I took turns beating our way through the snow so the rest could follow.' " End quote.

McGowan said they met the four-man Canadian party going up as they were coming down and reported they were probably at the 17,300 foot camp level.

McGowan felt that if they had had only one more day of good weather they would have made it to the summit; but the storm caught them.

The McGowan group also met the Hans-Gmoser ski expedition, and found out that they had become first to scale the Wickersham Wall, but had had trouble enough of their own, after the storm set in.

The Wickersham Wall, which was named for famed Judge James Wickersham, who failed in an attempt to scale the ice wall, rises fourteen thousand feet from the Peters Glacier. It is the greatest unbroken wall of ice in the world and is subject to all the fury of arctic storms and high winds which trigger many avalanches. Yet the party had perfect weather for the climb and their troubles did not come until after they had scaled the wall.

Although they disproved Judge Wickersham's belief that no one would climb the wall except in a flying machine, they still had the weather to deal with — which is often the greatest hazard in mountain climbing, especially in the Arctic.

After conquering the wall they were hit by a blizzard, and several of them became ill in the thin air. The continuing storm

87

prevented their climbing to the south peak — the summit; but Gmoser and two others did reach the north peak before being forced off the lower summit by the storm.

It was while they were descending the West Buttress on skis that they caught up with and passed the. McGowan group, which was devoid of snow shoes.

Led by thirty-year-old Hans Gmoser, Canadian Rockies Alpine guide, the first mountaineers to climb the Wickersham Wall are: Leo Grillmair, 32, Calgary; Gunti Printz, 27, Calgary; Hans Schwartz, 32, Jasper, Alta; Deiter Raubach, 26, Calgary; Pat Boswell, 39, Toronto; Tom Spencer, 28, Los Angeles; and Hank Kaufman, 25, Anchorage, Alaska.

By July there were so many parties on the mountain that they were meeting each other coming and going. There was a four-man collegiate team composed of track stars and the Anchorage Mountaineers, who proposed a 250-mile hike from Wonder Lake, north of Mt. McKinley, up the summit of both Mt. Foraker and Mt. McKinley, and south to Talkeetna on foot. This does not include the aforementioned Harvard team which hoped to be first to scale the Wickersham Wall; but was preceded by the Gmoser skiers.

The track star team, composed of Mike McCoy, 21, and Geoffrey Wheeler, '9, both of Boulder University in Colorado; Gerry Roach, 19, and Dick Springgate, 20, both students at the University of Washington, is believed to be the youngest age group to climb Mt. McKinley.

The track stars encountered four other groups, the Canadian, the Rainier Guide Service, the Hans Gmoser and the Adams Carter party.

Like most expeditions, the track stars did not make it without difficulty. Starting after the heavier snow and turbulences, they were fortunate weather-wise, but lost two of their stoves and damaged a third. On the upper reaches of the mountain, where the temperature stays below freezing, they were unable to melt snow for water. They managed to solve the problem, however, by filling their water bottles with snow and sleeping with them.

While climbing, one of their members, Dick Springgate, had two toes on one foot frostbitten. He was wearing rubber insulated boots and two pairs of socks, adequate footgear for the climb; but one of his boots was laced too tightly. The frost bitten toes bothered him a bit on the way down; but it was reported from Providence Hospital in Anchorage that amputation was not necessary.

The college boys reached the summit of Mt. McKinley on *July 4th at 10:30 P.M. in broad daylight. There was no wind* and it was sixteen degrees below zero.

From Talkeetna three of the group planned to drive back down the Alaska highway; and one, Gerry Roach, planned to go to the University of Alaska in Fairbanks to take part in a study of the July 20 solar eclipse, which would be total in this area.

Don had already ferried six members of the Adams Carter scientific expedition to the Kahiltna Glacier from which they would climb the 17,395-foot summit of Mount Foraker, for an unobstructed view of the total eclipse on July 20.

I was looking forward to this event, too, when scientists from all over the world would come to Talkeetna to study this phenomenon of nature. I had done several preparatory articles fc· publication and answered many queries concerning facilities ir Talkeetna. The Homemaker's Club planned tours, and my students were building a hot-dog stand. Special trains were to run into Talkeetna from both Anchorage and Fairbanks.

Another sadness, however, decreed otherwise. My sister Lela's husband, Emmett Lloyd, photographer and inventor, of Waco, Texas, lay near death in Waco. It was Emmett who had taught me to make and develop my first photographs. I loved him dearly, and of course wanted to be with my sister at this time. Lela was more than a sister to me, she was what my father termed my "Little Mother." It was she who washed and dressed me and my other sister, Annie, and took us to church when my mother was too sick to do so.

My mother, Mrs. Amanda Peoples (W.Z.) Latch, never failed to go to church so long as she was able to stand up; but for a long while she was quite ill. The old family doctor thought she had contracted T.B. after a hard siege of the flu which came to America during World War I. Since Lela was the eldest sister, many motherly duties befell her. In fact, when there were finally eight children in the immediate family and my father and mother had raised four others, three of them orphans,

Lela still assumed a portion of the guardianship and helped several of us through college, including myself.

At the time, in the early 1920's, when my Mother's lengthy illness was wrongly diagnosed, my father, William Z. (Will) Latch, who was then President of the bank and mayor of the little town of Chatsworth, Georgia, gave up everything, including our old plantation home and talc mine on old Fort Mountain, to come west to Texas for my mother's health.

I began my schooling as a first grader in Cisco, Texas and finished high school and Randolph Junior College there; before attending McMurry of Abilene and Texas Technological of Lubbock for further degrees.

But back to Talkeetna and the mountain climbers . . .

That 250-mile hike, longest traverse ever made over the McKinley range, was successful. The men making the hike, which included the first ascent of South peak of Mt. Hunter and both the North and South peaks of Mt. McKinley are: J. Vin Hoeman, David P. Johnson, Tom Choate, and Clifford Ellis, all college graduates who made the trip for scientific study as well as sport.

To have made such a lengthy trip with only two close calls is quite remarkable. In J. Vin Hoeman's words, it happened like this. *Fairbanks News-Miner*, August 15, 1963.

" 'Tom Choate, who was on the rope next to me when I fell through an ice cornice while climbing a northwest ridge of Hunter, did an arrest stop; but I was worried about the rope which had been weakened by the rock.'

"If the rope which broke the fall had not held, Hoeman would have fallen three thousand feet with the ice cornice which gave way beneath his weight. As it was he plunged only fifty feet into space, with only a rope and the skill of his companions between him and death on the rocks half-a-mile below on the vertical face of granite which had stopped all previous challengers.

"Luckily for Hoeman, much skill and training was back of him on the rope at this crucial moment. Choate, who was next to Hoeman, is a former Mt. McKinley ranger. The other companions, Ellis and Johnston, were also veterans of many successful climbs.

"While descending from the summit of Mt. McKinley on the Kahiltna Glacier one of the Mountaineers, Dave Johnston, fell twenty feet into a crevasse filled with water. Luckily the crevasse was narrow and his pack wedged between the walls of ice. His gangling height, 6'7", was of little advantage as he slipped repeatedly back into the icy waters of the crevasse. Despite the skill of his teammates, it took over thirty minutes to get Dave back to the surface of the glacier. Snow bridges continually gave way beneath their feet, dumping them into the slush.

"As they descended on the Kahiltna Glacier the mountaineers found several food caches left by previous expeditions. They ate from a can of sardines which had, 'no more keys will be made for the duration," printed on the label.

"While climbing Mt. Hunter they found a rope which must have been left by Henrich Harrer, the first to reach the summit of Hunter's north peak.

"From their vantage point on the north peak, the Alaskan Mountaineers became the first to traverse the middle peak and then climb the South Peak of Mount Hunter.

"Three of the group walked the seventy miles back to Talkeetna. Tom Choate, who has a Doctorate in Zoology, did not have time because he was scheduled to leave for England where he is to work on a research project.

"On the way out the boys stopped at some old gold diggin's where Rocky Cummins of Talkeetna, who laughingly reports that once he thought he would have the 'longest check book in Alaska,' fixed them some sourdough hotcakes and eggs.

" 'He'll never know how good they tasted,' was the version of the half starved climbers.' " Endquote.

"I'll never know how many eggs that long, lanky one (Dave Johnston) can eat," Rocky confided to me later. "I fixed him a dozen from my limited stock, but he could have eaten more."

Despite the food and encouragement given by Rocky Cummins, the gold miners and the 59'ers (remnants of a caravan of homesteaders who came from Michigan in 1959 to settle in the Susitna Valley across from Talkeetna) there was one hurdle too big to cross, the Susitna River.

Just north of Talkeetna the Chulitna and Talkeetna Rivers dump their silt-laden waters in the Susitna. At their confluence, the river is wider than the Mississippi, cold and swift. Luckily

91

for the mountaineers, Cliff Hudson, long-time bush pilot of Talkeetna, had kept a watchful eye on them since flying Choate to Mt. McKinley National Park, where his wife waited to join the ranger for their trip to England.

I'll never forget how those climbers looked when they reached Talkeetna with their scraggly beards, and that gangling 6'7" Johnston more gaunt and gangling than ever. Never saw boys any hungrier for something green and fresh fruit — nor more anxious for news of other climbers, especially the ones whom they had encountered on their 250-mile traverse.

They were especially good therapy for my sister, Mrs. Lela Lloyd, who had read all the stories I had written about mountain climbers but had never met one. After her husband's death I insisted that she come to Alaska with me. Coming to Alaska had done so much for me after my own husband's death, I felt it would be best for her. She agreed and came to spend the rest of the summer with me, but she would have to return to Texas in September, since she was a professor, teaching at Cisco Junior College.

She had heard so much about Don Sheldon and Mildred Campbell that it did her a lot of good to meet them. Village life was something new and helped her get her mind off her sorrow. Since she was a Journalism instructor, she offered to help me with my news columns, and did. Several times she wrote both "Talkeetna Topics" and "Talkeetna Ticky-Tac." Now she had mountain climbers to write about. I was glad, for this was the last opportunity of the season.

My sis escorted the climbers to my strawberry patch and cooked a meal for them while I pulled photos and stories from my file. Never did strawberries meet with a happier ending, nor food disappear more rapidly.

We enjoyed administering to their needs and made an excuse to leave the house for a couple of hours so they could relax — and take a bath.

The boys were clean shaven when we returned, yet still exposing their blistered feet to the healing air. When they told us that they still had a seventeen-mile hike into Montana Creek — there was still no road into Talkeetna — where they hoped to thumb a ride into Anchorage, my sister insisted we purchase tickets into Anchorage for them via the Alaska Railroad. The train was due within an hour.

How little did I expect at that time to be repaid in several ways. J. Vin Hoeman, who was to lose his life later while climbing Mt. Everest, gave me his book, "Mountaineering" from which I learned many of the terms for my news stories. The next spring, after the Good Friday earthquake of 1964, when I managed to get to Kodiak Island by sitting on a five-gallon can of milk in an emergency supply plane. I would not have been able to get into the disaster area except for the fact that my name, Mary Carey, registered with the young man issuing passes. I must have one to get past the guard.

"Oh, yes," he remarked with surprise. "Mary Carey from Talkeetna. Aren't you the reporter who bought my mountain-climbing buddies tickets back to Anchorage? Let me check. I believe we can manage a pass for you which will permit you to move freely through the destroyed area for photos and interviews."

Thanks to the friend of a friend, whose name I no longer remember, I did get an unusual story, "Panoramic Terror," which I compiled from stories given me from several sea captains.

Perhaps the most unexpected outcrop from the whole affair came in 1967, when the first winter assault was made on Mt. McKinley. This story comes later; but all the news media in Alaska, and some from "outside" seemed again to be in Talkeetna. Seven mountain climbers seemed in trouble, and it was falsely rumored that two were dead. These rumors came more easily, I suppose, since one climber did lose his life during the climb.

Battalions of reporters, photographers, lights and mikes intimidated the bewildered climbers as they crawled out of the huge Army helicopter which had set down on the mountain to pick them up.

"Remember my strawberry patch?" I yelled as the one-and-only gangling 6'7" Dave Johnston emerged.

"Yeah, we sure made havoc of that, didn't we!" came his answer while both of us were completely unaware of the fact that our comments were picked up on a nation-wide radio cast.

93

CHAPTER IX

THANKSGIVING AND CHRISTMAS

Another school year began, but not without change. With the new spur road being punched into Talkeetna, we had several newcomers. My eight-pupil enrollment jumped to seventeen; and a new high school teacher was added, Bruce Gilbert. Much to my delight, as well as to that of the students, this young man was a Peace Corps returnee from Africa, and what was more, a mountain climber. In fact, his love of Mt. McKinley was the determining factor in his applying to teach in our village.

My English students loved writing about Bruce for our little school paper, which I helped them publish and sell to the village folk to supplement our school funds. Our first earnings went to buy a plaque, upon which we had our thanks engraved to Mrs. Lena Morrison, who had given the high school its first set of encyclopedias.

Bruce had been on two climbing expeditions to McKinley, one of them successful, so we had a world-traveler and hero in our little school room — which was not partitioned, except for a row of shoulder-high book cases. Mr. Gilbert certainly had my sympathy, trying to teach over my voice because he was somewhat shy and soft-spoken. In fact, he was so timid that I wondered if he would ever make it as a teacher, or in our town.

But Bruce Gilbert and Don Sheldon were putty in Mildred Campbell's hands. They both enjoyed sweets and she liked cooking. Soon they were not only nibbling and sipping tea, but playing "Scrabble," a word game, at night. Don didn't have much time for playing, but another bachelor in the area, Milton Lictenwalner, was delighted to be counted in. Although Milton was well educated, with a degree in Economics, he was determined to fight it out on his homestead — to farm and raise chickens. He did, against staggering odds, and won. There was no road into his homestead, so he walked, over six miles, carrying a few dozen eggs in a pack on his back. Often he had difficulty keeping them from freezing while en route. Now he has proved up on his homestead and is teaching in the high school in Talkeetna. Earning a living on a homestead in Alaska, where there is no road, is a myth. If it hadn't been for Mildred Campbell, so help me, I fully believe that none of these bachelors would have come out of their shells; but here we are getting ahead of ourselves again.

I must admit that I was overcoming my own problem, too, thanks again to Mildred, who had shown in so many ways that she really cared. My love for her is boundless — but she's still a stinker!

Meanwhile a new and unexpected interest came to me in the way of a young couple who appeared in our town — Jay and Vicki Cornell. I'm not sure how I heard about them; but I believe it was Mrs. Alice Powell of the Talkeetna Motel who called and said, "There's a story for you down here at my place."

Although Jay and Vicki had lived in the area for some time, I didn't know that such a couple existed until they got into a seemingly impossible situation. At their place, twenty-six miles north of Talkeetna on the Chulitna River, there was no communication whatsoever with the outside world — and, of course, no road.

Vicki had gotten sick. Unable to attract the attention of a bush pilot, the couple decided to walk the twenty-six miles into Talkeetna. They tried. Tunnelling through all but impenetrable mountain alder, and clawing their way up and down and through the vertical canyon walls along the Chulitna River, they made it — almost: All except crossing the Susitna River where she was joined by the Talkeetna and Chulitna.

For three days they remained on a point of land within a mile of Talkeetna, looking across the big Su and trying to attract the attention of a pilot. Hunting season was on and planes buzzed. When they waved, hunters waved back. When they spelled out "HELP" with drifted logs, it attracted no attention. They tried to send up smoke signals, but were Chechakos themselves, and didn't know the distress signal was three campfires.

They tried to build a raft, tearing their underclothing apart to tie it together. It sank with their weight. Finally after resorting to eating berries, Vicki decided it was better to try the walk back home than starve. Fortunately, they found a deserted trapper's cabin enroute, with a little food cached away. After resting and fishing and regaining strength for a couple of days they headed back for their tent. The very next week, ironically enough, a bush pilot landed on the boulder strewn sand bar in the Chulitna canyon below their homesite and brought them out.

I was intrigued with their story, but that which was even more intriguing to me was the view from their homestead. Mc-Kinley was magnificent, and the Moose's Tooth dark against its breathtaking background. I had flown over this area several times not noticing their tent at all, but I kept wondering what the view would be from a butte which jutted out above the river. Surely it would make a mighty good observation point for Mt. McKinley from the south — better than the hard-to-get-to observation point from Mt. McKinley National Park, on the north side. The new Anchorage-Fairbanks highway would cut right through this area. *I wanted this land, this land with a magnificient view of the mountain which rears higher than any other in the world from its base.*

Whenever opportunity presented I flew in to see the Cornells. I began to talk of homesteading near them. It must have sounded foolish to the townsfolk. Me? A widow? Homestead in a fly-in area? Everyone seemed to think it a foolish notion which I would forget.

Meanwhile a Texas gal, Genie Chance, — now serving her first term in the state Senate, after two terms in the Alaska House of Representatives — invited me to join the Alaska Press Club which met in Anchorage. Genie, who is as enchanting as her name, is without a doubt one of the most vivacious and attractive women whom I have ever known. The following spring she made quite a name for herself over KFQD radio and television. Later, she won the nation's highest broadcast award for women, the "Golden Mike," for her fifty-nine hour marathon immediately following the 1964 earthquake.

I had heard of Genie before I left Texas. A very dear school-teaching friend, Miss Mariana McKee of Dallas, said that meeting Genie was a "must." Miss McKee was quite sure I would set the world on fire with my writing and that Alaska would welcome me with open arms — if I would only go to Genie Chance for an interview over television.

I appreciated Mariana's trust and thoughtfulness; but a writer is only as good as his next story, and when I came to Alaska my typewriter was dead. I had forgotten about Genie, and Genie had long since discarded the letter which her Auntie had written her about my being a writer and driving alone to Alaska.

Now that my newspaper columns and mountain climbing stories brought invitations to join the club and other news media, my outlook on life was a little brighter.

For my Thanksgiving column I was thinking of writing about my first Thanksgiving in Alaska. I do not believe another Thanksgiving could mean as much to me as the one I spent in the classroom with my students.

Together we planned an all-Alaskan Thanksgiving. All meat must be native to Alaska, and all trimmings, if possible. Many of our Alaskan foods I had not yet tasted. This made the planning even more exciting for me, to say the least. Susan Devore and Dorothy Marie Jones promised to do the cooking, provided the boys would bring the game, and I have never seen such variety.

The boys went hunting. Bruce Devore, Ronald Robeson and Gayland Wholgemuth brought back Arctic hare. Murphy Toughluck, my only native boy, brought in ptarmigan. James Kowske hunted with his father, a pilot employed by the local FAA station, and brought back moose and caribou. Ruby Dahl and Helen Atwater, who had just joined our class, brought "squaw candy" (smoked salmon) and wild berries for pie. We even made Eskimo ice cream, from snow and blueberries.

Never was food so good!

Yet Thanksgiving of 1963 was quite different. Although living in Alaska, our high school students and the people of our village were as stunned as the rest of the world with the assassination of President John F. Kennedy.

Perhaps the memory is more vivid since it came during our "opening exercises" on November 22, 1963. Each morning we would salute the flag, sing a song of our own choosing, discuss some current event, and then read a passage from the Bible or end the session with a short prayer. The Supreme Court ruling out prayer in our schoolroom hurt me deeply, although I have never been a devout Christian.

We got no daily newspaper, or more correctly put, no newspapers daily because of the transportation problem. Often we listened to the news on my little radio before school started. On the morning of President Kennedy's assassination we were listening to the account of the big parade in Dallas. In my mind's eye I was attending the parade personally because I had taught school in Dallas — journalism at North Dallas High School — when my husband, Dick Carey, worked for Texas Instruments there. So in spirit I was riding right along in that parade when we were all stricken by the news.

Since our time is four hours different from Texas time, it was 8:30 in our schoolroom, rather than noon. Regulation or no regulation, many prayers were said in our little room that morning.

President Kennedy's death was still heavy in my heart when school turned out for Thanksgiving holidays. Mrs. Campbell, Bruce Gilbert, and everyone else it seemed, had gone somewhere; but I stayed at home to catch up on my work. I had letters to write, paper to grade and newspaper columns to get into the mail, so I began there.

Perhaps this particular column, published in the *Fairbanks Daily News-Miner*, is the most personal one I ever wrote. Since it tells a great deal about my coming to Alaska, perhaps it will bear reprinting. Although Alaska is no doubt the friendliest state in the union; a person is not always handed a silver platter, nor should one expect it.

"During Thanksgiving," I wrote, "your columnist was grateful for an opportune time to think and write. Thankful that the world has grown mature enough to mourn its loss with a grim determination that John F. Kennedy did not die in vain. Thankful for concrete evidence that our government and the world is not easily plunged into chaos.

"Through the leadership of our late president, we feel that the world came nearer than ever to heeding the advice of the Master Teacher who walked the streets of Damascus over 1,900 years ago, admonishing men to beat their swords into plowshares.

"Sometimes one must wait to understand. Today we are anesthetized by the blow. But when the suddenness of the pain has subsided, the inertia which we now feel will build to a very high frequency for freedom from fear. Then, and only then, will world unity come about.

"Tomorrow, when man no longer fears his brother, history will begin. This is the beginning. Back of the twentieth century, the prologue. Today we compile miracles in medicine which will enable man to live long enough to absorb the learning of the past. Before this day is ended we will have explored the moon and other planets in our own solar system. Tomorrow and tomorrow there are thousands and perhaps millions of solar worlds awaiting our step into space. The earth will become our own hamlet, the moon and stars our neighbors. We will explore unseen worlds through uncharted light years.

"Fear and crime and violence will no longer exist when we accept the advice of the Master and fire our forges with the vigor of His disciple, John F. Kennedy. When we beat our swords into plowshares history will become, as it should be, a recording of man's progress which can and will transform this world and the worlds about us into a heaven of learning and eternal peace . . .

"This might seem like mighty "Tall Talk" from Talkeetna, considering the fact that your columnist was still in a state of inertia last Thanksgiving. Today this sadness and pain has somewhat subsided and new life comes with the wonderful things happening in our little village.

"How proud I am of the unified effort through which our town worked wholeheartedly for the betterment of mankind. Fired by last year's successful drive, Talkeetna again hopes to prove herself the village with the biggest heart in the nation, when the March of Dimes tallies are all in.

"I love my town, even though she's as wild and untamed as the wilderness about her, and as unpredictable as the three rivers from which she derives her name. I drink with her — and to her. I fight with her — and for her. I work with her — and for her. Best of all, I pray with her — and for her.

"Yet I am a stranger to my town and to Alaska. Until September of last year I had never heard of Talkeetna. I felt only a numb desire to come to this state of adventure — a desire which I previously shared with my husband, Dick Carey. We had a plan, an unusual means of reaching Alaska, upon which we lavished three years of our lives and much of our savings. We built a cabin cruiser and planned an extended adventure, leaving Texas and coming to Alaska via Panama Canal and up the West Coast. Then my husband fell, stricken by a heart attack. He died as suddenly as did our president.

"Although numbed by my personal loss, I carried on. I had two engagements which I felt I had to fulfill: one was teaching photojournalism in the Southwest Writer's Conference at Corpus Christi, Texas; and the other was teaching feature article writing at Indiana University. When I had done this, I headed for Alaska.

"Being left alone, I was unable to man the craft which we had built for the voyage, so I drove up the highway alone. Sometimes it seemed I was driving into a strange and hopeless world in which I had no purpose. I even thought of how easily the fears and loneliness which I had faced alone would all be solved if the car accidently rolled over a cliff — but it didn't.

"There wasn't time for me to secure a teaching position through regular channels before leaving Texas, but I wasn't concerned, not financially, to say the least. Furthermore, I had never had difficulty in finding employment as a teacher. Not so in Alaska. By the time I was turned down in Fairbanks and Anchorage I was beginning to wonder if Alaska was really a land of promise.

"With degrees from two universities and glowing recommendations, I had no fear of obtaining a teaching position. One thing, however, I did not know. There is a State law, and it is a good one, that a teacher must go back to college at least once every five years and gain six additional credits to receive and hold a valid certificate in Alaska. This I had not done, and the only way I could possibly have been hired was as an emergency teacher.

"School started the week I hit Alaska, and no emergencies cropped up in my field whereby those in authority could have issued an emergency certificate and hired me, so I was rejected.

"I was determined to teach, not because I was broke, nor because I had no other means of earning a livelihood, but because I was so lonely I felt I had to have the companionship of children. I looked further. I went to the branch office of state schools in Anchorage. There were two openings, both in very isolated areas where there were only natives. No telephones, no roads and no regular mail service. I did not feel I was ready for such complete isolation, so I turned them down. I went to

100

the Air Force base schools, with wholehearted cooperation from the heads of the Anchorage and State school system, but to no avail.

"There was no opening at the military base for which I was qualified. Besides, as the superintendent pointed out, I was grief-stricken. Conditions were different to those to which I was accustomed, and it could likely be assumed that I would soon be heading home. I would probably last one year, I was told, at the most. Teaching for so short a term, insofar as the school was concerned, would be lost because a new and younger teacher could add this year to her experience — and she would probably remain in Alaska. The man seemed to want to hire me, yet years of experience had taught him a hard lesson and he was trying to build a school system second to none.

"The door was closed. Alaska neither wanted me nor needed me. I would go back to Texas. I was spoiled, even pampered. I had received recognition, both as a teacher and as a writer; but here my reception was a skeptical one. I wanted no more of Alaska.

"I was tired, very tired, and it was late; but I started driving. I left Anchorage and passed the Air Force base where I had just been rejected — heading back to Texas.

"But I was too tired to get very far. I spotted a bar and motel sign. Why not? Drinking was not a habit with me, in fact it was quite a rare thing, but I was too lonely and disconsolate to face my misery alone, so I sought a bit of bottled courage. I tried for a room. There were no vacancies. The young couple with whom I talked as I had that drink invited me to stay in their house which was, of all places, on the base — if I didn't mind a housefull of children.

"Children! Suddenly I realized that more than anything else in the world I missed children. That night, with little arms around my neck, I made up my mind.

"Over and over I kept thinking of what I was told in the state office about a one-teacher high school which they thought might materialize in Talkeetna. I liked what I was told about Talkeetna, an historic little village near Mt. McKinley where Alaska's most colorful bush pilot lived.

"Thus far there were no books, no desks and no teacher's quarters. It could be an expensive venture because I would

101

have to stay in a hotel until the teacherage was finished, and this might be from four to six weeks. Besides, there were only eight students of high school age in the village, the minimum number required for a pilot school. If I lost one pupil, I was warned, I would be out of a job.

"This was the challenge I needed.

"That was last year, when I was stunned, as the world is today, with my personal loss. But things worked out for me as well as for the school, and life has purpose. So let it be with our nation.

"Let us rededicate our lives to that for which John F. Kennedy gave his last full measure of devotion. We bury our dead; but not their ideals." Endquote.

Every year of my life, the span from Thanksgiving to Christmas grows shorter. Perhaps the merchants have helped bring about this phenomenon, by shifting from pumpkin to holly overnight. Nevertheless, I was thinking about Christmas, as was the rest of the world.

The previous Christmas I had gone to Houston because of one of the biggest events in a woman's life. A grandbaby was born. For me nothing could be more wonderful than a trip to see my new granddaughter, Carol Ann Richardson, and her sister, Linda Jane. My daughter, Jean, is an only child, and I don't think I could have ever gone so far away from her except for the fact that my son-in-law, Frank M. Richardson, a rising young geologist of Houston, Texas, is as fine a son as any woman could wish for her only daughter. Of course, I wanted to see them this Christmas, but I had spent much of the previous summer with them. I just couldn't go back twice each year, however much I yearned to see my wonderful little family.

I would stay in Alaska, but what I would do during the Christmas holidays haunted me. Fortunately two events came to my rescue. Through my press club activities I was invited to visit St. Mary's Mission on the annual flight made to Nome by the Air National Guard each Christmas. It is their project. Each year they collect gifts for these orphans.

Then I received another invitation, this one to spend Christmas with my homesteading friends, Jay and Vicki Cornell, in their homesteading tent. I was delighted.

My Christmas column was also a personal one, but it was published in several different media. Sometimes I feel that anticipation of coming events is almost as gratifying as realization, yet an almost lost art because of our constant hurry. I was living this holiday in advance, and this is what I wrote:

CHRISTMAS IN ALASKA, ALONE BUT NOT LONELY

"Since coming to Alaska there has been a vague fear in my heart that the Christmas would come when I would be completely away from family and friends of long standing. This is it. Previously I have flown back to Texas to spend the holiday season; but this Christmas I will be alone in Alaska, or will I?

"CHILDREN! I'll have children, orphaned children, especially Eskimo children who will fill an empty heart with their star eyes as Santa on his sled makes a dash from the ski-equipped C-111 landing in Nome to St. Mary's Mission.

"I saw these children in October, during Arctic Airlift week, while flying Polar Deployment with the Alaskan Air Command for the press. How proud they were of a little book! Now I will see them again. These children will be made happy through the generosity of more fortunate Alaskans, and by the Air National Guard which makes an annual flight to the mission for this occasion.

"I am grateful for an invitation to go on this trip. Perhaps my personal motives are selfish; but I do hope to share this happiness in some small way. A picture, a word, a story!

"Already my arms ache and my heart yearns for fulfillment. Christmas to me will be the joy which will be shared not only by the Air National Guard, but by every person who gave a toy or helped in some way to make this mission a reality.

"Perhaps the Sisters at the mission will have the children sing. I hope so. Maybe there will be a story of Baby Jesus and a prayer. Needless to say, I will relive Christmasses past with my own family and friends. No tears. Rather let me thank God for the wonderful and gratifying experiences throughout the years. But now I am alone. Alone? These children are more alone than I, yet they are not afraid. They have friends. Friends and God.

"FRIENDS! When I return from the pre-Christmas flight to Nome I am going to make a shorter one. This flight will be made to see homesteading friends, Jay and Vicki Cornell. They, too, will be alone on Christmas except for having each other and God. They are young pioneers, alone in a wilderness. There's no way in or out except by plane, and this becomes expensive. Their mail is flown over once a month and dropped from a plane. They are living in a tent while building their cabin; but it is a warm tent. Christmas in a tent! Near the foothills of Mt. McKinley, the nation's tallest peak, in a tent? Will the temperature drop to 40° below? It may; but they're not afraid.

"Somehow I am looking forward to this visit with greater anticipation than of dining in a fabulously lighted hall decked with boughs of holly. I'll trade my dinner gown for the eider down of a sleeping bag; my golden slippers for mukluks; and roast goose for moose. Perhaps God will deck the sky with northern lights.

"My gifts will not be the conventional type. My jewels will consist of such things as ruby-red tomatoes and emerald green vegetables. Christmas! Of course it will be Christmas. Where I am going, fresh fruit and vegetables will be more graciously received than fine packages wrapped with glitter and gold.

"I'm not a good Christian; but sometime during the day I want to slip away by myself and snow-shoe to the top of a little knoll where I hope to file on some land and someday have a homesteading cabin of my own when the new highway comes through.

"I want to gaze at Mt. McKinley. From this vantage point I can see God's handiwork. Frozen rivers have inched their way between towering granite spires throughout the centuries. Above them a massive, white monument wrapped in pink ermine stands as resplendent today as when Christ was born. I am nothing!

"God and mountains, children and friends are forever! If you are alone, don't panic when church bells chime on Christmas. Hearts warm with sharing. Does it matter whether you know what eyes are made to shine? You are a part of the greatest pageant known to man. Your role is large or small, not according to your bank account, but according to what you have given of yourself.

"I will lift up mine eyes unto the hills and the agony and joys of the Holy Birth and the promise of a greater tomorrow will swell from peak to peak until my heart sings.

104

"Alone? I am one of the multitude. I am the present. I am a composite of the ages past. I shape the future.

"Majestic McKinley lies before me like a great bell, tilted to ring. Will she echo the chorus rising from hearts throughout the world — of peace on earth, goodwill toward men? So long as God is in the heart of man hope springs eternally.

Ring you beautiful bell
    On top of the world.
Ring with laughter!
    Ring for joy!
Man is but
    A grown-up boy.
Give us time
    As ages come and go
For man has just
    Begun to grow."

CHAPTER X

STRANGE RESCUE

After my first year of flying with Don, I knew what I must do. Teaching was fine. I loved it. Flying the mountain was one of the most exciting and rewarding experiences of my life; yet I could not suppress a deep desire to drink Mt. McKinley's beauty forever. Sharing "my mountain" with the rest of the world became as much of an obsession as flying her.

The thing I wanted most was to file a homestead and live near my mountain. I would have to give up teaching since this was strictly a fly-in area, if you could call it that. Landings had to be made on a gravel bar in a canyon, when there were no crosswinds. If one overshot this boulder-studded bar, he would no doubt find the glacial waters of the Chulitna River his undoing.

Although it broke my heart, I sent in my resignation in February of 1964, so that when teachers were re-elected in March, I would have given sufficient notice. I would finish the school year, of course, but when school was out and mountain climbing season over, my thoughts would turn to homesteading.

There was no doubt about it, the next year in our little school would be quite different. The spur road would be punched through, and enrollment was expected to double when the bus could run down to Montana Creek, where there was a one-teacher school. This teacher, Joe Heck, would be transferred to Talkeetna.

Already a handsome new high school was being constructed. A fine building with six classrooms and a library. It seemed so big at the time. Yet, when one punches out a road into the wilderness, the people flush in and the game out.

The new school was crowded by the time it opened, yet it has continued growing. By 1967 the Talkeetna school registration was ninety-six, and there were eight teachers. Mrs. Mildred Campbell, although she had reached her seventy-first birthday, had not missed a day of teaching because of personal illness, and remained one of the sharpest and best loved teachers Talkeetna ever had. By 1970, when COMSAT, an earth tracking satellite station, was built on the outskirts of Talkeetna, inadequate housing was again faced, but let's take this school problem as we reach it.

Days were filled with activity, planning and writing. There was little time for fretting about my decision. Throughout my life I have faced many turning points. This was one of them. I must homestead — and write.

Meanwhile I had plenty of writing to do, and as perhaps should have happened sooner, I discovered my sense of humor returning. More and more I laughed about the pranks and jokes and antics pulled in our village. But one of our greatest pranksters, Jim Beaver, had absolutely nothing to do with this anecdote.

Ever since Don Sheldon was written up in the May, 1963 *Reader's Digest* and *Alaska Sportsman*, some of us had teased, others rubbed it in, and many a hero worshipper tried in every way to meet our world renowned pilot, who Lawrence Elliot proclaimed "busiest pilot in the bush," in his *Reader's Digest* story. Envious pilots made light of Don's rescues. Lonely ladies, who had only read about our hero, wrote love letters making all sorts of absurd offers to this "poor lonely bachelor" who was most welcome by their fireside. Advertising agencies seeking endorsement of their products haunted Sheldon.

This anecdote fell into my lap; but I'll swear I would never have known about it if the school doctor hadn't been in Talkeetna giving physicals. Dr. Boyd Skille and his wife, Jean were very good friends of Mildred and myself. Dr. Skille had recently learned to fly and loved to get in flying hours between Palmer and Talkeetna. At night we played games.

On this particular occasion, just before school was out, Don Sheldon came rushing to the school to see if Dr. Skille was still there. I felt there was something wrong because of the urgency in Don's voice, and his "Hurry, hurry, we've gotta move!"

They took off the village strip like an avalanche down Mt. McKinley, and shot into oblivion.

Mildred, Jeannie and I could hardly wait until Dr. Skille returned to hear of a daring rescue, another strange and heroic adventure in the frozen northland, no doubt. Hours later, when he did return, Dr. Skille was laughing so hard that I thought we would never get the story.

"It all started when another pilot saw "HELP" stamped out in the snow," Dr. Skille finally started his narration. "This pilot, who was on a cross-country flight, spotted the distress signal some forty miles northwest of Talkeetna near a lonely cabin on a lake which he was afraid to try to land on. There was no other spot that looked favorable nor feasible for a possible landing in the wild stretch of wilderness surrounding the cabin. Disturbed, the pilot flew on in to Talkeetna and told Don Sheldon.

"Even more disturbing to this pilot," the doctor continued, "was the fact that he spotted no action near the cabin, although the snow was freshly trampled. Again this pilot looked over the small lake adjacent to the cabin; but the black ice, which had been swept clean by gale-force winds, appeared too thin for landing. So he left his troubles with Don."

"He would," Mrs. Campbell cut in, "everybody does; but Don doesn't seem to mind. He hovers over homesteaders like an old hen over a setting of eggs."

The arctic sun was already low and the winds had not yet subsided when Don Sheldon took off by himself for the spot which he remembered from a previous rescue run made last spring.

Reaching his destination, about thirty flying minutes northwest of Talkeetna, Sheldon spotted a lone figure standing beside the message stamped in the snow. He was waving a lantern wildly. In the gathering gloom all Sheldon could distinguish was the fact that only one person was visible.

Remembering that there had been two men at the cabin when he made the previous run, Sheldon did a few mental calculations. Perhaps the first pilot who had sized up the situation was right, the ice might be too thin for landing. But if there was someone inside the cabin who was injured he could need medical aid.

"That's when Sheldon thought of me," Skille said, "he knew I was giving physicals to the school children, or at least he had seen me there during the day, so he came sailing back. Medical aid would be avaiable much sooner; and besides, he could switch to a lighter plane, his new Super Cub on skis, which he could land on a willow limb without bending it too much."

"Roaring back in at home base, Sheldon caught me just as I was fixing to leave the school. I grabbed my pill bag and we raced for the ski-equipped Super Cub which he holds in fire-engine readiness for such emergencies.

"While airborne into the arctic night, Sheldon told me of the two chechakos from the East who were trying to make it as trappers. 'Maybe one of them is caught in his own bear trap,' Sheldon grinned.

"Closed in by shadows of black spruce, the ink-spot of a lake looked very minute as we approached it in total darkness. The lantern waved even more wildly than before. There seemed to be no alternative. A landing must be made."

Dr. Skille admitted that he held his breath as they glided through the saw-toothed cavern of spruce.

Hearing no sharp cracking noises and feeling no incoming tidal wave as they skimmed over the lake like a duck, the doctor resumed breathing again in time to grab his pill bag as Sheldon's lanky legs pegged the ice. Long accustomed to slithering across winter-horror lands without skates, the pilot and his companion, who had just made a four-point landing, were given a warm reception by a vicious hound that they later found out was named "Fierce," and rightfully so.

"The belligerent hound had slashed only a few chewy hunks from the toe of Sheldon's mukluks and siphoned only small quantities of vitamins through a rip in my pill bag before he finally subsided to his master's command," Dr. Skille laughed at the absurdness of the situation.

"Pushing past the gesticulating windmill with a lantern, we slid into the lighted sanctuary of the cabin — only to find it bare.

"Where's the casualty?" I asked.

"Oh, you mean my partner," the gaunt young man answered as the question finally registered. "He gave it up and went back East. I'm starved! No food for two weeks."

"Well, what are we waiting for?" Sheldon asked. "Let's get her moving. Hurry! No tea party here."

Before the plane could again be loaded there were a couple of would-be rescuers who were beginning to wish that the supposed "casualty" had eaten "Fierce." The very hungry young trapper refused to leave without his faithful companion, who seemed to have found one thing he had no taste for — aircraft.

"Two gangling six-footers can be folded into a Super Cub; but trying for three, plus a non-cooperative hound can present difficulties." Skille laughed.

"I crawled into the plane first and was going to hold the boy and dog; but Fierce tried making a new window. I bowled out of the plane in a very unsophisticated manner and declared in non-professional language that a very hungry lad could hold his own damned hound, and hold him back of the seat.

"This worked very well as we again folded in three-deep. But when Sheldon revved her up for take-off that hound bolted into a noggin'-knocking, instrument smashing orbit.

'A slightly exasperated pilot halted the taxiing plane, opened the door and invited the guest to either leave the hound or bring him under control. By now I was in a sort of horizontal sitting position, posterior exposed to a canine muzzle and face jammed against the panel, mouth ready to be probed by remaining instruments, in case I wished to open it."

After take-of from the sliver of ice, which seemed shorter than Christmas to New Year, the hound seemed to realize that it was too late to jump; and the boy pieced out his own story.

Although his companion had given it up and mushed out before the throes of winter set in, he was the more determined type and was going to stick it out. With abundant game and eight jars of salmon eggs he had it made. But the game was evasive and he had managed to catch only three Ling Cod through the hole which he had chopped through the ice.

Since he couldn't catch fish on his salmon eggs, and had six-and-a-half jars left, he decided to swallow the bait himself. The pale, very small, single-type eggs, a la formaldehyde, weren't too tasty, he reported, so he tried supplementing his diet with slightly fermented high bush cranberries.

"But I knew I wouldn't starve to death," the young trapper voiced with confidence. "I know Alaskan bush pilots. I knew sooner or later I'd get a ride with one, maybe a famous one."

There was no comment from the driver's seat. The silence grew until Don brought the plane in on the Talkeetna strip.

Given the Prodigal Son treatment at the Rainbow Lodge, the wayfaring stranger ate, according to reports, two monstrous T-bones, a bushel of salad, a peck of hash-browned potatoes and a pot of beans which he washed down with two gallons of hot chocolate and topped off with two-and-a-quarter apple pies.

"When the famished one had finished feasting," reported Dr. Skille, "he turned to Don and me, remembering a magnanimous suggestion which he had made on the way in:

"Oh, yes," the adventurer of the northland reported with a glow of admiration, "I almost forgot, I sure would like to buy you and Sheldon a cup of coffee." Endquote.

CHAPTER XI

THE ALASKAN EARTHQUAKE

There was much to write about. Again our little town became first in the nation, per capita, in the March of Dimes collection. An oil well was drilled across the Susitna River, west from Talkeetna, about thirty-five miles. The result we never knew. Like other test holes drilled from Palmer to the northwest of Talkeetna, the oil companies failed to put out a report, not for publication, anyway.

Downriver, about ten miles from Talkeetna, piers were being poured for a 10,500 foot bridge, which was to span the Susitna. Four young engineers and their foreman, John Schelin, were staying in Don Sheldon's bunkhouse below our kitchen window. These engineers, Ed Burgholzer, Ed Mulcahy, Dean Parks and Frank Lombardo and John Schelin, throughout the fourteen-year span of this book, play a major role in Alaskan highway history, as well as project engineer Sherman Powell and Anchorage District Engineer Jack Spake, who come in the story later. Now, back to our story.

Crews were coming into our town to finish punching the 14.6 mile spur road from near Montana Creek, on the new Anchorage-Fairbanks highway under construction, into our village.

The super on the job, Big Bob Swarthout, had a son of high school age, David, who became a favorite with his teachers as well as with fellow students. Big Bob was a colorful and humane hunk of humanity. He and his wife, Darlene, brought so much fun and good will with them that we dreaded, rather than looked forward to the day when the spur would be finished, because then they would be gone. Bob and Darlene were the life of every party — dancing, drinking, showing kindness toward all and malice toward none. Darlene never failed to help with school projects nor to bake goodies for the Homemaker's bake sales.

By March of '64 the little spur was passable, if the "Green Boys," as we called the Green Construction Company crew, were on duty to pull you out and through whenever you couldn't make it under your own power. I got my little red Rambler, which I had taken out of storage in Anchorage, stuck so many times on

Question Creek, that the "Green Boys" said they knew the answer. That seemed to be pulling me through the next trap, which they named "Answer Creek."

Easter holidays were coming up; but we would get no holidays from school because we had to make up a couple of days lost due to crippling snow. I was moaning and groaning, because now that we could drive to Anchorage — with luck — there would be very little time to spend there. Mrs. Campbell had visitors coming and said she had rather stay in Talkeetna.

Since the construction crews would not be working, Bob Swarthout advised that I should have someone with me who could shovel snow, in case I did try to make it out in my car. The ground was frozen solidly, but snow was falling and the road would not be bladed.

Our six-foot, sixteen-year-old student, Ronald Robeson wanted to go into Anchorage; and so did our other teacher, Bruce Gilbert. Why didn't I just ride with them instead of trying to get through with my own car? We would set a get-together time and place for the return trip.

Sometimes, but not too often, I do listen to reason. Two teachers in Anchorage, LaRita Heffner and Sanna Green, now president of the Alaska State Teachers Association, had invited me to spend Easter with them; and I was looking forward to it wholeheartedly. I had taken a short field biology course with them in August of '63. I took it because I wanted to become qualified as an Alaskan teacher, as well as to learn a little about plant and animal life. The camp-outs promised in the brochure, to Resurrection Bay and Wonder Lake in Mt. McKinley National Park, were especially inviting to me. Dr. Leonard Freese of Alaska Methodist University was the prof; and never was a class more enjoyable. After it was over I kept talking about it until Mrs. Campbell took it the following summer.

Bruce, Ronnie, and I had all promised to have our bags packed and waiting so that we could leave for Anchorage the minute school was out; but before we got off I was tempted to take my own car, disregarding snow conditions. Sanna and LaRita were giving a more-or-less reunion dinner for those of us who had been in the field biology class the previous summer. Some of the others, including myself, were bringing movies made on the trip. I was sure I was going to be too late for dinner.

113

First of all, Bruce had forgotten to get someone to take care of his cat, and he did love cats. Then his car wouldn't start. When it did Ronnie remembered we were supposed to pick up some things at the commissary on the military base for his mother, the widow of a Colonel; and he had to run back home for the card. Finally, about forty-five minutes later, we did get started, but we had a stop to make. Homesteader Milton Lictenwalner wanted Bruce to drop twelve dozen eggs, which were a rare luxury in this part of Alaska, by the Willow General store, which we passed en route.

Of course I was encumbered with camera, projector and film, as well as a bit of luggage, so I said I would try to work myself and my junk into the back seat. I was reading my autographed copy of *Glacier Pilot*, Bob Reeve's biography, which I had been trying to finish for several days.

The road — if you could have stretched your imagination enough to call it that — was a rough, one-rutted roller coaster. Snow banks on either side, which had grown to a height greater than that of the VW, seemed to leave only a tunnel-like trail between them in places.

"This road couldn't be this rough," I complained as I checked to see if I had broken a setting of eggs.

"No back seat driving," came the comment from the front as the fender of the bug scraped snow from one bank and lurched toward the other.

"I can't even keep my place in my book," I kibitzed, and with cause. "I thought you could drive this thing."

"I did, too," Bruce said meekly. "Must be something wrong with it. I can't even hold it in the ruts," he admitted as we hurtled downgrade from snowbank to snowbank. We were swaying and the car bucking so that Bruce started to stop, then said we would never make it up the next grade if he slowed at the bottom.

If we hadn't been in a snow tunnel we could never have kept on the road. As Bruce brought the bouncing bug to a stop on top of the grade and crawled out to see if we had two flats and the bottom had fallen out, a strong wind sprung up. At least that is what I thought. Trees were swaying and snow fell from the bank in places. Yet things seemed to be subsiding as Bruce came back to the car shaking his head.

114

"I don't see a thing wrong," he confessed, "but I could have sworn we had a flat and something had gone wrong with the steering gear all at the same time."

The sudden wind, which had sent trees to swaying and grabbed snow from the bank, subsided as quickly as it seemed to come. We all looked at each other sort of silly like, as if "is there something wrong with your imagination, too?" Bruce started the motor and all seemed well.

We sort of forgot about it for the next few minutes, until we got near Montana Creek Lodge. Just this side of the bridge a man flagged us down. His eyes were as big as Alaskan cabbage.

"Did you see it?" he asked. "I was crossing that bridge when that crack broke right in front of me!"

I don't remember any of the three of us saying a word as we crawled from the car.

"Didn't you feel it?" the man asked as if wondering whether it was he or we having "pink elephant" trouble.

"What's the matter? What's going on?" Bruce asked.

"You mean you didn't feel that earthquake? It's bound to have shook you. Look at that crack in the bridge!"

"So that was the trouble. It wasn't the car at all," Bruce mused.

"Didn't you see the trees sway?" the poor man pursued in disbelief. "The birch saplings almost touched the ground."

Here I believed him. What I thought a sudden wind must have been the subsiding quake. The falling snow must have been shaken, rather than blown, from the banks.

Together the four of us puzzled about the phenomenon, a hundred miles from nowhere in the Alaskan wilderness.

Which way did it come from? Was this the center, or did it come from back or in front of us? Finally, we decided there was only one way to find out: keep driving.

Bruce tried his radio. It was dead. The further south we drove toward Palmer and Anchorage, the larger and more frequent the cracks. This answered our first question, the direction the quake came from. Yet we didn't know whether it would keep getting worse, or whether we were near the center.

The cracks grew wider. There were no lights in Palmer. We pulled into a service station, and the attendant was all excited.

"There's no radio contact, no nothing," he reported. No one knows whether anyone was hurt here; but my oil cans and fan belts are all over the floor." This was evident.

"What about the Matanuska River bridge?" Bruce asked.

"I've heard it's holding," the attendant replied, "but the highway department headed for the Knik bridge and I haven't seen the truck come back."

A quick straw vote in the car brought three "yesses" for trying to proceed rather than turn back.

The Matanuska bridge seemed OK; but foreboding grew as we dodged larger cracks along the six-mile stretch between the Matanuska and Knik Rivers. The Knik bridge was always frightening to me. It was long, too narrow and marked "DAMAGED proceed with caution" the first time I saw it. From 1962 — when I drove over it on my first trip into Anchorage — until now, insofar as I know, the load limit and "DAMAGED" sign has never been lifted. Perhaps it will never be, since a beautiful new highway eliminates this section of the old highway between Palmer and Anchorage.

"Why don't you try your radio again?" I suggested to Bruce.

"It's been on all the time," Ronnie commented, giving the dial an extra twist. Suddenly came a voice,

"Power has just been restored to our transmitter . . ."

You know the rest. The whole world listened. What flabbergasted us most, however, was that the Knik bridge was completely demolished, at least this was the report we heard just as we pulled within seeing distance of the rickety span. The way it dead-ended, with a right turn at the base of Pioneer peak, was enough to frighten any newcomer, much less hearing of trouble.

As we approached the bridge it looked the same, except for a highway flare which had it blocked. In the deepening twilight we didn't see anything wrong with it, more than usual. We were curious. Of course I wanted to walk out on it myself. If this rumor was false, then others might be exaggerated, I hoped, because the reports were horrifying.

A few yards out on the bridge we realized we were not alone. A man approached from the other end. We waited.

116

"There's a big snow slide, must be a quarter-of-a-mile long," the young man spoke without our having to ask a question. "What's it like on your side? I'm Dr. Larry McKinley."

After introducing ourselves we explained it must be much worse, according to reports we had just heard, in Anchorage.

"My father and I just drove from there," he explained. "When the quake hit that huge slide came roaring down right in front of us. Looked like the mountain split and half of it slid into the river. We couldn't tell where the highway lay. I was with my father, Dr. Lee McKinley, an Anchorage dentist. We had started to Palmer to see my grandfather, Lee McKinley, Sr., who is ninety years old and quite sick. I walked across the slide and my father headed back for Anchorage to see about his wife and children. I need to get to my grandfather's house."

"Could we give you a lift?" Bruce offered.

"It's about eight miles from Palmer, out by the Butte," the young doctor explained.

"We're going nowhere fast," I commented as Bruce asked him which direction.

"You might get stuck, or run into something you can't get across."

"Four of us could carry this mechanized mouse," our brilliant ninth grader added in his usual quiet sarcasm.

It was rough, but we finally pulled up in front of the largest house I have seen in the valley — and huge barns.

"Come on in," the doctor invited, "I see the lights are out, but we'll find a way to make coffee."

We went in through the back door. A housekeeper, who was introduced as "Marie" gave an extra swipe with a mop and said, "You should have seen it before I got up the sugar and syrup and broken glass. Your grandmother and grandfather are in their room."

"Are they OK?" asked the young doctor who, we later learned, was a dentist from Kodiak.

"Them," the housekeeper shrugged. "Nothing shakes them. In fact, I believe your grandfather is even better."

Showing us into the living room, which was as long as a hotel lobby and looked sort of like a ski lodge, we were invited to make ourselves at home.

"Look at that fireplace," Marie explained. "It and candles are our only light, but we can't build up a fire. See those two rocks on the floor? The quake shook them out. And look at that poker, wedged right between the rock and hearth. Thought the whole thing was coming down."

We marveled at the phenomenon and looked around at impressive oil portraits at oblique angles, listening all the while to radio reports of death and destruction of unknown extent.

Larry returned to the room and suggested that if Bruce and Ronnie knew anything about a generator they could help in the basement, and we might get auxiliary power. They had been working only a few minutes when the lights came on. This was comforting, especially to Marie, who had been fretting about the deep freezes. I saw two, huge ones.

"Can we use the electric stove?" she asked.

"Better not," Larry thought. "But I'll bring some hamburger from the basement, and Mrs. Carey can broil it, if she doesn't mind, on the fireplace."

I was delighted to do so, hungry, too. It took a long while for the frozen patties, which were quite generous, to sizzle over the coals.

"There'll probably be lots of children and grandchildren here before long," Larry said, "so keep cooking."

About that time I heard a plane and saw landing lights blinking as it approached the house.

"That's my brother from Fairbanks," the young dentist explained. "He's a student at the University of Alaska. He lands in the field and taxis up to the barn which serves as a hangar."

Others dropped in throughout the long night. Our gracious hosts insisted we stay since we did not know what we might have to face if we started back for Talkeetna.

We were all shown to rooms. There were six bedrooms upstairs above the huge living room, but no one wanted to sleep. All night we hugged the radio.

When reports finally started coming in from Kodiak I studied young doctor McKinley's stoic face. Although his business could have been washed away and his own home hard hit, he took all reports as solidly as his ninety-year-old grandfather seemed to do. Grand family of Alaskan pioneers, the McKinleys.

Over the radio we heard no reports whatsoever from Talkeetna, nor any town in so far as that is concerned, north of Palmer, so we felt safe about things in our own little village.

I wondered how long it would be before I could get a message through to my daughter and sisters in Texas. Knowing that the telephone and telegraph communications would be tied up for days, perhaps I had best take a chance on scribbling a note. If I could only get it into the mail in Anchorage. Planes do fly, and although the tower at the Anchorage International Airport toppled and two men were killed in it, reports were that the east-west runway was usable. What if I could get out on a plane myself, to one of the harder-hit areas?

CHAPTER XII

PANORAMIC TERROR IN KODIAK

Being a freelance writer I wanted to get into Anchorage the worst way, but how? Would my press card do me any good? Larry McKinley was a doctor, and he was heading for Anchorage as soon as the snow slide was cleared from the highway. If I could just get in with him.

I asked Ronnie if he would get his mother to teach for me. I didn't know whether I could get anywhere or not; but this was news and I had to be there trying. Don't ask me how, but I did manage to get to all the harder hit areas.

Knowing that local and outside reporters would cover the Anchorage area first, I decided to try to get as far away as I could. Kodiak! That was a long flight. If I could only manage. Good reporters never inform on those who help them. Let it suffice to say that it wasn't Dr. Larry McKinley; but I did manage to get on an emergency flight. My seat was the top of a five-gallon milk can. All the passenger seats had been taken from the plane. It was loaded with huge spools of wire, medical supplies and food. It's the first time I've ridden an airliner sitting on a can; but I would have sat on a prickly pear for this opportunity.

Earlier in the book I told how I managed to get a Civil Defense emergency pass into the disaster area in Kodiak, through a friend of mountain climbers whom I had befriended. From there I was on my own, and I don't mind saying I used every trick in the book and then conjured up some before getting into all the harder hit areas. Most reporters do. We are despicable characters, for the most part, but working for you, to give you the news as it happens.

Over three hundred miles from the epicenter of the quake, it was not the shock, but the tsunami, or seismic wave which did the major portion of the damage in Kodiak. Nineteen persons lost their lives here. Three nearby native villages, Afognak, Old Harbor, and Kaguyak, were washed from the map. Afognak was one of the two villages where there was an opening for a teacher when I first applied with the state schools. I thought

120

seriously of taking this one, because it was not out on the Aleutian chain, like the other, yet this problem was solved with the school opening in Talkeetna.

Looking out over the destruction in the harbor and bay, I realized I was gazing into crumpled history which I knew not. Suddenly I wished I had read *Katmai*, by John Erskine of Kodiak, more thoroughly myself, rather than listen to the numerous reports made on this volcano by my students. This town had been destroyed before, in 1912, as wave after wave of volcanic ash buried her several feet deep, shutting out the sun for many days.

Trying to reconstruct in my own mind, I walked to a high point of land overlooking the sea and destruction which the tidal waves had brought. If I remembered correctly, the old Erskine house must have been on this point. The oldest building on the Russian coast, built by Lord Baranof, should be here too, but I didn't see it.

I was looking at a very old sun dial when an attractive, gray-haired woman walked outside the front door, probably wondering why I was snooping around the premises.

"Could you tell me about this sundial?" I asked hopefully as an entree to further conversation. "I'm a reporter, Mary Carey from Talkeetna, and this is my first trip to Kodiak, although I've always been intrigued by her history."

She introduced herself, Mrs. Betty Attcheson, and said that the sundial was taken from the Old Russian sea wall which it adorned before George Washington became president.

"The home you see across the way," she pointed to the impressive old structure across the street at which I had been gazing, "is the John Erskine home. Below it was the oldest frame building on the Russian coast, where you see what's left of that old sea wall. The tidal wave got it."

"You seem to know a great deal about the history of Kodiak," I complimented as she walked with me to show me the remains of the old building. Below it, in the wall, were two old anchors used as hooks for tying up Russian boats.

"I should," came her simple reply. "My husband, Robert, bought the oldest store, Donnelley and Attchesen, in 1948 from John Erskine, who purchased it in 1911."

121

I asked if this was the place where the old boat was tied up that was used as a refuge when Katmai erupted in 1912, plunging Kodiak into total darkness for seventy-two hours, and covering it with a coat of ashes from six to ten feet deep.

"This was it," she replied. "Refugees used lanterns as they beat a trail through the ash. The Father — (I never could find his name) — at the mission you see over yonder kept the church bells ringing day and night; and our citizens took refuge in the hold of the ship, which, fortunately enough, was loaded with fish and ice which served for food and water."

"I wish I had seen Kodiak before so much of her history was obliterated," I lamented honestly, before setting the hook. "You must know most of these people with wrecked boats and some of their experiences. Could you tell me which of them you think might make good writing."

"There's Dug Lohse, standing by his boat, the *Padilla*. He saved six boats."

That was intro enough. Here is Doug's description of the tidal waves.

"I heard the first one coming through the channel with an awful roar. I was under power and headed out to sea. I saw it bowling over houses, trees, stores and boats. There were three main waves, the highest better than thirty feet."

He said the current sucked boats out of the harbor. "I saw a man on the breakwater run for his boat, *The Yarsh* as she broke over it. They threw him a line. He missed it and no one ever saw him again."

I tried not to interrupt his story. He told of onrushing boats crashing over everything and into each other as they were sucked through the channel about twenty miles per hour. He saw a woman, the wife of a skipper, fall overboard into a king crab net. Her husband dived after her. They found him on shore, later, stark raving mad. His wife was never found.

"I understand you saved six boats," I stated trying to get his mind off the horror. "How did you manage that?"

"The harbor was full of boats, floating free. The bay was calm and I just tied them alongside. I couldn't see outside my pilot window because of the boats tied on either side. One boat wasn't a fishing craft, like the others, it was Bill Wright's 45' cabin cruiser, *Fancy Free*.

I left the beached *Padilla* with a great deal of respect and admiration for her skipper, thirty-five-year-old Dug Lohse, a native of Oklahoma, who saved six boats on the night of Panoramic Terror, March 27, 1964.

I had lots of boat-strewn beach to cover. The next captain I encountered was a real character, an old salt about whom someone should write a book. Let it suffice to say that Jim Veazey, a long drink of salt tied together with lean muscle, would have fit any movie version of a sailor who had circled the globe eighteen times.

When I asked him where he was during the quake he said, "Under the fu-fu (cosmetic) counter in Bert's Drug. Don't ever get caught under a fu-fu counter. First I was hit by a powder puff, then fu-fu water breaking all over. Even the dogs looked for a pretty leg when I passed them on the street."

I knew I had found a real treasure, and I was so taken with his tales of the sea that I forgot the disaster about me, although the burning rubble gave a dull-red overcast to the sky. Bulldozer operators were pushing splintered homes into piles, while still searching for the dead.

Jim came to Alaska in 1929 on a four-masted topsail schooner, the *Sophia Christenson*, owned by J. E. Shields. When the vessel put ashore on Kodiak Island to let off the man who "took the *Bear* with Admiral Byrd aboard, to the South Pole," Jim disembarked, too. He has worked in or out of Kodiak ever since.

Insofar as can be determined, Jim Veazey may have made the longest hike for survival, *sans* supplies, in Alaskan history. For ninety-six days he walked, from March 15th into June, with little food and no shelter. He lost nearly sixty pounds.

"I tried to write it," Jim confessed, "but it sounded like a Jewish Rabbi in a Synagogue."

I wanted to hear more.

"I hit a fog and cracked my boat up on the rocks. I walked out, from the Valdez area to Seward. I started out with my parka and rifle, but threw the rifle away the second day. I survived on 'uduck' a sort of sea biscuit which has bumps with a starfish pattern. I got them off the rocks at low tide with my sheath knife."

Of course I wanted to know whether he still had his ill-fated manuscript. In so far as he could remember, it must have gone down on his other boat, the *Hell Diver,* a thirty-foot crabbing boat which he had just bought and finished rebuilding.

"I had just got it livable and stored my 'goodies' on her when she was bowled over by other boats in the harbor during the tidal waves. Just disappeared."

"Goodies" to Jim were the irreplaceable items he had collected on his numerous trips around the world, probably each caching a bit of "faraway" nostalgia.

"Anything you can buy you can get again," came a bit of Jim's philosophy. "Money is the cheapest thing on earth."

I asked about the little craft he was working on, *The Seal* and how it escaped.

The *Seal* was in dry dock and he had been working on it, getting ready to go seal hunting. When the quake caught him under the fu-fu counter he headed for the docks, less than two blocks away.

"I was in a tidal wave on Okinawa, rebuilding after the war, and knew what to expect. I ran down the floats yelling for everyone to get out, there would be a tidal wave. I could see the tide fluctuating two or three feet and knew she was about to break.

"I ran to the *Hell Diver,* my boat that was lost, and secured the lines, then to my seal-hunting boat and put out a stern anchor and jammed and kicked it into the mud, another damned fool stunt."

I scribbled his tale as fast as I could, hoping I got no names mixed up nor misspelled; but this was no time to stop a story for such details.

"A fellow hollered and asked me to row him to the *Vagabond.* It was Mick Anderson. I rowed him out in my skiff to the KFC-6 and told him to get to hell out with it. His wife, Mary, and a deck hand were on board the thirty-two-foot beach seiner, rigged for crabbing. I saw them head for open water and rowed back toward the *Seal.* I was going to secure the bow line so it would swing out . . . then a hell of a racket, a grinding noise distracted me as big boats were over-running floats and smaller boats.

"I saw Bobby King riding the *Cindy* like a surf board on the first wave. He built her."

I asked him what time the first wave hit.

"Hell, I wasn't looking at my watch — but it wasn't quittin' time. The water was butt-deep to a tall giraffe, and I was scrambling like hell for high ground. When I reached the point I just stood and watched.

"The whole boat harbor moved out in one mass, tied to the floats, then it came back. Big boats came crashing in over the *Hell Diver.* The *Seal* floated up and bobbed up to Kraft's store, loose from its foundation. It caught and tipped her enough that the hatch cover came off and she took on water, then she righted herself and set down right in the middle of Benson's Road.

"A police car's horn stuck and it screamed out the full time, but it was drowned out.

"When the wave was out, I didn't pat my bruises. The Civil Defense gave me a complete outfit of clothes and Mrs. Margaret Emmons, whose husband, Don, was a bush pilot, gave me a place to sleep. Kodiak was dry for a week — the longest week I ever spent."

Ever since the quake struck I had been hearing about the *Selief,* an eighty-five-foot power scow which had landed in a school yard almost one-half mile inland, and of the heroic performance of her skipper, Bill Cuthbert.

It did look odd, seeing a monstrous boat tied to a telephone pole in a schoolhouse yard. As I approached, it seemed to tower three stories above me. Steps had been built. The boat was off-bounds and there were "Keep Off" signs; but the intermittent snow and rain must have blurred my vision — or was it the smoke boiling up from piles of debris on either side of the draw below, debris so recently called home by hundreds of persons?

I climbed the steps all the way up, then walked along the deck to the pilot house. Seeing it was occupied I climbed on up and knocked at the door, fully expecting to be invited off.

A quiet, well spoken man, probably in his late forties, invited me in and introduced himself. He was the captain, Bill Cuthbert, and the other two to whom he introduced me were Mike Economou and Pete Bergsagel, crew members.

I welcomed the cup of coffee and tried to explain my uninvited entry, saying that I thought the *Selief* had a great story, as well as being the lifeline of radio rescue when all other power in Kodiak failed. The *Selief* was the hub from which all messages were sent out and came in. For sleepless days and nights the captain had sat at the controls around the clock.

"They were sleepless enough," the captain commented quietly as he left the table and walked to the companionway, gazing through the glassed door at the destruction below, "but for more reasons than sending and receiving messages. Can you imagine a scow as big as this bowling over boats and houses and people and being unable to do anything about it? They dug a woman from that pile of debris this morning."

Evidently I had made a mistake and probably wouldn't get a story. This man was suffering.

"You can hardly blame yourself for an act of God. In the face of earthquakes and tidal waves man seems pretty helpless. I feel very differently about your story; but of course if you don't want to tell it . . . I shouldn't have come," I said rising, "I heard that you did not care to talk with news media."

"Keep your seat, you're here," he said simply as he returned to the table. "Pete, why don't you get Mrs. Carey a piece of your cake. This one didn't meet with such tough luck as the one you made just before the quake."

I saw both deck hands grin and waited for further explanation.

"We were berthed in our stall at the boat harbor and eating, Captain Cuthberth explained. "My first impression was that some drunken sailor had bumped into our boat. Then the whole harbor shook to the north. Rocks came rolling down the hill and waves rocked back and forth over the old Russian sea wall. Rats came pouring out — all came swimming. I hadn't known they were there before. When the lights went out we knew it was a bad one. Mike likes cake but I have never seen him eat a whole one before. He was so nervous that he ate the whole cake while things rocked around."

"Are you speaking of the tidal waves going over the sea wall?" I queried.

"No, this was just a rocking, from the quake, a warning. I put it up to the crew whether we should 'stay' or 'get off.' We stayed."

I waited for him to continue, or at least hoped he would.

"When the lights went out," he spoke a little more freely, "I started up my own generator. We were working on the clutch control and had only one motor at the time, so I knew we wouldn't have power enough to head for the bay. We had one motor running when a huge white wall came rolling in from the sea. We crashed over boats, but didn't feel them.

"Then, when the water drained from the bay, we were almost on bottom."

Pete recalled a man being washed overboard from another boat as it hit the seawall. "He probably broke a world record for walking on the bottom of the sea as he scampered for shore across the drained boat harbor."

I had heard about this bottom-walking bit, and was glad to have it confirmed.

"Then we were caught in two tides," the skipper continued, "one boiling in around by Woman's Bay near the Kodiak Naval Base to meet the other coming through the narrow channel at Kodiak. As the water came back in, the whole harbor went around and around, from three to five minutes, with boats smashing into each other. We hardly felt them hit us. Everything shook to the north," he commented for a second time.

I doubt that most persons would have been as observant. The churning second wave set the *Selief* where the Kraft's Dry goods place had been, and near Jim Veazey's stranded *Seal*.

There was time enough between the second and third waves for the crew to get out for a quick inspection.

"We had bent wheels and shaft to the rudder," Captain Cuthberth continued, "but we still had one motor and were going to charge out into the bay. We didn't have a chance. As the third and highest wave carried us inland I saw the *Yukon*, my son's boat, as it was pushed inland behind us. That's it you see right back there," he pointed to another large and impressive boat which looked rather intact, insofar as the hull was concerned.

"That third wave took us in and brought us back. Houses pushed against us, but I saw no one in the debris. As we settled in this schoolyard we put a line around a telephone pole, and here we stayed."

"Were there many boats being carried through the draw with you?"

"Yes, practically the whole fishing fleet was lost, in one way or another. The *Peril Cape* was up with us, but it floated out to Crooked Island. I kept calling other boats to find out who was hurt or missing. I had the only sending set powerful enough to get news out of the Kodiak area. An operator of the Alaska communications asked my location. 'Hitched to a telephone pole on the schoolhouse yard, across from the Elk's club,' I pinpointed. The operator laughed so hard she could hardly sign off."

As I left the *Selief* I saw a truckload of those tremendously large Alaskan King Crab being hauled away and dumped into the burning debris. The *Selief* dumped over 3,000 of them after the oxygen in her huge holding tanks failed. It was the weight of these tanks, two with a 1,250 cubic foot capacity each, that helped make the *Selief* so heavy that smaller craft and houses were hardly felt as she crashed over them.

I was warned before going into any of the harder-hit areas that there would be no place for me to sleep. But I didn't have to sleep in the street, thanks to a very fine host and hostess, George and Mary Cornelius, who lived in a new housing development high on the hill above Kodiak. George was a realtor, and Mary had been a Red Cross nurse in London during the blitz.

Neither did I have to walk all over town for my photos and stories. A kindly female horologist, Mrs. A. J. Anderson, took me under her wing and drove me wherever she thought I might pick up a good story. During this time Mrs. Anderson did not know whether her own husband was safe. He had gone in a boat to search for survivors on nearby islands.

As in all places where I visited after the quake, I can never thank these, nor the scores and perhaps hundreds of persons whom I can never get around to mentioning in these condensed versions of my earthquake experiences.

I did not know where I would go next. Wherever I could get a hop to. It happened to be Seward.

Chapter XIII

WE RODE IT OUT ON A ROOF

As our plane circled Seward, I could not have recognized the town except for the fact that I knew it was Seward. Only Resurrection Bay, far out, looked the same. I remembered my two previous visits there, once during the annual Salmon Derby, and when our field biology class from Alaska Methodist University camped there to study marine life. Those were such happy visits.

Now nothing looked familiar. Even the docks were gone. Books could have been written about the harder-hit Alaskan towns during the quake; but Seward and Valdez, perhaps, were the hardest hit of the larger towns. They suffered three major disasters almonst simultaneously: the earthquake, the seismic waves, and fires which destroyed docks and most of the industry in both ports.

There were thirteen deaths inflicted by submarine landslides and waves up to thirty-six feet high. About thirty seconds after the quake was felt in Seward, some four thousand feet of waterfront slid into Resurrection Bay, taking with it docks, warehouses, fuel storage tanks and the small boat harbor. There were several waves over thirty feet high, which were followed by ground swells. A freight train and railroad docks just disappeared, as did about seventy per cent of Seward's industry, almost immediately. Large fuel storage tanks along the waterfront quickly ignited, spilling blazing fuel which spread rapidly along the shore line and out into the bay.

The ring of fire around Seward, and wave after wave and swell after swell throughout the long night was enough to make the McRaes', whose story we will now tell, feel that they were clinging to a rooftop in a completely destroyed housing area across the bay, were sole survivors.

The McRaes' were at home, 614 Second Avenue, in Seward when the quake came. With Mr. and Mrs. Albert G. "Scotty" McRae was their son Doug, his wife Joann, their three-week-old son, Doug Jr., Scotty's ten-year-old son Robert and their sixteen-year-old daughter, Linda.

Scotty was a young grandfather. He and his wife, Margaret, were enjoying three-week-old Doug Jr. As a ten-year-old would be, Robert was playing with his poodle, Sussie and his cocker spaniel, Sugar.

The McRae home was a comfortable and well-built one. Scotty owned the Seward Lumber Co., and had been one of Seward's leading business men for many years. Yet suddenly their home quivered and shook until the chimney toppled.

Running outside the house, the family saw that the big Standard Oil tanks down at the dock area were on fire. Flames were spreading. A haze and smoke hung over everything, and they couldn't be sure what had happened except that there had been a terrible quake, harder than any of them had ever felt before.

Doug's wife was worried about her folks, who lived on lower ground in a new housing area about two miles around the bay, which was now hidden by bay-front wall of fire. If they followed the airport road, it looked as if they might be able to make it over to this new section of town.

"It didn't occur to me that we couldn't get back," Scotty stated. "I was in Kodiak in 1941 when that tidal wave came in, the year the Japs shelled Dutch Harbor, and it didn't amount to anything. We had warning here in 1945 and it didn't materialize."

The whole family, seven of them, and a friend, Mrs. Georgia Hensen, headed for the McRaes' new red Corvair. There were cracks and rough spots along the road and debris and confusion everywhere; but they made the two miles to Airport Heights, where Joann's folks, the Joe Lemas lived.

The house was intact; but a quick look inside and a resounding yell aroused no one. Everything seemed deserted. How could everyone have gotten out so quickly? Maybe previous warnings of tidal waves had never amounted to much; but there was an ominous feeling one couldn't shake. The fires were spreading. Another huge tank exploded. It was time to get home.

"We had only gone about one hundred yards," Mr. McRae explained, "when friends, Bob and Blanche Clark, who had climbed up on a crane sitting alongside the road screamed that a tidal wave was coming in.

" 'Go back! You can't make it!' " Bob screamed above the other noises.

"I slammed the Corvair into reverse. 'Up on the roof!' I commanded, 'over those oil barrels back of the garage.'

"No one needed urging. We could hear the crashing of the oncoming wave.

" 'On up! On up!' my son Doug called. He hardly touched the oil barrels as he leaped to the roof of the garage and reached for his wife and baby.

" 'On up! On up!' I urged as I helped the women and children from the bottom. 'And keep going, to the roof,' I urged as the oncoming wave looked higher than the garage. A dog whined. I saw my ten-year-old son turn back. 'It's Sugar,' he wailed.

" 'Up, go up!' I commanded, with the assurance that my son, who had always obeyed me, must now."

Scotty told me that long ago, when the family decided to move to Alaska, he had talked of the difficulties which might be faced, and the possibility that some day life or death might rest on a split-second decision.

"My family and I agreed," he recalled, "that in time of crisis there can be only one in command, and they have stuck with this, even though Doug now has a son of his own. It was always understood that if there was time, matters would be discussed and solutions worked out. If my younger son had not followed through with this training, I'm afraid he wouldn't be with us today."

Just as the others reached the safety of the roof and grabbed Robert's outstretched hand, the first wave struck, tearing the garage from the house. It floated away, carrying the red Corvair with it. The Lema's Cadillac was washed away when the second wave rolled in.

"Look!" someone screamed. "On top of the car!"

"It's Sugar!" Robert sobbed as the spaniel stood sentinel over the bobbing Corvair, trying desperately to maintain a foothold as the wave carried the bobbing car through the debris.

"To the very top!" Scotty cautioned as floating masses around them were sucked back out to sea. "The next one may be higher."

Two men, four women, a boy, a three-week-old baby and a poodle might be a strange crowd for a rooftop; but it was

Scotty's family, three generations of same, and the man in command was thinking fast as he shouted directions.

"The other end, Doug, lay across the eave, all of you, men on the ends, women between. Lock hands. Here she comes!"

The third wave crashed into the house, lifting it from its foundation. The house pivoted, pulling all the plumbing loose, hit a tree which snapped off the front porch, and was carried about two hundred feet inland.

"We were riding that wave like a surfboard until one of the gables smacked into a big spruce tree," Mrs. McRae recalled, "and we would have been shaken loose if we hadn't been clinging to each other so tightly."

"When we whacked that tree," Doug added, "it knocked a whole room right off the end of the house; but the roof remained intact. Then we swung broadside against two more trees, two huge cottonwoods. We had twice as much roof as house."

"The next wave lapped up on the roof of the house and water poured into my boy's boots," Scotty related, "but the house didn't go any farther. We were wedged, and it's a good thing. I felt the roof would hold. It was new, and I had furnished the materials and designed the house. When they buy from me, I intend for it to last," Scotty spoke with just pride in his own product.

"We saw all our neighbors houses go down on the first wave," Joann added. "My folk's house was the only one that stood. We were scared to death, and freezing. Doug hung on to Doug Jr. I didn't hear him cry. Maybe it was just too noisy."

"Making things worse," came Scotty's comment, "there were propane tanks, which had broken loose from houses, with jets wide open, shooting around like torpedos. I thought one would surely hit us. One did strike a house about fifty yards away. The propane set off the oil heater and the house exploded. It was a large, new house and it burned for hours. Each time one of those torpedos headed our way I thought, 'There she goes! Three generations of McRaes.'"

After the larger waves subsided, the Clarks, who had jumped off the crane and climbed a tall spruce, heard the McRaes calling and calling above the holocaust. As one of the swells went back out, they made a dash for the rooftop. All the other houses in the area were completely demolished.

As the time lapse grew wider between swells, Doug climbed down and tried to get a fire burning beside the house. Scotty tore insulation from the attic and wrapped the womenfolk in it. The temperature was near freezing. Intermittently the diminishing swells would put out the fire; but they were about an hour apart by 4:00 A.M.

Throughout the endless night Seward burned. So many oil tanks exploded that the bay burned. They were afraid the burning oil would drift across the bay to them, especially if the wind changed.

Doug Jr. slept throughout most of the night, but consumed the half-bottle of milk and was hungry again before dawn. His father found a can of peaches, and the juice was given to the baby, but he didn't go for it. No one else seemed hungry.

As daylight broke, the McRaes and the Clarks thought that perhaps they were the sole survivors in Seward. This was not true, as they soon found out, but from their rooftop they could see no sign of life, only a ring of fire around the town.

Later, during the day, when they did manage to get back into town, they found that much of the residential area had been spared.

How does one express appreciation to this type of family? Perhaps your admiration for their courage and clear thinking will deepen when I tell you, that among the other difficulties faced, both Mr. and Mrs. McRae were polio victims at one time. *In fact, Scotty McRae still walks with a cane.*

And the dog! Oh, yes, the dog. Robert wouldn't give up worrying about Sugar. On Easter morning, as you remember the quake came on Good Friday, Scotty walked back to the stricken area with Robert to search for the cocker spaniel.

Believe it or not, a few hundred yards from the house they heard a happy yapping as the cocker leaped from the top of the wayfaring Corvair into the arms of a very happy boy.

CHAPTER XIV

GONE ARE THE 700

Thirty lives were lost in Valdez. Devastation was so complete that the city had to be moved across the bay, to higher ground. The most complete destruction and tragic loss of life occurred in the dock area. The *M.V. Chena,* a 10,815-ton ship, was unloading and the area was crowded with people. Almost simultaneously with the first tremors, the entire dock area began sinking into the sea. Where there was formerly thirty-five feet of water, there is now one-hundred-ten feet of water. The docks, piers, huge fuel storage tanks, and small boat harbor just disappeared. Only two fishing boats, that were away from port, remained of the entire fishing fleet.

Today a new and beautiful Valdez, the terminus of the Alaska pipeline, has risen from the old, and it, too, calls itself the "Switzerland of America." It is located around the bay from the old site, which was built on an alluvial fan of unconsolidated sediments. During the quake a slice of the unstable alluvium, four thousand feet long and six hundred feet wide, slid seaward. This resulted in a violent upwelling in the middle of the bay. Within less than three minutes after the quake began, the *Chena* was lifted about thirty feet above the pier, which just disappeared in a whirlpool of mud and debris.

Capt. Merrill D. Stewart described it thus: "The ship was slammed on the bottom and rolled wildly from side to side like a rag doll. It heeled over landward forty-five to fifty degrees, then was lifted by huge waves and carried back to sea through the dock and cannery wreckage. Men in her hold were crushed by oil drums gone wild."

Although Valdez was more fortunate than Seward fire-wise, she was less fortunate quake-wise. Fire did not break out in Valdez until three hours after the quake, and this was a little over a quarter of a mile from town. When fuel storage tanks ignited, flames shot hundreds of feet into the air, yet by some miracle Valdez did not burn. The destruction to her business section and to the residential portion of town was enough within itself. Huge cracks and fissures, several feet wide and deep in places, ran across roads and undermined buildings. Structures heaved and shook violently. Many buildings were destroyed by the quake or the wake which sucked everything within its path seaward.

The damage was so intense that there were so many accounts in Valdez, as in Seward, perhaps presenting the holocaust through the eyes of one person will give a more vivid picture.

Maybe Dr. Boyd Skille won't mind my telling how I got into Valdez.

As I mentioned in an earlier episode, when Dr. Skille went on that 'canine' rescue mission with Don Sheldon, the physician is also a pilot. I'll leave you to your own deductions, but it was Mrs. Dr. Skille, 'Jeannie', who was with me in Valdez while that city was under martial law.

My story came from Mrs. Mary John Gilson: let it speak for itself. I called it "GONE ARE THE 700" because less than 100 of the 700 persons who left Valdez during the endless night had returned at that time.

"WHERE ARE THEY? On March 27, the longest night in history for many, the names of over 700 persons fleeing devastated Valdez were faithfully recorded. Where are they now?

"Stricken by the quake and bulldozed almost instantaneously by seismic waves, which carried the freighter *Chena* over the docks and back out to sea, scenic Valdez, known as 'The Switzerland of America,' was evacuated.

"Over the highway leading out of Valdez fled the 700. A checkpoint and temporary hospital was set up in a highway maintenance building at Mile 27. Cars were flagged and names of persons reaching this point were carefully recorded. Thirty persons who were in Valdez, tragically enough, never reached this checkpoint. But where are the others, those exiled by nature?

"If superlatives can be applied, perhaps Valdez was the hardest hit of any Alaskan village which remained on the map, in terms of loss of life and relative property loss. Her story may be typical of evacuees from many of the harder hit villages. Where are these displaced persons now?

"This reporter chartered a plane in an effort to try to find out. Valdez is still a town without water, except for that which is flown in or treated. There are no grocery stores, drug stores nor cafes open. This does not mean she is not functional to a certain degree. Although staggered, two hotels, a bar, a propane service, a charter plane service and a bank are open. It is reported that there are about 120 men, half that many women and a few children here.

"Civil Defense furnishes the food and patrols the streets which have been gutted by tidal waves, ravaged by fire and ripped by saw-toothed fissures. But no one complains. There's praise for the army and the many helping hands, much talk of rebuilding and speculation as to where most of the refugees are and as to when they will return.

"A most graphic account was related by Mrs. Mary John Gilson, R.N. and wife of Valdez banker, John Gilson. She explained, to some extent, the whereabouts of these persons. Her own family seems typical. Two of their three sons are in Fairbanks, and the other in Olympia, Washington. All are students, and there are no schools open in Valdez. Their school buildings are condemned. This reason alone, perhaps, will keep the devastated hamlet as lonely as Hamlin after the Pied Piper — until school is out.

"Since she is local agent for Cordova Air Lines, Mary John Gilson meets every plane which comes in. She records the name, time and business of each person entering Valdez, collects temporary passes issued such persons by Civil Defense, and records the time of their departure. She drives passengers to and from the airport, delivers messages, packages and supplies which weigh almost as much as she does, and stops en route to check the weather and call the report to Anchorage. The weather agent is gone, temporarily. Mary carries a pill bag, since she is acting Public Health nurse. When she is not giving shots she digs out her own office or helps her husband and those who work inside the boarded-up bank.

"Fortunately for all concerned, although a few inches of water did seep into the bank vault during the tidal waves, money and records remain intact. The building is a shambles; but the bank is open for business — in a new apartment house which suffered little damage. At least it looked fairly whole from the outside.

"Under the same roof as the First Bank of Valdez and on the same gutted street, George Gilson, John's brother, digs out the Gilson Merchantile, which he owns. Although George is not open for business, he is gracious enough to offer pop or fruit juice to thirsty persons. Ironically, their father, who was a banker, came to Alaska after going through the San Francisco earthquake in 1906.

"Between stops for pauses, deliveries, checking the weather twice, giving shots and a guided tour, Mary Gilson related this story:

"'After the quake and seismic wave, about 5:36 on Good Friday, Dr. Clarence Davis and a nurse, who administered to the immediate needs of those brought to the hospital, went aboard the *Chena* to help with the injured and dying. Soon the ship, endangered by burning oil tanks and oncoming tidal waves, was pulled out into the bay. The doctor could not get the injured off the ship and to the hospital. Nature, in her most violent mood, became sole dictator.'"

"Mrs. Gilson, although not a practicing nurse at the time, rose to meet the demand, as qualified persons all over Alaska did. Leaving her own family, she helped at the hospital. When word was passed that the town, even the hospital had to be evacuated, a startling revelation came to her. She was the only R.N. in the small establishment. She realized that the doctor and nurse who had gone aboard the *Chena* could not get back through floating debris. Eleven patients must be evacuated.

"'Someone had to organize, so we did,' she said modestly.

"Already every available vehicle was pushed into operation, picking up men, women and children and shuttling them to higher ground outside town.

"'We feared the Union and Standard tanks might blow,' Mary continued as she told of jumping gaping cracks in the road with cars loaded with patients. When wheels fell into crevasses there was always help. 'We all helped each other. We pushed, we pulled, we dug. I don't know how we made it, but we did.'

"'It must have been 2:00 A.M. when the highest tidal wave came in. Hoping that everyone in Valdez had been evacuated and that all homes had been checked for injured, the exiles, chilled by more than the weather, moved without panic, first to Mile 9 and then to Mile 27, where there was some protection from the elements.'

"It was here that Mrs. Gilson suggested to a high school girl, Sally Huddleston, that she record the names of each person from Valdez as they reached this point. Cots were set up for a temporary hospital and throughout the endless night the nurse administered to the injured as they struggled in.

"Sally manned her post faithfully, and the names of the living were recorded as her father, Raymond Huddleston, a maintenance head for the highway department, kept radio contact, calling . . . calling . . . describing their plight to the rest of the world, putting names of those saved on the air, helping unite families separated during the exodus, directing . . . pleading . . . helping.

"We wanted to talk with Sally and give you a photograph of this courageous girl; but she, like the other school children, was not in Valdez. Many of the persons with whom we wanted to talk were gone. Where?

"Who can trace exiles through a devastated land? They progressed along the old Richardson Highway throughout the night which turned into an eternity. The next day they were joined by evacuees from Cordova. Together the displaced mass of fleeing persons pushed inland. Together the exiles, from Valdez and Cardova pressed on to Copper Center and Glennallen. Some stayed. Some, with their own transportation turned to the west, north or east at the fork of the road. At Glennallen 115 of them loaded into three busses which carried them into Fairbanks. Here some of them took planes, others stayed. Reports from Fairbanks are happy ones, and many of the children are in school there — but where are the others?

"We flew out with Dave Kennedy who has had a charter service in Valdez for many years. Like many others with whom we talked, he had lost his home during the tidal waves. His family was scattered and much of his equipment was destroyed, but he still had a plane to fly and had no thought of giving up.

"He told of three men at the Granite Gold mine, which he pointed out to Jeannie and me as we flew over. We shuddered as he told us he landed on that crumpled glacier the day after the quake to check on them. They left a note, saying they had started walking toward Whittier. And they made it, eighty miles on foot through the torn land before they could be found. But where are Jack and Ed and John now? Those were the signatures on the note.

"Where are the hundreds made homeless by our greatest catastrophe? Scattered to the winds, but not forgotten. The whole world is looking for them, we hope, and many the helping hands.

And the 700 from Valdez? Friends got word — and they are coming back. They are made of sterner stuff than quakes. They are from the stock which helped build Alaska. From the town which tested the mettle of bush pilots who ushered in a new era; from the town which gave us founders of airlines and great industrialists; from the town which gave Alaska her first governor, William Egan, who served two terms as Alaska's first governor and was re-elected for the 1971-72 term."

For most persons involved, memories of the Alaskan earthquake are tragic. For me, a beautiful friendship was born under the most adverse circumstances.

The last place I visited was Portage. Fortunately, there were no lives lost in this little resort town, yet what the quake did not destroy, the highest tides of the year were expected to finish off, as the eighteen- to twenty-foot wall of water rushed in with icebergs as battering rams. I am sure the National Guardsmen on duty thought I had lost my senses when I proposed walking the twelve miles of broken pavement with all bridges out. If the tide came back in before I made it out, I would be trapped. The guardsman was right — at least half-right. I did get trapped, but not alone.

If there is a bigger fool than a reporter, it must be a photographer. Although it was almost twelve years ago, I'll never forget meeting Ivan and Oro Stewart — on what I thought was to be one of the loneliest nights of my life. The Stewarts are world-wide adventurers and photographers who established Stewart's Photo Shop in Anchorage during World War II.

Of course I stayed too long in Portage. Suddenly it was late, and the riptide came roaring through the crumpled bridge in front of me. Not knowing how far the water would rise, I was afraid and turned back in search of higher ground. A man and woman, with a battery of cameras, approached and introduced themselves as Mr. and Mrs. Ivan and Oro Stewart. They advised me to stay where I was. They barely made it across the broken pilings of the last bridge before the tide took it out. If misery loves company, this was it.

Ivan gathered splintered pilings for a fire; and that flicker was prettier than the northern lights. We shared a little bottled cheer, swapped yarns, and waited for the tide to turn.

Mrs. Oro Sewart was field chairman of the Chugiak Gem and Mineral Society. The club was planning a trip to Ivan's jade mine, Tin City and Little Diomede, near Russia. Would I like to join? Of course I would, and did. Some of my happiest and most rewarding trips have been made with the Gem and Mineral Club.

One which almost had a tragic ending was made to my own thunderegg and geode claim in the Talkeetna mountains. The area is so rugged that it is accessible by helicopter only. The Stewarts, Mr. Sandoz, Mr. Maurice and I were on the last chopper out. Coming through a six-thousand-foot pass, the chopper blade went "Whock! Whock!" and stopped.

I don't know what the others thought; but knowing my last fifteen seconds were lapsing I only thought "What a beautiful day." Just in time the blade took hold. Our pilot, Joe Petit, made a fantastic landing, about halfway between heaven and hell, mountains above, river below.

That was the second cold night I spent with the Stewarts. We were rescued at daylight. Yes, I spent a third cold night with them, too, at Summit Lake, when they were going to try out their new hovercraft. We're going to ride on that cushion of air, yet, if the three of us live long enough. I'll swear that if it hadn't been for Mr. and Mrs. Jim Caress inviting us into their cabin we would have frozen to death. Best friends are made under the most adverse conditions in Alaska, if you live to enjoy them.

Today there is a new Valdez, not on the old site, but on higher and firmer ground. In fact, this is the story of the same sort of courage which has helped with rebuilding that which was destroyed throughout the quake area.

Anchorage, being a greater metropolis, suffered the greatest property loss, about $200,000,000. Fortunately only nine lives were lost in Anchorage; but 215 residential homes were destroyed and 157 commercial buildings destroyed or condemned.

As I stated earlier, there were so many from the news media covering the Anchorage area that I thought my opportunities as a freelance writer would be better if I covered the harder-to-get-to areas. What I have related, of course, covers only a portion of the devastation. I have not mentioned the land-level changes which are difficult to evaluate.

The magnitude on the Richter scale was from 8.4 to 8.6, greater than that of the San Francisco quake, 8.3, and equaled or exceeded the largest individual shock, the 1960 Chilean earthquake, 8.4. The quake caused significant damage to structures and property over about 50,000 square miles and ice was cracked or buckled on some lakes and rivers within an area of about 100,000 square miles. Estimates of dead and missing range from 114 to 152. Probably the exact figure can never be determined.

CHAPTER XV
THE FRENCH EXPEDITION

For a month after the quake I was so engrossed with school, developing film, printing pictures, and writing about the quake, that Don Sheldon's wedding day arrived, and he and the former Roberta Reeve, daughter of glacier pilot Bob Reeve, owner of Reeve Aleutian Airways, were on their honeymoon before anyone could realize that Alaska's Number One Bachelor was wed. He had kept their courtship a secret.

Roberta, a twenty-four year old beauty and former airline hostess who flew the Orient, was certainly a blessing to our community as well as a good wife and inspiration for Don.

Certainly Mildred Campbell and I will never forget the day when she knocked at our door and humbly reported:

"I have everything a bride could ask for, the finest of silver and linen; but could you loan me a mop? With the spring thaw setting in and the store not open until Monday, I'm in trouble."

Mildred and I would open our window and listen while Roberta played classical music. She was really good on the "long hair" as well as rinky-tink. The whole town listened or joined in when she and Don made an appearance at the Rainbow Lodge or Fairview Inn. Don would wring his accordion for all it was worth, tongue in cheek and foot stamping vigorously to every beat. Often Jim Beaver joined with his harmonica; and sometimes Don would fly across the river and pick up Shorty Bradley and his fiddle. Happily, we would sing and dance a goodly portion of the night.

Yet I could not forget that a new mountain climbing season was rapidly approaching. My photographic experiences of the previous year, mostly bad, had impressed upon me that the thing I needed most to help with my stories was a darkroom. I had studied Press Photography at Texas Technological College in Lubbock and earned a degree in Journalism, back in the dark ages, 1945. For nineteen years this know-how had lain dormant because there was an easier way.

While living "stateside" my brother-in-law, Emmett Lloyd, who had a studio in Waco, Texas, did my work for me. He had won many honors in photography, and I could have no better ally. He taught me a great deal about photography, too, and

142

sometimes I did my own work in his studio. Yet as I stated earlier, Emmett, who came almost as near to being a father to me as my sister, Lela, was a mother, died the previous summer. Now my sister and I were both alone, in more ways than one. I knew that I must put in a dark room.

Mrs. Campbell swore I was buying out Stewart's Photo Supply in Anchorage, and that there wouldn't be a vacant corner left in our apartment, and she was right. The only place that could be made dark enough for developing film and printing pictures was our bathroom. Mildred said she wouldn't have a bit of it; and I'm sure she wouldn't — if she hadn't known I was setting up for mountain climbing season. There were a few small quakes in our apartment, every time my room mate wanted a bath and found people and boats and earth quake debris floating about in our bathtub. She fumed about it until every time we walked in the Fairview the first question Bill Price always asked was, "Who's in your bathtub today, Mary?"

But we lived with it, and the thought of leaving Mildred to homestead hurt.

A renowned group of French climbers arrived May 5, 1964. Again I was in the shutter clickin', story writin', school's a flittin' whirl of the previous year, and loved it.

The French Expedition planned to climb previously un-scaled Mt. Huntington and then try a new and unclimbed route up the South Face of Mt. McKinley. A German team, due with-in a week, would attempt the Moose's Tooth, that previously — unscaled vertical wall of granite rising two miles above the floor of the Great Gorge of the Ruth Glacier. Things promised to be exciting enough on this new international year coming up.

The leader of the eight-man French expedition, Lionel Ter-ray, had been described as "Absolute Tops" by Dr. Bradford Washburn. This alone would have made me want to know him, notwithstanding the fact that he was considered one of the four best climbers in the world. In 1950 he climbed Annapurna in the Himalayas, and in 1962 he was in the party which made the first ascent of Chacraraju, a 19,685-foot Peruvian Andes peak.

Don ferried the climbers to the Kahiltna Glacier, which grinds its way down from Mt. McKinley, passing between it and Mt. Huntington. Shadowed by the nation's tallest peak, 12,240-foot Mt. Huntington doesn't sound so impressive, but when I saw her vertical spires and snow plumes blowing from her summit, I realized she was the most beautiful as well as the most foreboding peak I had ever seen. Although little over half as high as Mt. McKinley, I had the feeling she would be twice as hard to climb.

One of my greatest thrills came when I got a spectacular shot of the climbers on a vertical ridge with a sheer rock face blocking their ascent. It came out in full 8 x 10 glory on the front page of the *Anchorage Daily Times*, May 16. Later the photo won a first place award as best action shot made in Alaska, 1964. Although I have won other photo awards, this is my favorite, and may always remain so.

But things didn't go so well for the climbers. On May 21st they were in the same spot, where they had been eight days earlier, calling over the two-way, which Sheldon had furnished them, for help. Here's a portion of the story which I sent to the *Fairbanks Daily News-Miner*.

"TALKEETNA (Special) May 21 . . .

"For eight days the eight-man French expedition has battled its way up previously-unclimbed Mt. Huntington with little or no gain from the spot on the north ridge where they were photographed at an estimated two thousand feet from the summit on May 12 by this correspondent.

"At a standstill on Wednesday, the French climbers made an emergency call to Talkeetna for hardwood stakes. This was accomplished through use of a high frequency two-way radio provided for emergency use by Talkeetna bush pilot Don Sheldon.

"No such stakes were available here. A telephone survey of Anchorage determined they were not available there, either, but that they could be cut to specification, with the grain, so that when pounded into the ice they would swell and hold. Metal stakes, we were told, absorb heat, which may induce melting and slippage.

"The French climbers, led by world-renowned Lionel Terray, are evidently playing it cool. By biding their time and taking every precaution, they may yet be the first to climb 12,240-foot Mt. Huntington, which has repelled all previous attempts . . .

"At the moment it is a waiting game. The stakes were cut and flown into Talkeetna Wednesday by pilots Fred Richards and Lynn Twigg, who are helping Sheldon with the ever-increasing number of mountain climbers.

"Adverse weather conditions prevented the stakes from being flown to Huntington immediately. A reconnaissance flight is being made at the time of this writing . . ."

From there I picked up on the German and Tacoma-Mt. McKinley climbers, whom I should like to mention, although there will not be room enough in this book for covering all the expeditions which followed: —

"Two expeditions are now climbing in the Alaska Range; and a third party, from Germany, is waiting in Talkeetna to be flown to the Great Gorge of the Ruth Glacier, from which it will attempt the previously unscaled Moose's Tooth, in the southeast shadow of McKinley. The Tacoma-Mt. McKinley expedition, led by John Simac, which was relayed to the Kahiltna Glacier May 5, may already have reached the summit of Mt. McKinley by the West Buttress route.

"Insofar as can be determined, their progress has been satisfactory. What was believed to be their snowshoes were seen at Windy Corner, at 13,500 feet. Ordinarily snowshoes are not needed above this point on the nation's tallest peak.

"With three expeditions here and seven to follow within the next few weeks, perhaps there will be more climbers in the McKinley area than recorded in any previous year.

"Members of the four-man German team are: Walter Welsch, leader; Arnold Hasenkopf, Alfons Reichegger and Klaus Bierl.

"Members of the nine-man Tacoma-Mt. McKinley team from Seattle are: John Simac, Dr. Robert Schaller and Mike Bialos. Tacoma members are: Stanley R. Engle, Bruce Galloway, Lee Nelson and Webb Sater. Gilbert Blinn is from Ashford and Dr. Paul Gerstman is from Puyallup."

Since Don was married he seemed less hesitant about flying me to the mountain for stories. In fact, Roberta was often with us. The trips I liked the very most were when she was along. Not only was she fun, but she helped with the photos. If it had not been for Roberta I would never have gotten my most prized movie, climbers in action on Mt. Huntington. She ground my movie camera while I tried for newspaper photos.

But this chit-chat, as Don calls it, will never get the Frenchmen off Mt. Huntington. Twice, when Don flew me in, I interviewed the Frenchmen on the glacier, none of whom could speak English, except Terray. Imagine trying to interview and make photos of men who do not speak English. I did, on two occasions — once when Lionel Terray fell thirty feet and dislocated a shoulder, and again when one of the climbers went snow-blind. Communication wasn't simple, but with the few words they had picked up, and one climber, Jacquis Botkin, understanding quite a bit of English and speaking some, we managed. Both Terray and Botkin have since fallen to their death. Terray in Switzerland, and Botkin on the first winter expedition on Mt. McKinley in 1967.

But again we are jumping ahead of our story and the Frenchmen are still on the mountain.

When Don took the stakes to the climbers I got my first full-page picture story on mountain climbers. This was something I had looked forward to for quite a while. To prove that I was there I set up a shot of myself sharing food with the Frenchmen in front of their tent. Self photos can prove points to disbelievers, as well as help paint a more graphic story.

On May 26 the Frenchmen topped Mt. Huntington. Here's a portion of my story to the *Anchorage Daily Times* which was picked up by the UPI out of Seattle. Quote:

"When a team of the world's best climbers tackled a peak which had never been scaled, the score was a mighty close one, and not without error.

"An eight-man French expedition won the score on May 26, but previously-unscaled Mt. Huntington, in the shadow of Mt. McKinley, demanded her toll. Leader of the team, Lionel Terray, who is considered one of the four top mountain climbers today, fell over thirty feet while trying to scale an overhanging ice fall, and injured his right shoulder and arm. Another of the climbers, Marc Martinetti, was confined to the tent with snow blindness for four days.

"Adding to the misery of the injured men, the temperature dropped from —20° to —40° repeatedly. Winds of hurricane force, estimated in gusts up to ninety miles an hour, all but tore them from the face of the peak . . .

146

"The first men to scale Mt. Huntington are: Lionel Terray, Paul Gendre, Marciel Cicquel, Larce Martinetti, Jacques Botkin, Jacques Soubije, Jean Louis Bernetat, and Sylvin Sarthous." Endquote.

Considering the great difficulty and hardship the Frenchmen had faced — enough to call it quits without trying Mt. McKinley — Don Sheldon dreamed up a scheme of all schemes, to put "Yetis" on the mountain. Up to this point I seemed to have been the only female to make repeated visits, but I had written so much about her that other fems got the whim. Sheldon made the most of it.

After Sheldon brought the mountaineers who were first to scale the Moose's tooth back to Talkeetna, I interviewed Walter Welsch, the only one of the German group who could speak English. His comment about Alaska and America in general is one which I believe well worth repeating:

"I cannot tell what I am thinking. It's a lot. But I can say, it's one of the finest countries I ever saw."

Thank you, Walter Welsch.

CHAPTER XVI

ARCTIC AIR LIFT

The summer of '64 was well spent before I could get around to filing my homesteading claim, Sept. 9, 1964.

Meanwhile, through the Alaska Press Club, I received three top honors at the annual awards dinner. Shortly after this I received an invitation to participate with other members of the press media throughout the world in Arctic Airlift week in October. This included many Alaskan activities, topped off by a flight over the North Pole to Sunderstorm Greenland, to Dye Base No. 1 and Dye Base No. 2. Who could resist such an invitation?

In Anchorage we had a full round of briefings and luncheons and intros to VIP's, as well as a trip to the Nike Missile Site and Mt. Summit.

There was also a most enlightening review of the Biathlon Skiers, Olympic champions who demonstrated many of the army's techniques developed for Arctic warfare. I could have enjoyed watching these skiers without the rifle-firing from standing, kneeling and prone positions, but it was all part of the course.

One highlight during this time was my meeting Alaska's first glacier pilot, Bob Reeve, now owner of the Reeve Aleutian Airways. Another was getting to know Colonel Bernt Balchen, who wrote *Come North With Me*. When I expressed my disappointment about the bookstores being sold out of copies, Colonel Balchen said he believed he could take care of that problem. To my sheer delight, on the night of the banquet in his honor, Colonel Balchen walked up to me an said, "I haven't forgotten your request."

I just couldn't believe it. With the big brass bowing and scraping, here he comes with the book I had wanted so badly. What makes a great man great? I sometimes believe that a prime prerequisite is humanity to man — a quality which, if lost, may well lead to decline.

The story of our North Pole flight, and of our reliving of Colonel Balkhen's epic rescue on the Greenland Ice Cap during the early days of flying was written by newsmen from throughout the United States to Norway, Colonel Balchen's boyhood home. These stories can be read elsewhere; and certainly anyone wishing a good picture of the Arctic should read Colonel Balchen's *Come North With Me*.

I guess I'll just have to blame my offbeat Arctic Airlift story on being a female. Why don't I tell the truth? Statistics and defense mechanisms leave me a little cold. These highly-precisioned instruments of defense are beyond my own comprehension, much less trying to explain them to others. Incapable of writing the big stories, I wrote about what I did understand and feel, an act of kindness, as we started our flight, which showed me that the military has a heart.

My story did not make the headlines, but it was published in the *Fairbanks News-Miner* and in the *Frontiersman*, a weekly newspaper in Palmer, the agricultural heart of Alaska. It was captioned "Talkeetna Is Arctic Airlift Guest" and I quote in full, with the permission of Publisher Bill Snedden of Fairbanks and then Mayor Theodore O. Schmidtke of Palmer, editors with whom I have enjoyed working.

I felt pretty small as I watched a snow plow and a jeep loaded into the C-130 in which we were to ride. I wondered what it would be like inside the plane when we were handed ear plugs. When we were given seats which pulled down from the side of the hull and faced the inside of the plane, I felt this must be more or less the way paratroopers ride. Certainly we encountered that which I did not expect. Here is my story. Quote:

"To aid a man who needed surgery, a C-130, in which newsmen from Europe and the U.S. were riding to view Top of the World Airlift capabilities, diverted its course and dipped four hundred miles southward, from the Nome area to Kenai, on a mission of mercy. This is the 17th Troop Carrier Squadron of Elmendorf Air Force Base, Alaska.

"To show the vital role which Arctic Airlift does, and must command over 58,000 square miles of our virtually uninhabited northern frontier, representatives from the news media were flown to Alaska to view and participate in demonstrations and Polar flights during the last week of October.' This is the Alaskan Air Command.

149

"To demonstrate the all but incomprehensible speed and efficiency with which the Military can strike, units from the U.S. Army and U.S. Air Force joined in King Crab VII exercises and Arctic Airlift Week activities, October 25-30. Major General James C. Jensen, Commander of the Alaskan Air Command, was aided by Major General Ned D. Moore, Commander of the United States Army, Alaska, and the 452nd Troop Carrier Wing, a Continental Air Command Reserve unit of California, in Airlift Activities and in transporting news media to Alaska. The 17th Troop Carrier Squadron of Elmendorf Air Force Base, Alaska hosted the press on flights via Polar deployment to Sonderstorm Air Base, Greenland, and to remote Early Warning Radar and White Alice sites in Alaska.

"Paramount among the observations made by this reporter is the fact that no task is too trivial nor none too staggering for the Alaskan Command. Big men stoop to serve, small ones to conquer. We saw retiring Major General Ned D. Moore share the first cut of a cake, baked in his honor, with a child. We saw the eyes of Eskimo children brighten as G.I.'s approached with bulging pockets. In our own heart we felt more secure when the huge C-130 Lockheed *Hercules* in which we were riding, changed its course to aid P.F.C. Mike Stischak, an M.P. from Toole, Utah, who is now recovering from an emergency appendectomy at the USAF hospital at Elmendorf Air Force Base, Alaska.

"The Alaskan Air Command plays an integral role in our lives. Previously the meaning was vague. Now we know that every man, woman and child in the U.S.A. is dependent upon its efficiency and maintaining of the lifeline to our scientific and defense installations in the frozen north.

"A joint paradrop involving the Alaskan Air Command and the U.S. Army, Alaska, was staged at Claxton Drop Zone, Fort Richardson. Airborne personnel and five C-130's from the Alaska Air Command's 17th Troop Carrier Squadron, commanded by Lt. Col. John H. Statts of Elmendorf, was joined by the 172 Infantry Brigade of Fort Richardson under the command of Colonel George W. Bauknight. Some 234 parachutists from the 4th Battalion of the 23rd Infantry made the jump.

"A team of Air Force paramedics parachuted to a simulated accident scene, gave first aid and hoisted the victims into an

H. 21 Helicopter of the 5017th Operations Squadron which hovered under simulated firing conditions.

"Although awed by the sky spectacular, amazed by the split second timing, half blinded by smoke signals and dazed by continuous firing as chopper after chopper churned overhead, we were thankful that it was only simulated warfare. We do not deny that in our own heart there was a continuing and non-suppressible prayer that it never happen, not literally.

"There is little doubt that the realization of the Air Command's complete ability to retaliate almost immediately anywhere on the face of the globe holds back the Red tide, which is within seeing distance from Alaska, across the Bering Straight. In a way we are all dependent upon the Alaskan Air Command's newest unit, the 17th Troop Carrier Squadron, which is the lifeline of two Distant Early Warning radar sites on the Greenland Ice Cap and remote A&W radar sites in Alaska. The 17th maintains Sonderstorm Air Base, Greenland, and is also responsible for search, rescue and air evacuation of the North Atlantic area.

"Flying within a few miles of a Russian air base is a sobering factors which makes one realize that the very existence of our world as we know it today depends upon the Air Force's ability to command Aerospace. Visiting the Army's missile site at Mt. Summit and watching Olympic Biathlons in a cross-country ski race combined with markmanship in sub-zero temperatures at Fort Richardson, makes us realize that the soldier in Alaska undergoes the toughest training under the most adverse weather conditions on the globe. We salute both the Alaskan Air Command and the U.S. Army, Alaska for a job well done.

"Our personal thanks to information officers Lt. Col. Elmer F. Edwards, U.S. Army Headquarters Fort Richardson, Alaska; Major Robert H. Reed, Director of Information, Headquarters Alaska Air Command, Seattle; and Capt. John Walton and A/1c Stan McDonnough, Information Division Headquarters Alaskan Air Command, Elmendorf Air Force Base, Alaska.

"To the C-130 crews who flew news media on various missions, to the Anchorage Chamber of Commerce and the Anchorage Press which hosted us for luncheons; to Major General Ned Moore of the Army; to Colonel Bernt Balchen, Air Force, retired; to Major General James G. Jensen, Commander of the Alaskan Air Command and to Betzi Woodman, Anchorage writer and former president of the Anchorage Press Club, who offered this freelancer her seat on a plane, and to many more persons whom we should like to recognize and the nameless thousands participating in Arctic Airlift Week activities. Our most sincere desire is to reward your efforts by transmitting these activities to the press." Endquote.

CHAPTER XVII

ME? GO POLAR BEAR HUNTING?

Winter came, but I was too busy to notice. Much of my time was spent in organizing centennial committees throughout our big borough, with a very small population. Although larger than most states, our borough has a population of 6,000. Most of these persons live in Palmer or along the road between Palmer and Talkeetna, and I kept it pretty warm. Each community along the route was planning for the Alaska Purchase Centennial in 1967.

Yet I had newspaper deadlines to meet, too; and all these things had to "go" despite the fact that Talkeetna was engulfed in a five-day white out. Knowing that several downed pilots were waiting it out at the Fairview Inn, I canvassed if for column material.

When in need of any sort of advice or information, there were always plenty of views at the Fairview, where world problems are solved and dissolved daily at the bar. This time I struck it rich.

Things were more interesting than I had even anticipated. With my editor's permission, let me quote this particular column, "Talkeetna Topics," in full, because it does present a fair picture of a problem faced by pilots and guides at the time. Fairbanks, Feb. 16, 1965:

"Sometimes one listens . . . and wonders.

"It's a poor white out that doesn't force some interesting person down in our village. This time there were several: two helicopter crews, one en route from Elmendorf to Fairbanks for Polar Strike, another from Fairbanks headed for the Chulitna River bridge site where they are drilling for abutments and piers, and incidentally, where this columnist has homesteaded.

"Among those forced down in planes were Bob Cooper, of Cooper Flying and Guide Service in Fairbanks, and Roy Stoltz, of the Missile Club at Clear, who seems to have fished every stream in this area. But three feet of snow on the ground and a white blanket extending skyward was not the proper setting for an angler. It seemed more conducive to thoughts of polar bear hunts, and Bob just happens to have a big one coming up the last day of this month.

"Previously this columnist has felt nothing but sympathy for the polar bear, with planes tracking him down and landing within a few hundred yards for the kill. What chance does the bear have? His tracks are exposed for miles and a plane can close in on him within minutes. There's no hiding. He's dead! He and the rest of his clan until man has sent him the way of the sea cow, the whooping crane and the bison.

"These were our thoughts. Now we're confused.

"When two of the greatest pilots and guides of the northland speak, one listens. Perhaps Don Sheldon and Bob Cooper are right. At least we believe these pilots more qualified to express opinions than one who reads a book and/or periodicals, as we have done. Perhaps their deductions are even of greater merit than those of bar boozing specialists who solve world problems daily.

"Our opinion, for what it is worth, is perhaps as valid as one who shook hands with Einstein in his day, thus declaring himself an expert on third dimension. But these facts become self evident:

"A man with the means to hunt polar bear is not looking for bear meat — this he gives to the natives. What's more, he is not looking for a sow with a cub, but a trophy. His selectiveness, sharpened, curtailed, and controlled by the game laws, causes him to pass many a tempting target.

"The hunting range of a small plane over the huge polar ice cap might be compared with one placing a dime at the base of the Empire State Building and saying he will step from it to the top. The poor polar, which we thought had no respite, happens to have the largest uninhabited area on the face of the globe as his retreat.

"Unless proven false, we'll take Cooper's word for it. Small plane penetration over the ice cap is nothing in comparison to the all-over size. The polar bear population could never be depleted by this method of hunting.

"We'll accept Sheldon's theory, too, that more polars are ruthlessly destroyed off the shores of Norway and Sweden from whaling vessels and fishing boats than will ever be taken by plane. A hunter in a plane is very limited, both in range and poundage. Hunters aboard commercial or pleasure craft cruising in icy waters are not so limited in range and tonnage. Many hunters are aboard. Polar hunting from a luxury liner is now a fad in the Eastern Hemisphere. All a tycoon has to do is come to the rail and shoot when a bear is spotted on an ice floe." Endquote.

Although we sat and talked of polar-bear hunting for a long while, I never realized why Cooper was discussing all this and perhaps he was just talking it over with the others because the Alaskan legislature was trying to stop polar bear hunting from light planes. Too many persons thought it inhumane. Cooper, as well as other guides, had several hunts coming up and was afraid they would shut the season down, thus causing all of them to have to cancel hunts.

"We need help on this matter, and we need it bad," Cooper commented as he sized me up like a computer, probably wondering if I could take it. "Would you be interested in going along, to Point Barrow, on a polar bear hunt? Of course you are to bring your cameras and typewriter."

He couldn't mean it! A polar bear hunt? At the topmost point of the continent? Surely he must have forgotten.

"But I'm a grandmother," I stammered.

"That hasn't kept you from flying with Don nor over the North Pole with the Air Corps, has it?"

"But what would the big game hunters think?"

"It doesn't matter what they think, so long as I ask you along. There'll probably be seven of them. They'll probably appreciate a few photos and a story themselves. Should get a good magazine article as well as newspaper material. Are you game? Do you want to go? Are you chicken?"

I hesitated.

"Of course," he said with a wink at Don, "you'll be expected to sleep with all seven men every night, melt snow for cooking and dishwashing, skin out the bear and do a few little chores."

"You're faded," I countered. "When do we start?"

"Meet us at the Nordale Hotel in Fairbanks on the night of the 28th of this month — and be sure to have eiderdown underwear, cameras, film and typewriter. And watch that weight! We're in small planes."

155

I still couldn't believe it, but nevertheless I wrote all the advance publication I could and looked up game and fishing laws and studied the legislation before the house. Had to know what I was fighting, if I chose to fight for these guides. Cooper had been fair enough: he said I could write it as I saw it, that I didn't have to agree with him nor any of the guides. I was on my own and owed them nothing. He just wanted someone who writes to see firsthand. I was flattered, of course, and felt this would be one of the biggest assignments ever.

As usual, all those who read my columns knew what was up, and I promised to keep them informed. I never missed a column. Sometimes they were written from Texas, on a plane, or from New York City while visiting the World's Fair; but my followers seemed to share my adventures eagerly. With permission from Editor Ted O. Schmidtke of *The Frontiersman*, perhaps this story is best told as the continuing story in my *Talkeetna Ticky-Tac* column.

On the first day I wrote:

"Just our speed! Your columnist is headed for a polar bear hunt out of Barrow, and the only strange animals we have seen so far is a live pig and a dead pheasant in a Fairbanks cafe.

"But we have faith, lots of it, otherwise we wouldn't have paid Kosloskys forty-seven bucks for a suit of underwear — and no black lace! Yet we're told that eiderdown and eiderdown only is recommended for going down on ice floes, in polar pursuit. Maybe it's because a mouth full of feathers frustrates bruin's chewin'.

"We'll keep you informed — via bottle a la bobble from an open lead on the Arctic ice cap. In case 'Ticky Tac' fails to show in the newspaper for one week, hold your breath. If we fail to sound off for a second consecutive week . . . you can relax.

"A jet has just juggled a couple of hunters, Bernard McNamara and George Brittin, in from Minnesota. One of our guides, Mike Ehredt, who has a charter plane service in Barrow, brung 'em to the Nordale where we are waiting for heap big hunter Bob Cooper to show with more Knights of the Nimrod. One local hunter, Don Obray of Anchorage, got polar fever last season when bit by a cub, and is back for a larger dose. We understand he gave the cub to the Seattle zoo.

156

"Since yours truly is the only Chechako on the hunt, we'll wait until we get to Barrow to harrow you with our tales of frozen toes and nose on ice floes. And just think, yesterday morning Alice Powell invited 'Ticky Tac' down to the new cafe and dining room at the Talkeetna Motel where she went to a great deal of trouble preparing eggs Benedict. Guess we'll just have to savor the flavor as we flow out to sea.

"Although we knew none of these hunters prior to their arrival in Fairbanks, we have every faith that they will be gentlemen enough to shoot that bear before his breath frosts the lens of our camera — if we manage to stay out of their hair. On the other hand, Cooper and Ehredt have mighty good reps as pilots and guides, and we don't believe they would let them open season on a shutter clickin' grandma. But come to think of it, maybe we'd best shush with the mush or they just might. We were invited along to take pictures and write, we'd never tell that we've tucked a tag in the bag because we have every intention of getting our own polar, and legally. This news we'll break to Cooper gently, while he debates with the hunter as to whether the bouncin' bruin below is Boone and Crockett. For your columnist, most any polar would do. Now we could wish for a cub to bring home as a pet for our grand . . . Shush, Mary Carey, you're always getting carried away on some tangent . . . on with the news." Endquote.

Then I brought in a little local news which I gathered on the train ride from Talkeetna to Fairbanks, about persons very near and dear to the columnist. Quote:

"Seeing Lloyd Wohlgemuth on the train did our heart good because we were not so sure but what he had taken his last ride when he went to Seattle, where he has undergone extensive treatment for cancer. The miracle of modern medicine has enabled him to return to his family. In fact his wife, Dorothy, met the train and taxied us to our huntin' headquarters. Lloyd and "Dotty" were our neighbors in Talkeetna for two years, and their son, Gayland, was one of the charter members of our first high school, composed of eight students and yours truly, as the total faculty. That was in '62-'64. Didn't know how difficult your columnist was to replace. It took four teachers. Of course we admit that the new road, forty-seven students and a new building might have a little bearing on the situation.

"But we loved it, and perhaps no other instructor was ever so effective in teaching Independent and Dependent clauses. Remember, Gayland, those implicit instructions I gave you when you were having difficulty? The clauses in your sentence were joined by the coordinating conjunction, 'but'. I had told you several times that if a clause made sense by itself, it was independent; but if it depended upon the rest of the sentence for its meaning, it was dependent. You hesitated. Then I came through with our never to be forgotten, "Go ahead, cut off your 'but' and see if it makes good sense." Endquote.

En route to Fairbanks I was looking through the newspaper when I saw the smiling photo of Dorothy Marie Jones. I was so proud of Dorothy that I just had to comment:

"Our Queen from Talkeetna, insofar as we are concerned, won the highest award at the Fur Rendezvous in Anchorage. Although Dorothy Marie Jones did not become 'Miss Alaska,' she was named 'Miss Congeniality.' This title, which is bestowed by the other pretty queen contestants, is for the one among themselves with the best personality and just plain old get-along ability. Anyone who knows Dorothy Marie would applaud their choice. Dorothy was also a charter member of our first high school class and we are justly proud."

Chapter XVIII

SO THIS IS THE YUKON!

On March 1, as planned, we started our flight for Barrow. Perhaps it would be more nearly correct if I said we started on a Cook's tour of Alaska, with Barrow as a final destination.

From the time I read my first novel I became enthralled with the works of Jack London and Rex Beach. Few names possess the romance and legendary quality of the Yukon. Now I was to see the river which is three miles wide when it reaches Ft. Yukon, hundreds of miles from its mouth. This mighty river was impressive enough when I saw it in Canada, at Dawson City, now I was to see what this Amazon of the north was like where it wound its way seaward.

For two days we flew on dead reckoning across tundra, through mountain passes and over contorted deserts of ice along the Yukon. In Canada, and in the eastern part of Alaska one can follow the winding, narrow, and treacherous road from Dawson City to the Alaskan border, with a mighty river a mile below. And believe me, there are places along that hair-pin where, if a motorist rolled over, I feel he might never be found; but where we were now flying, the river spilled all over the country in ox-bows and braids.

We accepted Cooper's explanation of "dead reckoning." "When you're flying 'dead reckoning,' if you reckon wrong, you're dead," he said as two planeloads of us began a tour of Alaska. We could have reached the "Top of the World" in half the distance and time; but all of us, of course, wanted to see Alaska, the part which was like she was during gold mining days.

Some two hundred miles west of Fairbanks we made our first landing on the Yukon at Ruby, a fabulous old gold mining center where there is still a little mining, considerable fishing, some trapping, and a little prospecting going on. Although Ruby roared during gold rush days, the village in the cleft of a mountain has settled to a complacent hum. Frozen fish wheels, sled dog trails and log cabins were a strange contrast to our aircraft landing on the frozen river, which must have looked just as it did during the days of Robert W. Service. We visited Jeannie's Cafe, which is reminiscent of her more picturesque days.

Only thirty minutes west of Ruby we landed at Galena, where, if we had not seen Uncle Sam's huge radar domes and put our wheels down below our skiis for landing on the long, paved strip, which would have accommodated anything from a Cub to a C-133 Hercules, we could have believed ourselves in Robert Service's Alaska. Most of our time was spent in the Yukon Bar, where one felt as if drinks should have been paid for from a little poke of gold dust.

The bartender, Hobo Joe, for whom there could have been no other name, was as colorful a character as they come. As Cooper, Brittin and McNamara repeatedly rang the bell to buy the house a drink the crowd increased, and tales of the Yukon began to match the size of the sixty-two-foot mural on the Shooting of Dan McGrew, which stretched around the walls.

"The dents in the bell," explained Hobo, "were put there last month by a crazy pilot — I won't mention his name, but it wasn't Cooper — who left forty-two bullet holes in the wall. He really tied a good one on. After the second fifth the only way he would ring the bell was with his pistol.

"After polishing off the third fifth he got mad at me and said: 'You so-an-so, I'm going to shoot your teeth right out of your mouth.'

"'Not while they're in,' I told him as I grabbed the upper bridge, which I acquired after a fist fight, and threw it into the air. That damn plate hit the floor in three places."

Bullet holes back of the bar confirmed the shooting, to say the least.

Meanwhile Hobo Joe had sent for Singin' Sam to serenade us. Strumming his guitar like a wrangler, Sam sang in everything from his native tongue to English and Spanish. He had picked up melodies and lyrics from wayfaring strangers throughout his thirty-one years, and it was his birthday. He had triplets and was expecting twins. Although Sam was already the father of eleven children, his wife was only twenty-six years old.

The singing was unexpectedly good, and a beer would get you any number, until Sam got a little too close to Cooper's ear with the volume revved up and asked for a request.

"What about Silent Night, Western style?" Bob asked.

Singin' Sam faltered. Frustrated for a few seconds while you could see the wheels turning, Cooper prodded with, "You bastard, you said you knew all the songs."

Immediately an Indian version wailed through the smoke rings.

Quite a contrast to the local coloring was Yvonne Worthington, a freelance artist of Anchorage, who was free-handing the last verse to "The Shooting of Dan McGrew" in Old English with a print so perfect that one would not have believed without seeing. Formerly a graphic illustrator from Boeing in Seattle, Yvonne says: "Have brush, will travel."

So personable her character and intriguing her work that hunger was forgotten until Leonard Veerhesser walked in and announced that Betty had our steaks ready at the Yukon Inn. What chow! Real Alaskan-sized T-Bones — off Texas steers — no doubt, baked potatoes and the works, except for salad. That and milk are harder to find than gold nuggets, and probably worth more. Thus far we had found neither.

As the DEW Line domes and multiple spires of White Alice communcations faded behind our prop wash on March 2, we left the Yukon River and headed up the Koyukuk River, into the vast uninhabited waste of a new world. Flying over valleys pocked with spruce and loaded with moose — McNamara counted 32 — we saw little else of life, except for one herd of caribou, for some 250 desolate miles.

Kotzebue was a different story. Here, although the Eskimo women fished through a hole in the ice for shee fish and Tom cod by jiggling a barbless treble hook from a line maneuvered in a sort of dexterious knitting motion which dropped or took on line, hotel accommodations at the Arctic Inn were modern. Here, too, T-Bones overflowing huge platters, with all the trimmings except salad, were served at the immaculately clean Field's Cafe.

During our day in Kotzebue I met Jack H. Jonas, a strapping six-foot grandson of Colman Jonas, founder of the Jonas Brothers in Denver. Jack, who was stalking his own polar bear as well as seeking pelts, deduced that this writer was interested in native craft as well as hunting.

"There's a place down the beach that just opened today," Jack suggested, "where they do their own carving and lapidary work. Would you like for me to introduce you to Mr. Spikes?"

My parka was already on, so I just flipped up the ruff. I had wanted to see Eskimos carve ivory since I arrived in Alaska, almost three years ago. Thank you, Jack, for this introduction. Inside the S&S Crafts shop a native named Joe was etching as well as carving. John Spikes was utilizing some beautiful lapidary equipment in an anteroom. Huge saws with diamond-edged blades for slabbing the native jade — which came from nearby Jade Mountain in the Kobuk River area — hummed as they consumed electricity from a city plant. Vertical lapidary units, with sanding wheels which graduate from coarse to fine sandpaper until the stone is finally ready for buffing with jeweler's rouge on leather, stood ready to receive and polish cabochons. I was in a strange, yet familiar world, having been a rock hound for several years.

As hand-carved ivory bracelets, polar bears, seal and birds tempted me to rob the cache which must carry me through a bear hunt, I compromised for a ceremonial mask. This small, translucent mask, in the form of a pendant which was made from a caribou hoof and inlaid with gold, dangled from a delicate chain of gold. Matching earrings were irresistible.

Ivory birds perched on a terra-cotta rookery revealed the ingenuity of these craftsmen. A bit of worm-eaten driftwood cast upon the beach was transformed into a work of art.

Constant callers were almost as interesting as the craft. There was "Mr. Reindeer," Dick Birchell, who was in the area to inventory, protect, and help the Eskimo with his herd. Out of Kotzebue there were seven herds, and the results were not as good as hoped. Often the Eskimo did not keep close watch over the herd.

There was B.N.C. Robert Trammell, with the Coast Guard, whose duties ranged from teaching the Eskimo how to vote, to giving instructions on safety requirements for boats. Even the Eskimo must register his boat and carry life preservers.

"Registering a boat and giving it a number is not difficult," says Trammell, "but did you ever try to describe them? They think I'm sort of nuts when I say 'skin upon bone and skin upon skin.'"

A man, very great of stature, who I thought must surely wrestle polar bear with his bare hands, walked in. Imagine my surprise in finding that "Old Red," as Mr. Richmond called himself, wrestled with bipeds rather than quadrupeds. The son of this school principal, David, was learning to carve ivory.

Mr. Spikes began pulling artifacts from beneath the counter, explaining their use and the area where they were found. Soon Mrs. Spikes — Ada — came home from the hospital where she was employed as a secretary. Together they gave me a verbal tour of the Kobuk River. Both of them had worked with the Bureau of Indian Affairs for five years as teachers and counselors. In my mind's eye I saw real, native Alaska, where the tallest tribe of Indians lives completely away from civilization. I was assured there was much jade in the area.

'I found a pair of mastodon tusks," said Spikes, "and this summer when Dr. Dorothy Jean Ray, an anthropologist who has been digging in the area for some time comes back, we are going to unearth them."

"You would enjoy Dr. Ray," Mrs. Spikes remarked, "and she is one of the greatest. Would you like to come along? Bring your sleeping bag, rock hammer and down underwear. The temperature may hit 90° during the day but it gets mighty cold at night and we will be sleeping in tents."

You can bet I boiled with anticipation. To go where white man has seldom trod, to visit remote Indian villages, to hunt jade and artifacts, as well as to have an anthropologist along with a treasure of the ages waiting to be unearthed. Accept such an invitation? Who could resist?

Mrs. Spikes suggested that I see the mineral collection of another rock hound, Evan L. Nelson, an engineer at the Kotze-Hospital. She asked if I would mind walking a few blocks. In Kotzebue everyone walks, almost.

I though Mr. Spike's drawl was unmistakable, so I asked him.

"You bet I'm from Texas," he replied, "Waco. I barnstormed all over the state and did wing walking on planes when flying was young."

Before we reached the Nelsons, Ada filled in a few details. Major Spikes had been a meteorologist in the Air Force. His specialty was long-range weather forecasting.

"And tomorrow," I asked, "will we take off for Barrow?"

"It will be fair," he predicted.

At the very comfortable apartment of the Nelsons there was running water, wall-to-wall carpeting; and in fact this very pleasant and modern unit was as comfortable as one would find "stateside". Mr. Nelson was at a Boy Scout meeting. We had coffee while we waited. No one calls to announce visits in the Arctic; but one is always welcome and time is of no great import.

When Mr. Nelson returned we went to the basement, which was also heated, where he had a shop. For thirty years he had been collecting rocks, beginning while prospecting in McKinley National Park.

"You collected in a National Park?" I asked in amazement.

"Under permission granted by the U.S. Senate," he replied.

I asked about some carnelian agate and a thunderegg, "Are they from the park?"

"No," he answered with a slow grin, "they are from the Talkeetna Range, right under your nose. You did say you live in Talkeetna?"

I felt like a fool, but not quite so badly when he said the only way to get into the area was to fly in.

"That's the story of stone, ivory, and artifacts in Alaska," he made comment which I have found quite true, "you take a boat to where there is no dock, or a plane to where there is no landing strip."

It was getting late. Tomorrow, if the forecast of Major Spikes was right, our party would be flying. Again, according to our pilot and guide, Bob Cooper, on "dead reckoning." Yet, having flown the Yukon River with Cooper for three days there was little worry insofar as I was concerned. Tomorrow, if Spike's weather forecast and Cooper's flying were both as good as I believed, we would be landing at the "Top of the World" for a polar bear hunt.

As predicted, the morning broke bright and clear. Eskimo women were already fishing through holes cut in the ice before our planes got underway. The temperature stood at —34°.

As the menfolk refueled and warmed up the motors of the Cessna 180 and the Super Cub, I observed the ancient method of fishing used by the natives; and of course I kept clicking and grinding away with press and movie cameras. Through the hole in the ice, which was about three feet thick and used as a runway for several light planes, the woman maneuvered the line much as one would knit and purl by a dexterous movement of two sticks, notched at the end. The catch, which she shook from the barbless hoof, froze as it fell to the surface of the ice beside the sled upon which she sat.

I wanted to watch longer, but purring motors told me it was time to start on the last day's journey northward, to the "Top of the World" for a polar bear hunt.

Previously little time had been spent in observing the flying techniques of our pilot and guide, Bob Cooper. Having landed on glaciers in the Alaska Range to cover mountain climbing stories and rescues, this reporter is not the squeamish type.

For the first hour all went well. The Baird Mountains were no sweat. Off our right flank, Mike Ehredt, who was flying cover on the hunt for Cooper, piloted a red Super Cub. Below us there was little sign of life; but the red plane against the white peaks was quite picturesque.

The Delong Mountains were a different story. Flying through a pass we hit squirrely winds, down drafts and some zero-zero visibility. At times we lost sight of the plane flying alongside. When we glimpsed it now and then it looked as if an invisible Rat Terrier had caught a mouse and was giving it the works. Our pilot was talking into the headpiece but we could not hear what he was saying.

We hit an air pocket, then our dropping Cessna hit hard on a squirrely current. Cooper did not seem in too great a sweat. As big and as sturdy as they come, he seemed as well in control of the situation as the elements allowed. One of the hunters looked a little green.

Just as one of the Chechakos from the East asked if it would be wise to turn back, Bob broke through and over the mountains to the frozen Chuckchi Sea. Below us lay Cape Lisburne. Bob looked for Mike. We did not see him.

"I told him we would land here for refuelling," Bob explained. "We'll find a smooth spot beyond these pressure ridges and bring her down."

We were over two hundred miles north of Kotzebue. Although the Cessna in which we were riding might have flown the six hundred miles to Barrow without refuelling, the Super Cub was only good for about four-and-a-half hours. We were hardly out of the plane before Mike came sailing through the clouds. Bob motioned for him not to land too near our plane: — "too much weight on one cake of ice is not too good," he explained.

As they refueled I took a look at the strange Chuckchi Sea. Smooth in some spots, as where we landed, yet broken and contorted pressure ridges around us spoke of the endless struggle of the restless water below to escape the ever-hardning encasement of ice. I wondered how it would sound to hear the sea break through the ice, and how high she would spew house-sized blue-green boulders. How long would it take, if she split, for the non-relenting cold to seal these breaks, which ran further than the eye could see? Someone said the temperature was —42° I could have believed it —62°.

I was suffering. I just had to relieve myself, and it may have been half-a-mile to the nearest pressure ridge. There was absolutely nothing to hide behind except the slender body of the plane. I was sure the men must have relieved themselves on the opposite side of the Super Cub. But I had to squat. I had no choice. I got as close to the side of the plane as I could, and unzipped three layers. Cold! I forgot I was in the prop wash and I don't think my rear end thawed out for two days after we reached Barrow. I'll swear it was 100 below in that wash. Blown past the tail of the plane, amber icicles clinking to the frozen sea taught me what not to do.

Lifting from the ice of the Chuckchi we headed up the coastline for Barrow. Determining where land and sea met was difficult. We followed what Bob said was a spit of land for over 150 miles. From Naohok to Icy Cape, a deserted military installation, we saw little sign of life. Suddenly there were many tracks and wallows on the tundra. Then they were below us, hundreds and hundreds of caribou.

Nearing the village of Wainwright, we saw many heavily-loaded dog sleds headed homeward. It was not difficult to guess what they were carrying. Our pilot circled to give us a better look. Outside every hut many dogs were staked. Our guide said it was caribou we saw stacked on top of their houses — where it was kept away from the dogs in nature's deep-freeze.

We would have liked to stop; but we had no choice other than making Barrow before nightfall. Bearing inland again to the northeast we flew over Skull Cliff and Peard Bay. Our guide told us that soon we would be passing the Wiley Post-Will Rogers memorial. Flying so low that we could have read the inscriptions, it wasn't difficult to imagine obituaries being written here.

Again there were caribou below us.

"About five minutes out," Cooper remarked, "there's Barrow."

I could have believed we were at the end of the world rather than the top of it. In relief against a red sky the radar domes of Point Barrow marked man's last outpost. Communication spires were suddenly above us and wires barely below us as we came in for a landing. Barrels by the hundred were scattered over the barren landscape. Before I could ask why, lights blinked on down the snow-covered runway.

We were landing in Barrow. The temperature was —34°, but it didn't matter. Tomorrow we would go polar bear hunting.

Chapter XIX

BARREN BARROW

Could this be Barrow? This hovel of plywood box houses, with caribou and reindeer carcasses on flat roofs, and sled dogs staked out without shelter, for the most part, in the granulated snow? Shy children with big dark slant eyes and oval faces peeped curiously at strangers as they passed, but said nothing.

To get anywhere, we walked. There was one taxi in town; but it was broken down at the moment. We always walked down the middle of the street, and were rarely challenged for this advantageous position, except when a military jeep came in from Point Barrow; but Barrow was off limits for the military, and it didn't take me long to know the reason.

As we walked toward town Cooper pointed toward a plywood structure not too far from the end of the runway saying, "That's the Bore's Den, where the menfolk stay. I've made arrangements for Mary to stay at the Top of the World hotel. There was a hotel with bath and running water in Barrow, but it burned to the ground last year. There's nothing to be afraid of or worry about. I know these people here and they'll take good care of you. I brought you here for you to make up your mind about polar bear hunting. You don't have to take anything off anybody. You're here to write and you're on your own."

I didn't see how anyone could be much more fair.

The lobby of the Top of the World, an unpainted shotgun affair, must have been 10 x 12 or even 12 x 14. It was furnished with an old divan and one table and four or five chairs. One corner was blocked by a counter which served as a desk, and there were stairs leading to a second floor, where I never visited. One floor was enough. But the proprietors were kind, especially the ladies, who were sisters, I think.

I was shown my room and the bathroom, if one speaks benevolently. Although there was steam heat, and my room was always quite warm, there was no room in the room. What little space there was was usurped by bunk beds, upper and lower against one wall, and a night stand upon which was a pitcher of water and a wash pan. Since the stand was not large enough to accommodate my typewriter, I asked for a table. The card table which was brought to me would hardly squeeze between my bed and the next wall. The bunk above mine, a real head banger, served as a storage spot for my miscellaneous gear.

The bathroom was of the variety which I have never seen before and hardly wish to visit again, although far preferable to the prop-wash on the Chuckchi Sea. It had three enclosed stalls, each with a regular commode seat on a square, or rather oblong, concrete base. Below the seat was a five-gallon "honey bucket" as they called the removeable containers. These were collected, weekly, and replaced by empties, much as garbage is collected in cities. There was running water in the wash basin, from an overhead tank. Paper towels and running water were luxuries: for them I was thankful.

The drinking water in the hotel, as in cafes, was something else. It was stored as cakes of fresh ice, usually outside the front door, until needed. Some places kept it covered; but for the most part these cakes of fresh water must have made good stand-ins for city fire plugs, in so far as the roving malemutes were concerned. They could never resist heisting a leg. These canine-flavored blocks, when brought inside, were rinsed off and dumped into containers to melt. In the hotel they used a five-gallon insulated tin and zinc water barrel, with a large pull-open lid at the top and a push-in spigot at the bottom. I had seen many of the same type used by oil crews out on the Texas plains for keeping their drinking water iced.

As Cooper promised, before leaving to help Mike get the fellows straightened out at the Bore's Den they came by and picked me up for dinner.

The cafe, I've forgotten the name, wasn't bad. The waitress, Elizabeth Thibadeoux, was most attractive and seemingly well educated. When I asked her for water she suggested that I just drink coffee or hot tea. No one drank water, and she didn't have to tell me why. Those who did not drink coffee disguised the flavor with cool ade or some sort of powdered drink mix.

I found out later that Elizabeth's husband, who was a pilot and guide, had been lost on an ice floe while on a polar bear hunt, and never found. Part native, Elizabeth had chosen to stay in Barrow to raise her children, one of whom was in college, although Elizabeth was only in her thirties. Her children were beautiful, native and French. I believe she told me her husband was from Evangeline country in Louisiana, although I am not sure.

The food, which was served in generous quantity, was fair, about like that of an average cafe, except for lack of salad and milk, which was understandable. Only liquor and staples seemed precious enough to be flown in on the one Wein airliner, which arrived daily — at least once a week — if weather conditions were right, which they usually weren't.

"If the weather is right, we fly tomorrow, but the taxi should be in operation and we'll come by for you, so don't worry," Cooper admonished as he and the hunters said goodnight at the doorway of my hotel.

But the weather wasn't good, so I visited the school. The school and church were the only attractive buildings I had seen in Barrow. In fact, the school looked much like any other from the outside, and I was quite surprised to learn that, despite the fact that the children go to and from the school in total darkness most of the winter months, the percentage of attendance in Barrow was the best in the United States. Perhaps warmth, cleanliness, free hot lunches, and absolutely no place else to go, were contributing factors.

You can imagine my surprise when, walking into the attractive hallway, the first thing which I saw was a bulletin board featuring bluebonnets and Texas Independence day, March 2. It could have been on any Texas bulletin board at this season, but here — surely there must be teachers from Texas. There were, a mother and daughter, and the music teacher and her husband, who was scout director. I made photos, but much to my chagrin, have misplaced that set of notes.

I went to the principal's office, explained my mission and was given a cordial welcome, as well as an attractive high school girl as a guide.

The only green thing I saw growing while in Barrow was in the Texas teacher's room, where plants of various varieties were thriving under a flourescent light. The children, fourth graders, were most proud of the vegetation and overcame their shyness in their eargerness to tell me the names of the plants. It helped, too, when their teacher told them I, too, was from Texas and had seen bluebonnets grow.

170

They called me "Missie Carrie" and I spent half-a-day with them, enjoying every minute of it and amazed at the high scholastic standing maintained in their school. Their teaching and learning experiences were very similar to those of fourth graders I had taught in Wichita Falls, Texas, before my late husband and I moved to Dallas, where I was employed as a Journalism instructor at North Dallas High school.

Since the wind was still blowing hard and visibility low, I accepted an invitation to lunch in the cafeteria. Here they had milk, made from the powdered product, but it tasted good. All vegetables were from cans, but they were much the same as children ate in school cafeterias throughout the nation. We had chocolate pudding for dessert.

After lunch I visited the teacher's lounge. It was much like any other, with one exception. It, too, had "honey buckets" in the rest room.

I expressed a desire to visit the other teacher from Texas. I could have found her without a guide, except for the fact that she was in another building. As we walked down the spacious hallway, strains of "Home on the Range" greeted us from an open transom. My guide introduced me to the music teacher, who in turn introduced me to the children, telling them I was from Texas. They delighted in singing cowboy songs. "These are their favorites, anyway," explained the teacher as they swung out on "I'm an Old Cowhand, From the Rio Grande."

After school I went to the scout meeting, and then I knew beyond a doubt why school and its activities meant so much to these children. It was their life and they were making the best of it. I fully believe that when this generation has grown up, living conditions in Barrow will be much better. The school was new, and their mothers and fathers, who grew up during territorial days, knew no such luxury — as indeed it was for Barrow and the Eskimo.

The next day it was still blowing hard and white-out conditions prevailed, so I wrote.

On the third day there was still no change; but I was never one for staying inside. I had heard of a local missionary and her husband who had built a youth center in town and were doing a great deal of good work in Barrow, as they had done in other

171

outposts where they had built missions, chiefly from their own funds and whatever they could raise.

Mr. Kenneth Garrison was out of town on business; but no one could have been more gracious than Beatrice Garrison, who was a teacher in the public school, giving everything which she earned to the furthering of Christianity. She and her husband had furnished most of the funds for the Youth Center, which she showed me. Her husband had directed and done a great deal of the building himself, here and elsewhere. When they have finished a building and have trained local converts to take over, they move to a new territory where there is no mission.

I accepted her invitation to come back during the evening for Bible study. I was amazed at how much the natives knew, especially about the New Testament. Once, during high school days, when I had stars in my eyes, I had dreamed of the mission field — even thought of studying for it.

On the fourth day in Barrow it was still blowing, but on the fifth day, March 9, the wind had subsided and it was clear. Surely this was the day we had all been waiting for. Perhaps what really happened can be told no better than at the time through my column, "Talkeetna Ticky-Tac," from which I quote:

"After five days of wind that slapped canine flavored ice particles into the ruff of my parka, however tightly I drew it around my eyes and nose, it let up and yours truly was exuberant. Surely, now, the day had come for a polar bear hunt. Offshore winds brought huge open leads to within seeing distance of Barrow. This would be the day. At 9:00 A.M. the town taxi would pick me up for the hunt. This was the standing agreement for pick-up time, if flying weather came.

"At ten I was still at the hotel. The sun was shining. What a rare sight! I tried to overlook the fact that it was a little white seaward, and that black steam was boiling off the open leads. But it was quite clear overhead and the sun was really bright. Perhaps the only taxi in Barrow had broken down again or would not start because of the extreme cold. By now the planes should be warming up.

"In near panic, 'Ticky Tac' pulled on the feathers, (our apologies to Koslosky for complaining about paying $47 for a suit of down underwear, with no black lace) parked parka over-

172

all and headed for the airfield, about three-quarters of a mile from the hotel.

"Before I got there my ruff, which was wolverine and not supposed to frost, did. The planes lay half buried in the snow-sand. The cemented white stuff sounded hollow and I made no tracks. I hardly knew which way I disliked the Arctic snow the more, blowing or so cold and crusted that it had to be cut with a knife before melting, if you wanted water.

"Unable to feel my feet, I debated walking to the hotel again without warming them. The menfolk, I knew, were at the Bore's Den, just off the end of the runway. It was really Mike Eherdt's place, built to accommodate hunters. I stubbed it down there, hoping they were not still sacked out. They were.

" 'Female,' I sang out hopefully as I banged at the door.

" 'Come in,' came the reply; but there was no one in the combination living, dining and kitchen area which was centered by a big, warm stove.

" 'Are we going out?' I asked of the surrounding walls.

" 'And why did you think we would go out this morning?' growled a voice which I recognized as that of Bob Cooper. 'Don't you see that layer of white stuff out past the steam boiling off that open lead? You think you could see a bear through that?'

"Feeling pretty small and talking to the wall, I tried to make amends by offering to make a pot of coffee and wash yesterday's dishes.

" 'Warm yourself and get back to your Tee-Pee. It's —43. We'll send for you when it's flying weather.'

"Then came a pounding on the plywood walls separating the bunk rooms. 'Larry,' Bob boomed at the taxi driver who also stayed at the Bore's Den. 'You have a passenger.'

"My eider-down feathers seemed a little warm, even singed."

173

CHAPTER XX

TROPHY POLAR BAGGED

On the following day the taxi did arrive and I was never more excited. I must have looked like a stuffed Teddy bear with my feathers on under my parka and all the other rigging I could stuff on. But I wasn't too warm, not a bit, even though the fellows teased me and called me "fatty." To make things worse, my cameras cached underneath my parka to keep the lenses from frosting, made me look as if I were overdue at the maternity ward. I guess the fellows couldn't help but howl.

"Christ," Cooper kibitzed, "do we bring back a bear or a bare baby?"

The guys were still laughing and George asked to feel it kick as we sailed out over the frozen sea. Below us on a point of land, northmost on the continent, lay the military base, Point Barrow. Domes and radar and communication spires were quite a contrast to the cracker box houses of Barrow.

A few miles further north over the broken and contorted frozen waste, then nothing. It was impossible for me to distinguish sea and horizon at a distance. It was difficult to believe the frozen mass was the Arctic Ocean. Below us pressure ridges and open leads ran for miles and miles.

"Look at the seal," Cooper observed as we zoomed in lower. "Good sign. Keep your eyes peeled. Polar bear are a pale yellow against the snow."

"Stop!" I yelled, trying to get my movie camera from beneath my parka to zoom in on the seal.

"In midair," Cooper teased as he circled.

Zooming in with the plane aroused more than the seal.

"Bear!" George Brittin yelled. "Behind that ridge."

Never was I more excited. I heard them debating the size of it, and Cooper saying, "no"; but I guarantee that bear sure got shot with my zoom. Seeing him swaying as he ran beneath us was worth the full trip.

Farther out we sailed. For an hour we saw no sign of life, except seal, and very few of those. The cold came right through the thin skin of the plane. The thermometer on the wing read —54°.

"Mike has spotted one," Cooper sang out as the red Super Cub dipped its wing. "He's circling it. Look the way his wingtip is pointed."

"Christ! It's a monster!" Cooper observed in a most enthusiastic tone, "Mike will keep circling him while I look for a landing area close enough to bring it down. Are you ready, George?"

George Brittin had been ready since the bear was spotted.

"When I land, jump from the plane. I'll try to get within range."

We did get within range, but barely. George didn't bring the rapidly disappearing monster down without difficulty, and a full volley of rifle cracks, first behind, then leading the bear until he had dead aim.

The bear went down; but George had to pump another slug into the brute when he reared as we edged toward him.

"Wait," Cooper warned as I went plowing through the snow with them toward the bear. "You can't always tell."

Crimson spreading over the snow dulled my enthusiasm a little, but not enough to keep me from heeling in. Cooper watched both me and the bear; but it seemed to be dead and he relented, after he had poked it with his foot, rifle ever ready.

I had never seen anyone skin out a bear before, nor did I realize it could be done so fast. Bob and Mike were experts. I wondered why Bob had bound a package of twelve pair of gloves together and brought it along, but I soon found out. The blood would freeze on their gloved hands and the gloves became so stiff they would have to be thrown away. We were all excited. Perhaps this polar was a record. We measured its paw prints and took photos. The guides measured its head, as is done for Boone and Crockett, but no decision could be made officially until the skull was sent in. We would not know for some time; but I had my story — more of a story than I thought when we landed and found out other hunters might be in trouble. I wrote the story. Quote:

"One of the largest, if not the largest polar bear on record was taken today by George Brittin of St. Paul on the first hunt of the season, some twenty-five miles north of Point Barrow. Piloting the plane was Bob Cooper of Cooper Flying and Guide Service, Fairbanks.

"There is some possibility, however, that other hunters going out in another plane from Barrow at approximately the same time may have met with serious difficulty. Unable to get their plane off an ice floe where they landed to attempt a kill, a pilot and two hunters from Texas,· Ray Cook of San Antonio, who hoped to kill a polar bear with a '44 pistol, and Tex Sorrel of Houston, are adrift in the Arctic Ocean.

"As reported by the covering pilot, these hunters are in no immediate difficulty, except from the elements. Visibility, which was practically unlimited earlier in the day, quickly faded into a white-out. When one of their planes failed to start, the other, piloted by Bill Ellis of Anchorage, returned to Barrow for plumber's pots (heaters) to get it started. Just before reaching the downed hunters on the return trip, however, an incoming frontal system forced Ellis to turn back. Weather conditions permitting, aid will be flown to these hunters at day break." End-quote.

On March 10 all pilots in the area were out and hunting, but not for polar bear. Target for the day was a Helio, No. 4163-Delta, piloted by Ralph Marshall of Anchorage. Pilots joining the search with Ellis were O. J. Smith of Wein Airlines, Bob Cooper of Fairbanks, and Mike Ehredt of Barrow.

The day was as long as I have ever spent. Toward noon I took my chances and headed toward the Bore's Den at the end of the runway where Cooper and Ehredt kept their planes. Mike couldn't stay aloft much over four hours in the Super Cub. He would be forced to return soon.

This time my reception wasn't bad at all. The hunters were as worried as I. What's more, two new ones had been added to the group, Bruce Harrison of Fairbanks and Bob Elinskas, from New York. They had arrived on the noon airliner, just in time to be greeted with the bad news.

Hardly two cups of coffee had been gulped when we heard Mike coming in and saw the red cub. We all rushed out for news, but he shook his head.

"Maybe Cooper will have better luck," he encouraged.

But Cooper's news was no better when he arrived, about forty minutes later. We were wondering whether to alert search and rescue; but it was decided that all search planes should be in before doing so. Smitty (Smith) and Ellis were still out. Ellis carried extra gas.

It was getting late when Smitty came in. No news. Again search and rescue was discussed; but Ellis had not yet returned. Then he came in, less than an hour before dark. He was beat. There was nothing else to do. Ellis didn't have the heart, Smitty was elected to turn it in.

Of course I had my story ready and asked to go along. There was only one way of getting any message out of town, over the communication maintained by Wein Airlines.

Smitty said he would put me through to the newspapers; but I would have to call collect. I listened and made notes as Smitty called Search and Rescue at Elmendorf Air Force Base in Anchorage, giving wind velocity, drift of current and areas already searched. A plane was to be sent immediately, with flares to be dropped over the ice for a night search. Other planes would join by morning if the hunters were not located. Smitty called Wein Airlines and asked for a plane he could fly on instruments.

As Smitty stayed on the phone, coordinating search plans, a plane droned overhead. Leaving the receiver dangling, Smitty rushed outside. It couldn't be! But there was no other plane out. It was dark and there was warning of icing conditions.

Fuzzy balls of light blinked overhead. A plane circled the field. Over a radio, which had been of no use on the ice floe because of the drained battery, bush pilot Ralph Marshall called for landing instructions. With him were the two Texas hunters, Cook and Sorrell.

Being on the scene, nothing but a first person account could have pleased me, and Cook was plenty ready to talk, as soon as he stopped shaking enough not to bite his words off between syllables. Here's the story that went out over the Associated Press lines. Quote:

Barrow, Alaska, March 10. "We had to get off that ice floe and the Good Lord was just with us," said Ray Cook of San Antonio, Texas, who spent two days and a night in a plane down on the Arctic ice some twenty-five miles north of Pt. Barrow. "'All night,' Cook said, 'we listened to her crunch and groan and pop. By morning the floe we were on had broken loose from the pack and turned completely around. We were surrounded by open leads and there was water within fifty yards of the plane.

" 'The water was getting closer to the plane all day. It came up in our tracks wherever we stepped. It would get the plane before another night and it was beginning to get dark,' Cook said as he still shook with a bone-deep chill.

" 'I was plenty glad to get back, too,' said Ralph Marshall, pilot and hunting guide from Anchorage. 'That plane had to start. I kept propping her with a rope.'

"By some strange phenomena, or the grace of God, the temperature which had been ranging from —30° to —54° rose to +18°. This was unseasonably warm for the Polar ice pack off-shore from Pt. Barrow, a military installation at the 'Top of the World.' In the nearby native village of Barrow, the warmest day of the year brought the temperature to above the freezing point and light rain fell.

"When the men adrift on the ice pack in the Arctic Ocean were not back by 5:00 P.M. of the second day, Air Search and Rescue was alerted and a C-130 4-prop Turbo Jet from Elmendorf Air Force Base, about 900 miles to the south-east, was dispatched with flares which would have been dropped over the ice along with a sonic grid pattern which would have been used to pin-point the hunters, as had been first tried successfully when Don Sheldon was down during a white-out. Before the Turbo Jet reached its destination, however, the men on the ice got their plane started.

"In the sub-zero temperatures of the day before, the men had run the plane's battery down in an effort to start it. Having difficulty killing a polar bear, they stayed on the ice a little too long. The motor of the Helio Courrier No. 4163-Delta froze up on them. The Super Cub, flown by hunting pilot and guide, Bill Ellis, who was flying cover for Marshall, did start. Only a few minutes from help, Ellis headed back for Barrow to pick up a plumber's pot. The weather was clear when he left the other hunters on the ice to fly back for the heater.

"Ellis was on his way back, almost within seeing distance of the Helio, when hit by a blanket of swirling snow. The white-out condition made it impossible for him to land. On the ice there were pressure ridges taller than trees and many open leads. Ellis had no choice. Climbing above the incoming clouds he raced the frontal system, which brought the warm weather, back to Barrow. Winds with blowing snow and gusts to sixty miles per hour prevented further flights.

"By daylight on March 10 winds had died and the temperature was on the rise. Again Ellis sailed out over the ice floe with the much needed plumber's pot. No trace of the downed plane. Searching until he neared the point of no return, Ellis nosed her Toward Barrow, his gas expended.

"Perhaps no one alive has much better knowledge of how it feels to be adrift on an ice floe than Bill Ellis. In May of 1963 he and Ralph Marshall, the pilot out on the ice waiting for him, drifted on a diminishing floe for four days after their plane crashed. They drifted some seventy-five miles and the ice pan they were on was less than half a block long when they were rescued . . ." Endquote.

On March 11 it was —54° and blowing like hell.

March 12 was beautiful, but cold. Flying the open leads all day, Cooper made two trips but came back without a bear. No one else got one either. We did spot three, a sow and a cub and perhaps an eight footer. These were spared because Benard McNamara was trophy hunting. We came back empty handed. The plane, in which this reporter rode, a Cessna 180, was flying cover. In it was Mike Eherdt, Bob Elinskas, Mike Obray, and myself.

March 13 was an exceptionally clear but cold day. Two trips over the icepack of the Arctic Ocean netted two polar bear, both of them good but not of trophy size. Thus far no other kills are reported from the area.

Figure the odds yourself, twenty-three hunters, ten days, three polars, three men down on the ice and six days unfit for flying. Match this against polars which have never been counted on the largest uninhabited wasteland of the earth, the Polar icecap, and do your own deducing. Personally I was beginning to wonder what the big squawk was all about. If we want to protect the polar, why don't we look to the East where the hunter is allowed four bear per season. Some sort of conservation which would regulate more than one portion of the icecap would present a more logical answer.

And then the winds came. She blew and blew and blew. On March 14, 15, and 16 she blew. On St. Patrick's day it was still blowing. This was a white-out of the meaner type, not snowing, just blowing snow. Stark little stems of stunted grass stand naked on the barren tundra, breaking beneath your feet. White dunes rise wherever obstacles block the flying mass. Everything would be buried except for the fact that it's too arrid for that much snow to fall. Flying weather didn't come.

Suddenly I realized I wanted to return to Talkeetna. This was spring according to the calendar; but there was nothing except granulated snow in Barrow. In Talkeetna the snow would be melting, and green peeping through. What's more, I was being a poor president for the Matanuska-Susitna Centennial Council. I had postponed a meeting to come to Barrow, and set one up for March 30. This was to be a joint meeting; and the state director, as well as representatives from surrounding towns were to join us. We were planning a May Day Centennial Caravan, from Anchorage to Talkeetna. 1 had worked it out with community and committee heads and with Carl Sullivan, Centennial director for Anchorage. Potentates from Anchorage would get the caravan rolling, and it would snowball, picking up more cars and Centennial boosters, all the way into Talkeetna. Bumper stickers were printed.

On March 25 I wrote. Quote: "Who wants a polar bear? Not 'Ticky Tac,' not if it isn't gotten before the next plane leaves out of here. In so far as I am concerned it can stay on the polar ice forever.

"The things your columnist wants most are: a bath, a drink of clear, pure water, a green salad and milk. Throw in a few green trees and the temperature above zero and we'll swear allegiance to the banana belt forevermore.

"Your columnist called a meeting of the Matanuska-Susitna Centennial council for March 30, and we plan to make it, polar or no polar bear, that May Day caravan will be coming your way." Endquote.

I had no way of knowing whether my columns were being published. I was in a lonely world. The hunters who had gotten their bear had been stateside two weeks, and the others were growing impatient. I was beginning to fear pilots and guides might fly in doubtful weather, if pushed too hard by man and nature.

Why did I want a bear? I loved seeing them in the open, but to have a rug to step on every night, or a trophy for my wall? I could shoot one, of this I felt confident. If I didn't bring him down the guides would finish him off for me, as in the case of other hunters. What would this prove? I had killed a moose. I didn't particularly enjoy it, except for sharing the meat. Bear meat was lousy, to my own taste at least.

Yet I would get my polar, the next trip out. It was my turn, of this I was assured. Realization and materialization were within my grasp. The conquest had been great and an experience in life which could never be taken from me. I had my photos and stories. The hunting season had been extended ten days, rather than curtailed; but I had little to do with the extension. In fact, at this time I didn't know whether I was being published or not. Mail is so slow in getting to Barrow.

I love nature, the wilder the better. Anticipation had been great, yet somehow realization had lost its charm. Why kill that which I loved in its natural state?

On March 27 I crawled on a Wein Airliner, no doubt the one which had the spark plugs aboard. I arrived home a month from the day I had started. My reception in Talkeetna was great, yet I could hardly wait until I got to my own little cabin where I flushed and flushed the commode, just to watch. Never realized the miracle thereof, previously.

CHAPTER XXI

DEATH ON THE MOUNTAIN

I made that Centennial meeting, and many more. We planned projects for the villages throughout our borough, to commemorate Alaska's Centennial of Purchase from the Russians.

Before I realized what had happened I got tangled up in so much civic work that I found little time for homesteading and working on this book. To make things worse, I started another newspaper column, "Along the Mat-Su Trail." Mat-Su is the short name I gave the real chocker, Matanuska-Susitna Borough.

This new news column, covering activities in our borough, gave me plenty of news coverage for my new project, Centennial planning. Although half the size of the state of Texas, our borough still has less pavement than Harris County, Texas. In 1965 we had two paved roads. One was a portion of the Glenn Highway, which passes through the southeast corner of the borough, through Palmer and into Anchorage, thirty-six miles to the south. The other pavement extended north from Palmer to Willow, a distance of forty miles. Our borough can not be crossed in any direction on a roadway. When the Anchorage-Fairbanks highway is finished it will bisect the borough, north to south.

I was greatly concerned when that portion of the highway north of Talkeetna was not let in time for the construction season. The two-million-dollar Susitna River Bridge of which we were so proud would be idle a second summer. I asked why, extolling the merit and need of such construction through my columns. I was assured by highway officials that the bid would be let later in the summer, so I turned to coverage of mountain climbers. Already the season was well in progress.

Most of my summer was buried in Centennial planning and trying to get a cabin built at my homestead. I did a very poor job of covering the '65 mountain climbing season.

Before going to Texas, I had done stories on four Harvard climbers who were brave enough to tackle the west face of Mt. Huntington, which had never been climbed, and was equally as tough or even tougher than the east face climbed by the Frenchmen the previous season.

The day I returned, the news broke in Talkeetna. Here's my story. Quote:

"TALKEETNA-August 8. EDWARD BERND, 20-year-old mountain climber from Upper Darby, Pennsylvania, was killed in a 4,000 foot plunge from Mt. Huntington on July 30, yet it was not known until three Harvard companions climbing with him were spotted by bush pilot Don Sheldon of Talkeetna, who returned them to civilization.

"Fellow climbers, all of whom reached the summit by the previously unscaled route up the west face are: Dave Roberts, 22, Boulder, Colorado; Catt Hale, 21, Alexandria, Virginia; and Don Jensen, 22, Walnut Creek, California.

"The climbers planned to hike back to Talkeetna from their climb. Glacier pilot Don Sheldon, who landed them in a small, foreboding basin of the Tokositna Glacier where no man has been known to set foot previously, much less land a plane, felt there was something wrong when he saw only three men walking out. Known internationally as 'Keeper of the Mountain,' Sheldon spot checked the boys many times and knew they had reached the summit of seemingly unsurmountable Mt. Huntington, although he waited for the climbers themselves to break the news. The wrong story broke.

"On the way down from the summit a carbiner (snap link of chain which was supposedly impossible to open accidentally) did come open. These snap links are made to withstand 5,000 pound stress and supposedly will not come open if turned upside down and backward; but it did, hurtling Bernd 4,000 feet into open space.

"The climbers were rappeling at the time and Bernd was suspended on a rope from an overhang when, in some freakish manner, the carbiner opened. Helping him was utterly impossible. Within a split second he was hurtling into a white vastness and his body may be completely embedded in the snow, almost a mile below.

"For a search party to go into this inaccesible area would be suicidal. Companions saw no trace of the body. After such a fall down the rocky precipice, there could have been no hope of life, even if the remaining climbers could have found or reached him.

"A student of architecture at Harvard, Bernd had been mountain climbing for one-and-a-half years. His home was at 69 Maplewood Drive, Upper Darby, Pennsylvania.

"Edward Bernd reached his goal, setting foot where man has never climbed, then fell victim to a seemingly impossible accident. Perhaps he will remain enshrined forever in the beautiful and foreboding vastness of the Alaska Range. With him, no doubt, are the hearts of three fellow conquerors, who would gladly have exchanged places with the companion whom they were powerless to save." Endquote.

CHAPTER XXII

A HOMESTEADING CABIN BUT NO HIGHWAY

The eleventh hour had come for building my homesteading cabin.

Building where there is no road and no landing strip does present a few problems. Just getting the material to the homestead would be difficult, to put it mildly.

A new hunting and fishing guide in Talkeetna, Ken Holland, had a long river boat. He believed he could get all the material, which was now delivered and stacked on the bank of the Susitna River, up to my homestead in three trips, provided it was done immediately, while the water was still high. Nothing could have pleased me more; but I needed someone to do the building, too.

Luck was with me. I hardly knew Don Bennis; but Alice Powell of the Talkeetna Motel recommended him highly, so I hired him. Without his help I'm not so sure that cabin would ever have gotten off the ground. I admired this fine-looking and well-educated man from the first time I saw him. The longer I have known him, the greater my admiration. But back to the business at hand.

Up the river we started — Ken, his wife Doris, Don Bennis, and yours truly, all perched on top of plywood sheets laid across and over a boat load of two-by-fours. The thirty-one-foot river boat was completely covered, except for pilot space in the stern, which Ken needed to man the huge outboard motor.

The current was swift and our progress slow, despite our fifty horses. We did quite well, however, past the swells at the confluence of the Talkeetna and Susitna Rivers, until we hit that mile-and-a-half wide stump yard where the Chulitna and Susitna join. It seems to change channels every time it rains. We lost it. The river was cold and swift and laden with glacial silt. If you capsize in this river, your chances of getting out alive are about as good as that of a condemned man arguing with his executioner, as Don Sheldon would put it.

The water is so murky, during glacial run-off, that it is sometimes difficult to tell whether you have eighteen inches or eigtheen feet boiling beneath your boat. Suddenly, as Ken swerved to miss a floating log, we realized it was nearer eighteen inches when the prop snagged, zing-zing-zing-against the rock bottom. We sheared a pin and the propeller stopped zinging. Powerless, the boat was caught by the current — goodbye boat and lumber.

Having grown up around boats, I read Ken Holland's mind. He went over the stern; Don and I went over on opposite sides of the bow, just before she hit the snag. When the waves tried to inundate the boat from one side, Doris tipped it the other way.

When we had maneuvered the boat to where it came underneath the high end of the snag, rather than lodge against it crosswise, Doris and I both grabbed. The current was deeper here, and it's a good thing that both Ken and I were swinging on to the boat.

"Jump in and hold on!" Don yelled as my feet were washed from beneath me.

It wasn't easy, with no footing and trying not to tip the boat, but with one arm swinging on to the limb and the other on the boat, I bellied up.

"We've got her!" Doris screamed, as she caught her breath. "Do you have an extra shear pin?"

As Ken got a leg into the boat, we hung on for dear life, with thirty-one feet of boat swinging behind that limb like a lure working on a swivel.

Ken dug into his tool box for a shear pin and raised the motor. Far out he leaned over the now horizontal shaft, inserting the pin. I was never so glad to see a cotter key go into place in my life.

"Hold on until I get her started," Ken yelled as we took on another dip of water over the side, "and don't let go until I'm under power."

These instructions were a little unnecessary for either Doris or myself, for neither of us had any intention of letting loose until the nose was splitting the current.

After dodging a forest of stumps, Ken managed to beach her on an island. Don was off the boat and pulling her up by the rope on the bow. He was making sure that the current didn't catch her again. A goodly portion of my homesteading cabin was aboard. We all crawled out and for a few minutes none of us said a word.

"May as well start bailing," I said as I got up on unsteady pegs. "Got to keep your lumber dry!"

Mechanically, we lifted off the plywood from the top of the boat. Those 4 x 8 foot sheets had made the trip doubly dangerous. We bailed her out the best we could, from either end, without removing the 2 x 4's stowed in the bottom of the boat.

"From here we go into the canyon," Kenny said, "and there's no danger of losing the current; but there are a few boulders and the current is mighty swift. Just watch and sing out if you see a rock."

One ride like that was enough. White water and sheer canyon walls above us made for spectacular scenery and thrills and chills. Here and there a waterfall spilled over the cliff above. The rock strata was almost vertical, for the most part. The old earth really heaved and strained here at one time. I hardly had time for thinking I would like to check a dyke and contact zone for possible quartz veins, because all eyes were needed to watch for boulders which might be cached just below the undulating current. More than once Bennis sang out, just in time.

I just can't imagine Doris not wanting to go back home by boat. She and I stayed with Jay and Vicki Cornell while Ken and Don brought in more lumber. They had better luck on the next trip.

I selected a cabin site on the first rise above the moose flats along the river. There was a good view and a crystal stream of water.

It took a while to cut a trail through the willow flats to get to the side of the hill; but it was an advenure like I had never lived before. If there was a neighbor within a hundred miles to the north, I didn't know it. I couldn't see the Cornell's place from mine; but just knowing there was a cabin down that unbridged river, helped.

"You just keep working," I told Jay Cornell and Don Bennis, "I'm quite capable of carrying these two-by's." And I did. I'll have to admit that I needed help with the plywood sheets and the door; but the rest of it I tugged up the hill while they were felling huge spruce for the foundation and clearing some cottonwoods which were in our way. My job lasted four full carrying days, and there were blisters on my hands; but I kept ahead of them, even to the roofing, and this made me quite happy.

It was such a little cabin — 12' x 16' — but completely wonderful and doubly insulated against the cold. Jay and Don teased me about the windows and the glass in the front door. They said it was just right for bears to break in; but I said it was just right for seeing Mt. McKinley. To date a bear has never tried to break in, although they sometimes fish where my little stream joins the river. One little blackie raided my garbage pit now and then. If he gets too bold, I'll have that bear rug yet.

The cabin was hardly finished when bad news came. The bid for highway construction, which would bring the new highway to my homestead, was not let.

To me this was a triple blow. There would be no pavement leading to some of the villages where I was doing Centennial planning and there would be no road to my homestead the following year. To solve this problem, I bought a Super Cub, N-9471-Delta, and resolved to learn to fly.

But this would not help with my clearing problem. With no road to my homestead the following year, there would be no heavy equipment in the area. How would I get my clearing done? Ordinarily, construction companies cooperate with homesteaders in virgin areas by renting D-8 Cats with operators, by the hour.

My loss would be minor, of course, in comparison to what the delay in construction would cost the borough and the state. Maybe there was still time, if I gave her full bore through my newspaper columns, for the governor to reconsider before the 1966 construction season.

At the time, I was writing four newspaper columns, for the Fairbanks, Palmer and Anchorage papers. If two of these columns, "Mat-Su Menu of the Week" and "Alaska Recipe Round-Up," hadn't been menu columns featuring Alaskan-grown products and foods, I would probably have tried getting a few blows in through them, too.

Although I was disappointed when the federal funds for new construction were used for reconstruction after the earthquake, the reason was apparent, imperative, and understandable.

188

Yet, since federal funds were again allocated, I could see no reason for the bid not being let.

Vainly I sought the reason through the highway department and the governor. No answer was given. For several months I challenged through correspondence and through newspapers.

The Anchorage-Fairbanks highway was Alaska's greatest undertaking since statehood. Over five times the purchase price of the territory of Alaska had already been spent on it. Why work suddenly ceased along this portion of the blueprint highway seemed a mystery. I tried to awaken the citizenry through articles like this, published in *The Frontiersman*, Feb. 11, 1966. Quote:

"If Alaskans understood the vital effect which the Anchorage-Fairbanks highway, now under construction, will have on the state's economy and realized that this construction actually brings prosperity to us because Uncle Sam foots 95 per cent of the total cost, perhaps they would realize that Alaska's most important undertaking since statehood is jeopardized.

"Nothing under construction will mean as much to the citizenry of Alaska as a whole and to the projected influx of tourists, as completion of this sixty-five miles of highway which would cut about one hundred miles from the distance now traveled between Anchorage and Fairbanks by the motorist. This would mean a direct truck line from the docks at Seward to Fairbanks, with connecting links to all major towns in south central Alaska. It would open a circular route for the tourist whereby he could visit the more populated areas of the state without doubling back. It would give both the Alaskan and the tourist a close-up of magnificent Mt. McKinley and the virgin wilderness, with its vast potential, which would encourage economic development.

"Insofar as the tourist is concerned, we could probably plant daisies on either side of any pavement we now have and he would still consider it "lousy" in comparison to what he has at home. According to a graph compiled by Alaska's Tourism Department, eighty per cent of the persons questioned listed the nation's tallest peak and scenic wilderness as Alaska's top attraction. Why not give them McKinley? A good highway through

189

this area is of inestimable potential. A short cut between Alaska's two major population centers has long been needed."

Here I will not bother to quote the cumbersome figures which I used in my articles showing how much money had already been spent on various segments of the road. It may be of interest, however, to know that by 1970 the cost was estimated at $147 million. There are many places along the route which cost over a million dollars per mile. The most difficult stretch of road thus far completed, a distance of 4.8 miles through Nenana Canyon, cost $6.7 million. But again we are jumping ahead in our story. Back to our newspaper article of 1966.

"Do we leave the $35,722.50 already expended, lying practically useless insofar as most Alaskans and the tourist trade is concerned?

"The magnificent two-million-dollar bridge across the Susitna River west of Talkeetna remains useless for a third season. Already the 28.5 miles between the unused bridge and the projected Chulitna River crossing has been cleared twice. Will it be left to vegetation and erosion? If the bid for this job were let as soon as September this year, construction season would be over. The first projected completion date of this highway was 1967. Will Uncle Sam continue to bear with us indefinitely and allocate more money as we lag years behind projected schedules for which the federal government absorbs 95 per cent of the cost?"

This and similar articles brought assurance from the highway department that the bid would be let. I fully believed it would be let in time for the 1966 construction season. I was so busy with Centennial planning and with homesteading and writing that I was temporarily quieted, more or less, by the promise which invoked this truce.

I was so proud of the work being done by my Centennial committees throughout the borough. Talkeetna was planning a museum; Willow, a replica of a gold mine; Montana Creek, Houston and Big Lake, adequate camper parks; Sutton, reopening an old gold-rush trail; Palmer, a log cabin tourist center; and Wasilla, the restoration of Old Knik, Alaska's chief seaport on Cook Inlet before Anchorage, where they began anchoring huge ships across the bay, bringing it to life as a tent city during World War I.

My Centennial groups worked hard, and I especially want to thank the following leaders who, as chairmen of their community committees, traveled many miles at their own expense over a two-year period of time: Curly Sutton, Palmer; Mrs. Dorothy Page, Wasilla (who refused to give up and carried on for this author when all hope seemed lost); Mrs. Helmi Blank, Big Lake; Mrs. Bernice Sellens, Willow; Mrs. Hazel Silfven, Mrs. Carol Sik and Mrs. Minnie Swanda, Montana Creek; and the Talkeetna workers. Let's not forget Carl Sullivan, the Anchorage Centennial head, or Bob Arnold and Herb Adams, Centennial coordinators for the state of Alaska, who were helpful, not only with organizational planning, but attending meetings and pre-Centennial functions as well. To each and every committee member and every person who helped, and there were hundrds, our sincere thanks.

In January of 1966, my Centennial castles toppled — because our hopes for the new highway were taken away. Federal funds allocated for this project were transferred by the governor to other construction projects.

To say I was unhappy is putting it mildly. I fired this and similar missiles at the governor through the Anchorage, Fairbanks and Palmer papers one week, then declared war on him and his administration the following week.

This particular letter to the Editor appeared in the *Anchorage Daily Times*, March 1, 1966. Similar ones were sent to editors throughout Alaska. It was headed, "AMBITIOUS UNDERTAKING SCUTTLED."

"Dear Editor,

"Anchorage has been robbed of her Centennial tourist in a steal so clever that many persons are yet unaware of the fact.

"The Anchorage-Fairbanks highway was first projected for completion in 1967. From 1960 to 1964 it was given highest priority. During those years we have spent over five times the purchase price of Alaska on connecting links along this route from Palmer to Nenana.

"Then, suddenly and without apparent reason, work was stopped on the south end of this route. The $2 million dollar bridge across the Susitna River, over which heavy equipment was to roll northward to join the 65-mile stretch with Cantwell and the Denali Highway, has remained idle since the last span was bolted into place in 1964.

"Without any apparent reason, the governor of the state of Alaska has failed to answer any of the questions repeatedly asked by this reporter concerning delay in construction on this "high priortiy" route. projected completion date 1967.

"Without any apparent reason, the long delayed bid for the the twenty-eight-mile stretch north of the new Susitna River bridge failed to appear on the list of those let for bid last fall.

"On January 14, the reason became very apparent to this writer. This bid, which Governor Egan evidently held up in hopes of talking the federal government into letting him spend the money elsewhere, was the sacrifice now on the altar for "half-soles" patching sub-standard highways.

"Last fall I challenged the highway department, the governorf or anyone in authority for a reason as to why the bid was not let with the others, but received no answer.

"There was no answer. It is my belief that this information was withheld from the public because those in authority knew a howl would go up from those who would suffer most by the loss.

"I further believe that the 'Centennial' soft soaping issued simultaneously with the announced 'transfer of funds' for which the governor states in a four-page telegram of explanations to the newspapers, 'but until rather late in 1965 the Federal Government would not agree that the work involved,' (evidently referring to maintenance and 'half-soles' for existing highways) 'qualified for funding under the Federal Aid Highway Act.'

"It is apparent to this writer that Alaska's most ambitious undertaking since statehood has been scuttled. It is up to the people to figure out why." — Endquote.

Practically every person in the Matanuska-Susitna borough was backing my fight—yet no response came from the governor. I may as well have been non-existent, insofar as getting an answer from him was concerned. I was completely ignored. This made me madder. This was election year. If I couldn't defeat the Governor of Alaska one way I would try another. One of my editors, Theodore O. Schmidtke of the *Frontiersman* in Palmer, seemed without fear, so we lowered the boom.

Chapter XXIII

I DECLARE WAR ON ALASKA'S GOVERNOR

In a full-page spread, February 18, 1966, I declared WAR on Alaska's Governor William A. Egan, and all those in his administration who had been responsible for robbing the Matanuska-Susitna borough of federal funds allocated for highway construction on the Anchorage-Fairbanks highway. My publisher used the map given by the highway department showing the sixty-five-mile gap where there was no construction activity. It also showed the parts paved and unpaved along the new route. Below it was a petition signed by residents of the borough.

On the following week, February 24, there was a full page petition signed by residents, and another full page which I had written explaining the situation quite fully. This is taken from The Frontiersman, Feb. 24. Quote:

"To The Honorable
WILLIAM A. EGAN
Governor of Alaska
"We, the taxpayers and voters of the Matanuska-Susitna area, feel that your recent decision, transferring federal aid funds, allocated for highway construction in this area, to maintenance in other parts of the state should be reconsidered.

"We do not dispute the fact that a certain amount of repaving is necessary and desirable; but to sacrifice earliest possible completion of the direct Seward-Anchorage route to Fairbanks is unnecessary.

"We believe that this decision, if allowed to stand, will work irreparable economic harm, not only to the Matanuska-Susitna Valleys, but to the entire state of Alaska.

"We, the undersigned, petition you, the Governor of the State of Alaska, to restore federal aid construction funds allocated for work on the stretch betwen Talkeetna and Cantwell, thus allowing continued progress from both ends of this new highway route which will cut approximately one-hundred miles off the motoring distance from Palmer to Mt. McKinley National Park."

"Signed by:

Signatures poured in. Petitions were placed throughout the borough. Here's the full page story, verbatim, about the:

"TRANSFER OF FUNDS FROM THE ANCHORAGE-FAIRBANKS HIGHWAY

Mary Carey

"For want of VISION a VALLEY is lost,
For want of HIGHWAY the TOURIST is
lost,
For want of TOURIST the STATE is
lost.
For want of "HALF SOLES" our
Seven-LEAGUE boots are lost.

"One who has never flicked a switch to illuminate his home does not miss the miracle of electricity.

"One who has never seen Mt. McKinley except from a distance does not experience the electrifying grandeur of nearness.

"Endowed with an intimate knowledge and respect for the nation's tallest peak, this writer would be doing an injustice to fellow Alaskans, the tourist and posterity if failing to present potential within our reach. Only sixty-five miles of construction is needed to close the gap which will cut approximately one-hundred miles off the motor route from Anchorage to Mt. McKinley National Park and Fairbanks. Yet construction from the Anchorage end of the new highway is halted because federal funds allocated toward completion of this miracle of modern engineering have been transferred to maintenance or so called "half sole" jobs on existing highways, thus prolonging the delay and hastening economic disaster for the Matanuska-Susitna area.

"The plea for continuing construction from both ends of the route stems from more than love of a mountain. It is an acute sympathy for those along this promised highway who have been forced to give it up. It is an admiration for the stamina and courage of those who have stuck it out long after the "blue print" highway was scheduled to reach them. It stems from the utter tragedy for those who have stuck it out this long only to find that the roadway which was cleared when his child was born *will not be passable when that same child is of school age.*

"For want of a road his crops were lost.

"For want of a school his homestead is lost.

"My sympathy is with the farmer of the luxuriant Matanska and Susitna valley area, robbed of the magnificent highway over which his produce could flow, at reduced trucking rates, to existing and potential markets. My sympathy is with every Alaskan who must pay more for the necessities of life for years to come because of this delay.

"For want of a road the market is lost.

"For want of a market the economy is lost.

"Yet this is only the beginning of a chain reaction. My sympathy is with the school board of the Matanuska-Susitna Borough, because, after being robbed of the promised highway, some means must be devised for getting children across the Susitna River where the useless $2 million dollar bridge terminates in swampland. Only very strategic moves thwarted the building of a schoolhouse. My respect goes to those who were clever enough to import one woman from across the Susitna River into Talkeetna. A woman with a college degree and several children in school, a homesteader who is now on half-day assignment.

"For a borough with a sagging economy which already gives twelve of every fourteen tax mills to school support, this was a very strategic move. Half a day's teaching compared to that of a full-time teacher and building a new school is a real saving for the interim—until a school bus can roll across the new bridge into this area. But the road was scheduled to reach this area two years ago.

"What will you do now? Sacrifice educational opportunity which is proposed for students in larger communities for a few in the bush who have no school at all? At the present rate of delaying action there will be no road for at least two years to come.

"A teacher at the time, this writer attended a school board meeting where a study was made of the cost involved in flying these children into Talkeetna daily. This was BEFORE we were robbed of funds for bulding the new highway upon which you depended.

"Since the borough could not afford such expensive transportation at that time, two years ago, for what was considered or hoped to be a one-year interim . . . what can it do now? The *cost of building and maintaining a one-teacher school across the Susitna River from Talkeetna alone would offset the $200,000* which is the projected five per cent the state would have to pay for construction of the adjacent twenty-eight miles of roadway. This is the section of the Anchorage-Fairbanks route, for which Uncle Sam allocated federal aid funds which were transferred by the governor for maintenance.

"FOR WANT OF A ROAD
A BRIDGE IS LOST

"By the time the bid (for which federal aid funds were allocated and transferred) is let, there is the likelihod of every business and every homesteader along this route, from Palmer to Cantwell, being frozen out. This is the land of PROMISE. The land where promises never materialize.

"FOR WANT OF ECONOMIC OPPORTUNITY
THE MATANUSKA-SUSITNA VALLEYS ARE DEAD

"Continuing work on the new highway will bolster our sagging economy. Stoppage hastens our economic death.

"Half sole, if we must; but remember, the new highway symbolizes our seven-league boots. Our next giant step will cut one-hundred miles off the motoring distance from Anchorage to Mt. McKinley, an eternal attraction for all mankind.

"Reconsider! Let the bid! Let it in time for the 1966 construction season. Bring this matter before your legislative body now, while there is yet time for amendment.

"If such consideration is not given, I, Mary Carey, backed by those petitioning said restoration of funds, hereby challenge the Honorable William A. Egan, Governor of the State of Alaska, to public debate on the senate floor in order that the people of the Matanuska-Susitna area, who have no senator to represent them, may be heard." Endquote.

As I stated earlier, this was election year. In the same February 24 issue of the *Frontiersman*, from which I have just quoted, Wendell P. Kay, for many years a prominent practicing Anchorage attorney, who was running against Governor Egan for the Democratic nomination, came out with this statement, which was given a banner headline. Quote:

"KAY JOINS FIGHT FOR ROAD COMPLETION
CALLS SWITCH IN FUNDS 'UNTHINKABLE'

"It is unthinkable that the so-called "planners" of the state administration could spend over $35 million of our tax dollars on a major project and then suddenly decide it is not important enough to finish now. This vital artery should be completed and in use by the 1967 Centennial Year!" Endquote.

Kay listed the advantages of the new highway and urged Alaskans to make a determined and concentrated effort to convince the Governor to "reverse his stand before it is too late."

Republican-hopeful Walter J. Hickel also used completion of the Anchorage-Fairbanks highway as a campaign issue. I was pleased when he asked me to organize campaign tour for him in the Matanuska-Susitna Borough. Hickel not only won his campaign for the governorship of Alaska, but he later became Secretary of the Interior for the United States of America.

The Governor did relent, on the very next day, February 25. Jalmar Kerttula, State Representative from our area and speaker of the House, announced that construction on the highway would continue.

This was good. The road would soon reach the long suffering '59'ers, and their children could be bussed to Talkeetna to school.

I have always appreciated Representative Jalmar Kerttula— "Jay" as I came to know him—since the year I arrived in Alaska. He wrote me several times during my long bout with the Governor, although he was a strong Democrat and backed Governor Egan all the way. Jay and his wife, Joyce, who was on the school board before our borough was formed, helped me to get books and desks for our eight-pupil, pilot high school in Talkeetna. Later our area did gain a seat in the Alaskan Senate; and in 1975, when this book was published, Kerttula was Majority Leader of the Senate.

Retrospect is a great crystallizer: in 1966 it was difficult

197

for me to see, but I know now that our former governor always worked toward what he thought best for the majority of Alaskans. The longer I know Governor Egan the more I appreciate this truly great statesman. He is a kind man, a selfless man, a man of fine and unquestionable integrity. Even at the time I felt no elation when he was defeated in his bid for a third term for the governorship.

It was not until October 14, 1971, at the ribbon-clipping ceremonies of the new highway, that William A. Egan, who was again our governor, after being out of office for four years, told me how proud he was of the new highway, that it was he who initiated construction of the new route, during Alaska's territorial days. He said that no one, not even Mary Carey, could be happier to see this artery opened. There were tears in my eyes, and his were misty, too.

Although every word I said, and everything written was true, I did have an ulterior motive, my homestead. For this I wish to apologize, but not for my feeling toward the importance of this highway to the State of Alaska.

Perhaps, in time, I can even ask Uncle Sam and the Good Lord, Himself, to forgive me for gaining federal land under false pretense. I never wanted to farm at all; but I did want to share Mt. McKinley with the world, and this was my only way of procuring the best view of the most magnificent mountain on our continent. Later both the State of Alaska and Uncle Sam saw they had erred by not embracing the southern view of Mt. McKinley. By 1970 Denali State Park engulfed my homestead. By 1975 enlargement and proposals for extending Mt. McKinley National Park to join Denali State Park on the Southern approach have been made and will no doubt be finalized soon. In case you do not know the meaning of the Indain word Denali, it means "Great One", as Mt. McKinley was once called.

Chapter XXIV

GRAND OPENING IN THE CLOUDS

Meanwhile much was happening in Talkeetna. A daughter, Janice Holly, was born to Don and Roberta Sheldon on March 26. Don was so happy that I believe he could have topped McKinley without wings. Mrs. Campbell swore he was going to land the mountain climbers on the moon.

Don had been flying pretty high for some time, and building castles in the clouds. Perhaps it would be more factual if we stated that for months Sheldon had been flying building materials to the six-thousand foot level of the Ruth Glacier, where he was building a glacier chalet, and not a castle in the clouds.

At the starting point for most climbers of Mt. McKinley who take the West Buttress route, the least precarious way (if there is such), Don was building a refuge. The glassed-in hostelry would also serve as an observatory and headquarters for skiers, those who wish a twenty-mile course.

Aided by a Talkeetna resident, Chester "Chet" Price, Don built a hexagonal observatory on an outcrop of rock on the moraine of the Ruth Glacier. This outcrop, jutting some 1,500 feet above the glacier floor, gives a close-up of Mt. McKinley which can only be experienced by one who is actually on the mountain.

To get to the glacier house one must climb a steep snow incline from the landing area below. When reaching the top, it is quite startling to realize that the next step could be 1,500 feet down. Sheldon had this area roped off; but I was wondering how many such mis-steps one might encounter while climbing McKinley. Sometimes I think mountains are made to look at, and not to climb. McKinley's treachery was not fully realized at this time, certainly not by your author, who has thrilled to glacier landings and frolics. It was not until 1967, when eight climbers lost their lives, that I realized how fully cruel and how cleverly "Denali" caches her traps.

I am glad these tragedies were still in the future on May 11, 1966, when the "Grand Opening in the Clouds," as I termed my story, took place.

Perhaps there has never been a party like this one. The decor was furnished by nature, an extravaganza of dazzling peaks and frozen rivers of time, as if in a different world. On the day prior to the arrival of thirty-nine guests of note, Sheldon, with the help of world-adventurer Lowell Thomas, Jr., now Lieutenant-Governor of Alaska, airlifted a six-man instructor squad, led by Hans Metz, to the glacier observatory, where they remained overnight.

Six sled dogs were used to pull supplies up the hill to the glassed-in cabin. The only furnishings in the 16' x 16' hexagon were the six bunks around the wall and a central heater. Nothing else seemed needed: the bunks served as divans, the stove for cooking. Outside, a little way down the hill, was a Chick Sales, the first such wooden structure upon Mt. McKinley. Built in full half-moon glory, with a Sears Roebuck catalog hanging from a chain, the nostaligc effect made one forget the snow below.

Throughout the following morning guests were shuttled in from Talkeetna and Anchorage. I was happy to see so many of my friends at the grand opening, and to become acquainted with a few persons whom I had wanted to meet ever since coming to Alaska.

Betzi Woodman, President of the Anchorage Press Club, who offered me her seat on a Polar flight during Arctic Airlift week, was there. Carl Sullivan, Anchorage Executive Director, who had helped me organize the Mat-Su Centennial Council, was present. Both Carl and Betzi were among those who had traveled in my May Day Centennial Caravan from Anchorage to Talkeetna.

Don Sheldon's mother-in-law, Mrs. Tillie Reeve, of Reeve Aleutian Airways — whom I had come to love through her visits with Roberta and Don in Talkeetna — was there, as well as Roberta's sister, Janice Reeve. Roberta was not there, and with very good reason, a new baby. Dr. A. Clair Reen, obstetrician from Anchorage who had delivered Roberta and Don's firstborn, said she was reveling in nature's white rather than the white of the maternity ward.

Herb and Miriam Hilscher, who had co-authored a book, *Alaska, U.S.A.*, which I had faithfully studied before heading north, were there. I had read and reread Hilcher's chapter on an upcoming young business man, Walter J. Hickel, who they predicted "the most likely to succeed." The book dealt with Alaska as she was in the year of statehood, 1959. Now this man, whose ability was lauded seven years earlier, was Republican candidate for the Governorship of Alaska. I have since wondered whether they were surprised when President Nixon appointed him Secretary of the Interior.

Among the persons whom I recognized from Hilscher's book was "Muktuk" Marston, founder of the Alaskan Scouts, who later gave me an autographed copy of his book, which I cherish. MukTuk, who reportedly got his name from eating whale blubber with the Eskimos during his younger days while organizing and training Eskimos to defend Alaska, was as colorful as the Hilschers pictured him.

Lars Johnson, director of the State Division of Aviation, whom I knew through the Press Club, was there, as well as Martin Ridener, Ski Editor of the *Anchorage Daily Times*, and free lance writers John Grady and Jim Balog.

Two men whom I had known or read about many times, Dr. Rodman Wilson and professional photographer Paul Crews, no doubt relived a less-pleasant experience on Mt. McKinley in 1960. Both had reached the summit on May 17, the same date as the John Day Party. Then followed the four-man-on-a-rope fall which broke John Day's leg, and Helga Bading's high altitude sickness, which led to the seemingly impossible rescue and care of the sick and injured by these men and Don Sheldon, when he made the highest fixed-wing landing ever recorded. This rescue was discussed earlier in this book in conjunction with the account of Don Sheldon being down, and in the chapter on Dr. Bradford Washburn.

Adding color and beauty for the photographers were two Reeve Aleutian Airline hostesses, June Stanford and Toni Abbott.

Appetites were sharpened by the clean, crisp air. Huge "wolverine" steaks, as Don called the Alaskan-sized sirloins, with baked potatoes, barbequed beans, and salad was served out in the open. There's little dust and no smog in Alaska. On the mountain you breathe deeply of the cleanest air on earth.

There were many V.I.P.'s, photographers, and friends from the news media with whom I should like to have visited; but I kept thinking that this was Wednesday noon and that if I could get back to Talkeetna and get my photos developed and my story into the Palmer paper, which was a weekly, I might get a scoop because the other reporters planned to stay throughout the day.

Lowell Thomas, Jr., had a dinner engagement in Anchorage to show film on his Alaskan adventures. I got this bit of information from Mrs. Miriam Hilscher, who said her husband was riding out early with Mr. Thomas.

What if I could get back ahead of the other reporters? I wanted a "SCOOP" for the *Palmer Frontiersman* which had backed me so faithfully in my war for continued highway construction.

"Do you have room for another passenger?" I asked of Lowell Thomas, Jr., as he and Hilscher headed for the plane.

"Why would anyone want to leave this party?" Thomas asked. "You're not ill, are you?"

"Oh, no! Just anxious," I confessed, blurting out my desire to get a scoop for a weekly newspaper.

Fortunately enough, Hilscher had once worked for a weekly. "Give Mary my seat," he responded graciously. "My appointment is of the 'if I can get off the mountain' in time variety. It can wait."

Thanks to Herb, Miriam and Lowell, I did get that scoop; but not without added excitement.

As we tried to take off from the wet, sticky snow on the glacier, the skis on Lowell's plane failed to shake loose. The further we plowed down the glacier the deeper they seemed to dig. When Mt. McKinley holds you down, you're stuck.

I feel that Lowell Thomas Jr. could have lifted without additional weight, and he probably would have lifted with my added weight; but he just isn't a pilot who takes unnecessary risks. Already we were beyond the strip used for landing. There were snow bridges and crevasses on this glacier; and no one was more acutely aware of this fact than Thomas. Cutting the motor, he said he would ski down in front of the plane to check.

Having been stuck on glaciers previously, I crawled out and started tramping down a runway in front of the plane's skis. Hopeless, for one person without snow shoes, but one has to try to help, to say the least.

Lowell must have been half-a-mile down the glacier when I looked back toward the glacier house, wondering if they realized we were in trouble. Soon I saw specks gliding toward us, six of them. Hans Metz and his ski instructors were en route. They reached us shortly after Thomas got back. He was shovelling snow from the plane's imprisoned skis when the men on the boards offered helping hands — and feet — as we tramped out a runway. This was fun. I thought back to the time I had joined the Frenchmen in tramping out a runway for the previous year, when Don brought me in for a story.

Thomas said there were no crevasses ahead; but he doubted that he could take off in the sticky stuff with additional weight. He said he felt he could make it by himself if I didn't mind walking back to the better packed runway at the observatory.

Of course I didn't mind. I had always wanted to take a long walk on a glacier. I sank mini-skirt deep in the snow, but I didn't mind since I was wearing ski pants — without skis, darn it. I must admit that the melting snow clogged inside my boots taught me what kind of foot gear not to wear on a glacier.

I must also admit that I was plenty happy to see Carl Sullivan bringing snowshoes for me. How wonderful! It must have been well over a mile back.

The gang at the glacier house had set up a ceremonial ribbon for me to cut at a goal line, just for me. They gave a rousing cheer when I made it, huffing and puffing. I'll never make a mountain climber, not even a snow bunny, so help me!

Our second try for take-off was more successful than the first. And to top it off, I need not have worried at all, nor rushed, for the others got closed in by a white-out and twenty-five of the party remained in the 16 x 16 overnight. Oh, well, that's what comes of sticking to duty, always missing fun.

Did I forget to tell you how scared I was when our plane failed on take-off? Excuse me; but I wasn't. Not at all. We simply failed to lift. If there had been a crevasse in front of us large enough to trap a plane, Thomas would have seen it. If we had hit a snow bridge the wings would no doubt have spanned it. We weren't even in danger of tearing out landing gear. Sorry, folks, but our position was less precarious than if we had been in a car stalled on a freeway, and it was much more exciting because I admire Lowell Thomas Jr., greatly.

I had my scoop; but the editor had a story, too, which begun thus, the previous day:

"For those still listening to radio reports on Don Sheldon's glacier party on Mt. McKinley, *Frontiersman* columnist Mary Carey is back in Palmer with the first pictures to be published on the world's most unique 'Grand Opening,' even though she gave listeners a few suspenseful hours while stuck on the Ruth Glacier in a plane piloted by Lowell Thomas, Jr. of Anchorage."

Chapter XXV

UP THE RIVER IN D-8 CATS

According to federal land laws, homesteaders must clear and cultivate 20 of the 160 acres, as well as build and live on the homestead, before applying for final proof of possession. Since I filed as a widow of a veteran, the terms were a little more lenient, insofar as the amount of time I had to live on the land is concerned, but I still had to clear and plant 20 acres within the first three years.

Despite winning "the war," the new highway would not reach my homestead in time to be of help insofar as bringing in heavy equipment is concerned. Furthermore, I couldn't homestead in the bush where there was no communication whatsoever with the outside world and keep four newspaper columns.

My first editor, Dave Galloway of the *Fairbanks News-Miner,* suggested I keep my column, "Talkeetna Topics," which I had written for five years, turning it in whenever convenient. This I am still doing.

After writing farewells through my other columns, which had become an intimate part of my life, and explaining how impossible it would be to keep them while homesteading in an isolated fly-in area near Mt. McKinley, my thoughts turned to the seemingly unsolvable problems at hand.

Imagine clearing and planting where there is no road and apparently no feasible means of getting equipment into the area. This law is as outmoded as a reindeer for transportation in Alaska. When a homesteader has cleared and planted his twenty acres, how does he get his crop to market, if there is no road? Invariably the consequence, unless he has a fortune backing him, is going broke.

If I had my way, the last choice for use of the land in this magnificent wilderness area where I homesteaded, would be to push down the tall, virgin timber for farming. But homesteading laws must be obeyed. I had to homestead, as well as file an eighty-acre Trade & Manufacture site, to have enough acreage to reach the top of the butte where I want to put a Mt. McKinley observatory. Yet, without these homesteading laws I could never gain his land. I am humble for this opportunity to try for it, even though I complain of outdated laws which I feel should be amended.

To get a D-8 Caterpillar into this virgin wilderness to clear land, and put in an air strip — since the road would not reach it for the next two years — seemed a virtual impossibility. Yet nothing smaller was capable of handling this type of work. Size of equipment was really no factor since there was no road and no bridge across the Chulitna River, anyway.

I had a problem. No one seemed eager to risk such an expensive hunk of equipment as a D-8 on such a "damn fool adventure" in the Alaskan wilderness. I had little choice. Now I must buy a D-8 Cat — which I couldn't operate — to add to my Super Cub — which I couldn't fly — to clear and plant crops — which I couldn't harvest — or give up homesteading. Never had any sense, anyway, so I found a second hand Caterpillar and started looking for operators.

Fortunately I found a man, Jack Silven, who said he would risk his cat since I would have another along. This was great. Finally I found four men who believed they could walk two D-8's up the twenty-eight-mile clearing, if you could call it that, which would later become a part of the Anchorage-Fairbanks highway. They would have to cross the unbridged Chulitna on the winter ice. Could they make it?

There was eight to ten feet of snow on the ground. No highway equipment had been on the road clearing since last fall, when a D-8 broke through the muskeg and sank to her stack. The operator managed to get a cable around the blade and hitch the cat to a large spruce tree. This cable and stack were the only reminders of the depth of the muskeg, fed by warm springs which we would have to cross. How well I remembered, from way back in 1962, when the first clearing was done in this area. The construction crews laughed about a swampy area, rightfully named Rudy's Lake, because a very determined cat skinner named "Rudy" sunk three mechanized monsters there before making it through the muskeg to higher ground.

It was a terrible chance to take. Such an Odyssey had never been attempted previously; but I had to try.

With much foreboding and fear, I plunged my life savings into a seemingly impossible dream in the Alaskan wilderness. A huge twenty-one-foot sled was built and loaded with twenty-four 55 gallon drums of diesel, two drums of aviation fuel and materials for building another cabin on my homestead, this one for hired help. Cached between the fuel and lumber was a sleeping-room-only area, which was covered with a plastic tarp and warmed by a small heater. Here the four men: Jack Silfven, Earl Ray, Gene Richardson, and Jim Sibert, Jr., would sleep.

Since the blade on the machine which Earl Ray was operating had a higher lift than that of Jack Silfven, Earl was to break trail and Jack would pull the sled. This wasn't as simple as it sounds. Twice Earl was stuck in areas where warm springs kept the muck soft all winter. Much cable and time was expended extracting the cat from such wallows. Always there were snow bridges to be filled in over open streams by the lead cat. These bridges had to be substantial enough not to wash out nor break through before the cat pulling the overload sled could follow.

It took the men eleven days to make the first twenty-two miles. Temperatures ranged from ten above to minus twenty degrees. I became desperate.

Nothing could hold me in Talkeetna any longer. Although it was against his better judgement, I persuaded Don Sheldon to fly me in. We saw the cats, within three miles of my cabin. They seemed to be making good progress along a windswept ridge. I asked Don to land on the river bar below my cabin, so I could walk back to meet the men. Landing here was less dangerous in winter than in summer. I would never have attempted such a landing myself . . .never did. It is precarious enough, flying down this canyon, any time of the year. Yet in winter, if you overshoot the postage stamp bar below you will at least skate out over the drink rather than being dumped into it.

Knowing I'm nuts, Don didn't argue. Down through the chute we fluttered, landing like a duck as the skis skimmed the snow. He argued with me in silence, as he sometimes does, while I reached for the snow shoes.

"If you just have to go," he finally relented, "maybe you'd best carry my rifle."

"Why? We didn't see a thing except moose and they were concentrated below, on the willow flats. We flew up the clearing and I can see all the way back to the cats from the top of that ridge."

"O.K., Kid. You'd probably shoot a toe off anyway."

As Don took off I saw him flying low over the trail, again checking and perhaps routing any game within hearing distance of the plane's roar. Bear had long been in hibernation and moose didn't care for deep snow. If I met a cow and calf, which I surely had sense enough to watch for by now, I could get out of their way faster than the cow could get to me, since I was on snow shoes. Moose have a great deal of difficulty "swimming" in waist-deep snow and avoid doing so, sticking strictly to well beaten paths most of the time.

I was so happy when I made it back to the cats that the fellows probably thought I was some type of idiot or that I had gotten "cabin fever" as one sometimes does in a frozen world away from civilization. I later learned that Gene Richardson, whom I hardly knew at the time, said, "Good God, not a woman! What will we do with a woman?"

At this time I had every confidence that the men would make it to the cabin. It was 10:30 A.M. and shelter was less than three miles ahead.

It is quite evident that I did not know what was involved in those three miles. Earl Ray invited me to climb on the lead cat with him in order that I might make photos fore and aft. The big blade bit into the deep snow all the way, and pushed or pulled it to the side. Once when we stopped, I forgot and jumped from the cat without snow shoes, and sank waist deep in the fluffy stuff.

We came to a grade which seemed insurmountable. Thirty-four passes were made upgrade, dragging back a snow fill. The incline was so steep that Earl stopped and suggested that I ride on the trailing cat. Its long cable, which was attached to the lead cat for extra pull and protection, in case either machine should plunge out of sight into soft muskeg or into a snow-bridge ravine, was now disconnected. The grade was so steep, it was explained, that the front cat might slip backward, as it had done on previous inclines.

208

It would be difficult for me to speak my admiration for these men. There are more kinds of pioneering in Alaska than is done by dogsled or plane. My prayers must have helped support that cat. With each drag it made to the side I was sure it would go over the cliff and plunge into the river, which we now parallelled. On the thirty-fifth drag back, Earl made it to the top. Triumphantly the big cat held its footing as it clogged in reverse to the rear cat.

Downgrades were worse than upgrades. The sled back of Jack's cat, kept sliding down and bumping into his D-8. The heavy guard rail which they had built in front of the sled was not heavy enough. Fuel barrels were punctured; lumber and materials toppled overboard with the terrific impacts.

Adding to these delaying miseries, some of the longer two-by-fours had to be sawed off because they extended too far over the rear of the sled. When turning a corner they would bang into trees. When crossing a narrow ravine the 2-by's bridged it and seemed to suspend the whole sled. There was little or no fill along this part of the clearing and there were drop-offs where streams cut through.

The nearer the river, the steeper the down-grades. The men put on snowshoes and walked to the top of the final ridge. It was too steep. They backtracked, then walked down a ravine to the river. They drilled the ice with an auger brought along for this purpose. It seemed thick enough to support the cats. Eighteen inches of ice will support a lot of weight, but each cat weighed about twenty-four tons, and that sled was no feather.

By pushing over a few trees, the fellows deduced we could reach the river by heading straight down the ravine. From there we would go up-river the rest of the way, on the ice. There was open water in places along the river where the current was too swift for the clutching fingers of ice. We would have to chance it, there was no other possibility for making it, and this was not a crew for turning back.

I thought I had been quite a few places and done quite a few adventuresome things, but nothing like this. Going down the steep ravine, the only way I could stay on the bulldozer was to swing to the crossbar overhead. The temperature was dropping and my gloves seemed to give little protection against the sticky-cold iron. Earl gave me some heavier gloves, which I pulled on over mine. They helped.

When we finally reached the river I held my breath as we inched the iron monster out on the edge of the river ice. It held.

Gene Richardson took his turn on the snowshoes, as he and Jim Sibert had done all along, leading the way. The snow was not so deep on the windblown river ice and the going was much easier. Ahead of the cats, the fellow kept the ice auger in constant use whenever the ice looked thin. Again the gigantic invaders were coupled together by cable. This time the span was lengthened to avoid putting too much stress on the ice in a concentrated area. We were almost within seeing distance of my cabin across the river; but getting to it would be a different story. There were open spots in the river, and overflows. She was too deep and swift in this canyon area to freeze solidly all the way across. If she did freeze, the current would cut away under the ice until it escaped and overflowed. On up to where the glaciers had done their own bulldozing, the river was wider and not so deep. Ahead, the nation's tallest peak loomed closer, pinker, and colder as we trespassed her virgin southern flank with clanking iron monsters.

It was —22° and late in the evening when we made it to where the men thought we might effect a crossing. The ice was thinner, but there was little choice. Earl sent me to the back cat again. They were roped with a long, black cable, like climbers on a mountain, just in case.

Earl seemed doing so well, when suddenly, down the cat plunged! There was slack in the cable, and we hardly felt the lurch as the front end of the lead cat slid into the water. We yelled and waved at Earl Ray to jump; but he rode her down, scotching the brakes before swinging on the overhead beam and leaping to the shattered shelf ice which had broken away from the rest of the pack.

It was a strange, as well as a horrible, sinking feeling, seeing the motor of the cat underwater almost to the stack, yet hearing the motor put-put as it kept running. The back cat would not budge her.

"Quick, the chain saws," Earl directed, "the blade has caught on shelf ice and she's holding. If we can cut an ice ramp, maybe I can back her out, if she keeps running.

I had not realized that the cat was suspended by the huge blade which bit into the ice and held as the motor sank. A test made with a steel rod carried for this purpose showed fourteen feet of water underneath the blade. If the ice gave way, no more cat.

Ice and snow flew as the men sawed through the frozen shelf and kicked it down on a firmer footing. Water sloshed up and froze on their gloves and clothing. They would surely freeze to death. I had been no colder in the prop wash on the Arctic Ocean. This was it!

Our drama was so intense that we hardly noticed a plane circle overhead, until it landed. The men did not have time to stop work. It was Talkeetna bush pilot Cliff Hudson who saw the predicament we were in and landed on the river ice to see if he could be of possible aid. It was getting late. Although it was twenty-two below, the men were working so hard and fast that they were wet and sweating despite the ice which clung to them where it did not get knocked off.

Cliff offered to take a chain saw; but Earl thought it would be of more help if he flew me back to Talkeetna, where I should stay, sending back dry socks and gloves for them while there was still light enough for a landing. If they got the cat across, they would stay in my cabin.

My spirit was lower than the cat. My feet had long since ceased to have feeling and I wondered if one could tell when he had frozen toes. The meat had been frozen in the sandwich which I had eaten for lunch, and my stomach felt as if the meat never thawed up. Yet I didn't want to leave.

"We'd better hurry," Cliff encouraged as he offered to help me through the snow to the plane, "the trading post will be closed and it will be too dark for me to get back."

The store was closed, but I managed to buy eight pairs of gloves from Carroll Close at the Roadhouse, and a jug, of course. Quickly I begged socks from anyone whom I could find.

Mrs. Christine Flescher was headed toward her home down the runway. Knowing how precious minutes can be in case of emergency, she didn't let me look elsewhere. Like the old pro which she is, she came up with the goods immediately.

I ran with my contraband for the plane, which Cliff already had revved up. He took off in the gathering gloom.

I returned to thank Christine.

"Sit down and warm yourself and relax," she invited. "Cliff should be back within forty minutes. You'll be right here on the runway to hear the news."

"But it will be dark."

"He's landed in the dark before. In Alaska one does what he must."

Mrs. Flescher made me a little ashamed of my own anxiety as she talked of her fishing days in Ketchikan, when she had owned her own fishing fleet of four boats, as well as a charter cruiser. She knew what it is like to be in trouble, especially in the water. It was difficult for me to imagine her in such a role, so immaculate her dress and so soft her speech.

Soon after dark I heard the drone of a plane. I rushed to the airstrip. Before the prop stopped turning Cliff climbed from the plane and beat me to the draw by asking:

"What's the matter, Kitten, worried about something?"

"Tell me," I pleaded.

"They're O.K. The cat's out of the water. They're headed for your cabin and I bet there'll be a little party tonight."

I could have cried with joy and admiration.

There was no doubt in my mind now that the necessary clearing would be done. The worst was over.

CHAPTER XXVI

FIRST WINTER CLIMB ON MT. McKINLEY

On January 28, 1967 I flew into Talkeetna to do a very strange story, about the first winter assault on Mt. McKinley. It was known as the Centennial Expedition, a sort of kick-off to Alaska's Centennial of Purchase exposition. Much to my delight I knew four of the eight climbers through previous stories and climbs.

Jacques Batkin and Dave Johnston were among my favorites, as mountain climbers. Jacques was with the French group which scaled Mt. Huntington in 1964. He was the only man among the French climbers, except for the leader and now-deceased Lionel Terray, who could speak English enough to be understood. He had helped me with interviews on the glacier when Terray's shoulder was dislocated and when one of their group was snow blind. Dave, bless his heart, was the gangling 6-foot 7-incher who ate my strawberries and a settin' of eggs prepared by gold miner Rocky Cummins when Dave and his buddies made the long traverse of the Alaska Range and were walking out. Ray Genet and Shiro Nishimae I had met and photographed when they made previous climbs.

The first midwinter climb was a scientific expedition. The University of Alaska's Institute of Arctic Biology ran a series of physiological and psychological tests that were to be carried out during the climb. The men would be returned to Fairbanks, as soon as the climb was finished, for further testing. The climb was expected to take about forty days, in sub-zero temperatures.

The team was composed of Gregg Bloomberg, 25, Denver, Colorado; Art Davidson, 22, Anchorage; Dave Johnston, 24, Anchorage; George Wichman, 39, Anchorage physician; Shiro Nishimae, 31, Anchorage; Ray Genet, 35, Anchorage; Jacques Batkin, 36, Anchorage; and John Edwards, 35, Cleveland, Ohio. Blomberg and Davidson were leader and co-leader, respectively.

The climbers arrived in Talkeetna on the 29th of January and Don Sheldon airlifted them to the six-thousand foot level on the Kahiltna Glacier.

In height it was a heterogenous crew, Dave towering six-foot seven and Japanese-born Shiro Nishime, who was a school teacher in Anchorage, standing only five-foot-four. Regardless of weight or size, however, each member would carry a total of between fifty and sixty pounds.

Their food, according to Dave Johnston, the man in charge, would be for the most part, "super market stuff." There would be six or seven different types of high-protein breakfast foods. There would be cheese, sausage, hard candy, a bread stuff called "logan bread," and four ounces of chocolate per man per day. The diet also included liquid jello, and high-protein orange drink, tea, and cocoa. A touch of home cooking was added by Mrs. Gregg Blomberg, wife of the team leader, who prepared various delicacies such as apricot coconut balls for the climbers.

On January 30 the mountaineers started packing their loads from the base camp at the 8,200-foot level to camp two. It was a beautiful day. The team was traveling with neither snowshoes nor skis. The glacier face was hard packed and made for good walking. Four of the climbers had reached the second camp. Johnston and Batkin followed in their path. When the other climbers looked back there was only one man on the trail.

Dave Johnston was with Batkin, when suddenly and without warning, he just disappeared into a tiny hole, breaking through a snow bridge into a small crevasse about two feet wide. His pack remained on the surface, jammed across the crevasse, but the straps broke and he went on through, falling about fifty feet.

Batkin's body was taken from the crevasse at 4:30 P.M., about an hour after the fall. He was pronounced dead by Dr. George Wichman at the side of the crevasse. He is reported to have sustained severe head injuries in the fall.

In hopes that Don Sheldon would be flying in the area the mountaineers stamped out "LAND" on the snow.

Jim Cassidy, a member of the Mountaineering Club of Alaska, saw the sign about noon Saturday as he was flying by the mountain. He landed and subsequently relayed the message to Sheldon in Talkeetna, who arrived about forty minutes later to remove Batkin's body from the glacier.

District Ranger of McKinley Park, Wayne Merry, had flown over the group about 9:00 A.M. on the morning of the day the climber died and said the weather at the time was clear and "fairly calm". Merry said the McKinley climbers were an extremely strong team — "thoroughly experienced."

Merry said, "It's really ironic that one of them should drop through a small hole and be killed on a flat glacier."

Ray Genet, who helped Sheldon bring his fallen comrade back to Talkeetna called it a "one-in-a-thousand accident."

Asked if the climb would be continued, Genet replied: "Once you've started, you've got to continue. This is not a little afternoon climb — when someone has died for it, you've got to go through with it."

An official release, signed by expedition leader Gregg Bloomberg, had this to say of Batkin's death:

"The remaining members of this expedition express heart felt sympathy to the family and friends of our companion.

"Farine died in pursuit of the winter ascent in which he truly believed."

"After serious consideration, the remaining members of the expedition have concluded that we should continue. The extensive preparation and support vested in us and the program of work we have undertaken are major factors in this decision.

"We continue the attempt with Jacques Batkin's spirit and presence very much in mind."

Batkin was known as "Farine" or "flour" which was a nickname derived from an occupation which he had in France, carrying sacks of flour for a living. He was a tremendously powerful and highly experienced climber.

Batkin was the fourth climber to die on McKinley. Elton Thayer fell from Karsten's Ridge on the north side of the mountain in 1954. Two other climbers, Allen Carpe and Theodore Carpe, died when they fell through a crevasse on the Muldrow Glacier in 1932. Harvard climber Edward Bernd fell four-thousand feet to his death while descending Huntington, in the shadow of McKinley, in 1965.

After making what arrangements he could for Batkin, Ray Genet was flown back to the mountain by Sheldon, where he rejoined his team for the continued winter assault of McKinley.

The climbers made good progress; and all was well until February 28, when they headed for the top and were struck by bad weather. Three of the climbers, Ray Genet, Dave Johnston and Art Davidson, stuck it out and made the summit on March 1, at 7:00 A.M.; but they were pinned down by bad weather and could not return to the 17,300-foot camp.

The four climbers waiting below feared their companions were in trouble when they failed to make it back by March 3. It was decided that Bloomberg and Edwards would head for the lower camp where their two-way radio had been left, to try to contact Don Sheldon. Dr. Wichman and Nishimae would wait in the middle camp for the climbers who had tried for the summit, then descend if they did not appear within two days.

On March 5 Edwards and Bloomberg had not heard from any of the other climbers. Six days passed. The international distress signal was stamped in the snow.

Paul Crews, a pilot and photographer, flew over and saw the three climbers at the higher level, but where were the others?

Because of the distress signal great fear was expressed for the safety of the men on the mountain. Search parties were called in.

I arrived at the Rainbow Lodge, information headquarters, just about the time J. Vin Hoeman — later buried beneath a snow avalanche while descending from a successful climb of Mt. Everest — and his wife, Dr. Grace Hoeman, also a climber, returned from a reconnaissance flight which they made with Don Sheldon. They reported winds over 100 miles per hour were hitting the plane so hard that it was like backing into a threshing machine. Sheldon said his speed indicator was at 160 miles per hour and they were making little visible headway. They had spotted three men at the 17,300 foot camp, but everything was blotted out below.

Talkeetna was swamped with rescue personnel as the anxious days of March 5, 6, and 7th clicked off. Art Hames, of National Park Services, was Director of Operations, and Wayne Merry, District Ranger, was rescue coordinator. The Alaska rescue group, as well as Colonel Bennett and two helicopters and crews from Ft. Greely were on hand.

Five climbers from the Mountain Rescue Council had arrived from Seattle: Glenn Kelsey, Lee Nelson, the Whittaker twins, Jim and Lou, and Dick Pargeter.

Rescue coordinator Gary Hansen stood by with Barney Seile, Clarence Serfoss and the Hoemans, waiting to go in if the weather cleared.

An airdrop was made to the men at the 17,333-foot level, where the mountain was clear. A radio, oxygen, food, and instructions to go down to where a possible landing might be made was in the drop.

Via two-way communication, rescue operations were set up. Helicopters were ready to pick up these climbers when their position and weather permitted. Yet where were the other climbers? Word leaked out, falsely, that they were dead.

Major James Okonek of Elmendorf talked to the climbers over the two-way in Sheldon's office. The mystery deepened. The names of the climbers at the upper and lower camps were not revealed to the press. All that anyone knew was that somewhere, between 14,500 and 8,000 feet, two of the seven were missing. What had happened to the two men supposedly at the 10,200 foot level?

March 9 broke clear and two helicopters were dispatched to the mountain. Johnston, Genet and Davidson were picked up at the upper camp, Bloomberg and Edwards at the lower. When they arrived in Talkeetna the whole world knew. No sign and no trace was seen of the men, now known to be Dr. George Wichman and Shiro Nishimae, at the camp level where Bloomberg had left them when he and Edwards went to the lower camp to get to the radio. In fact, not even a tent was spotted.

Again Rescue went into conference. In the morning, weather permitting, the Whittaker twins would be carried by copters to the lower camp level, Lee Nelson and J. Vin Hoeman to the upper camp level. They would work toward the center camp in an effort to find the other two climbers. Lee Nelson had climbed the mountain with the Seattle-Tacoma group, and was an old friend whom I was indeed happy to see. I did not know Louis and Jim Whittaker since their climb with the Day party was made before I came to Talkeetna.

Every foot of the trail would be searched between the upper and lower camp. The parties would meet at the center camp, where the lost climbers were last seen. A chopper would wait at the center camp.

Imagine the surprise of everyone concerned when the chopper landed where the center camp should have been, and two blinking mountain climbers crawled out of a shallow crevasse where they had taken refuge when their tent was blown away during the height of the storm.

"Where are they?" the bewildered mountain climbers asked.

"Where are who?" asked the equally bewildered rescuers, still stunned by the unceremonious appearance of the lost climbers as they crawled from their hole in the mountain, around which there was no sign of life.

"Where are the b —" somehow the mountain climbers couldn't bring themselves to saying "bodies" because this is what they seem to have deduced when the three climbers failed to return from the top.

When the situation was explained one of the rescue team asked,

"Didn't you hear us? Didn't you know the mountain was alive with search and rescue operations?"

How could they? With winds of hurricane force blowing above them and a constant overcast at their ten thousand foot level, although it had cleared on the upper and lower reaches of 20,320-foot Mt. McKinley. Under the circumstances a whole army could have been within a few yards of them without their hearing a sound.

Although I was not working regularly for the newspapers any more, I could never resist a "scoop"; and it looked as if this was my opportunity, since the last two climbers were rescued on Thursday morning, the day the *Frontiersman* is published.

I flew into Palmer, posthaste; and while my film was being developed I wrote the story, which I had already written a dozen times in my mind.

"I should again like to thank Park Rangers Hames and Merry and Information Officer Sgt. Herrington of Elmendorf, who were most cooperative under trying circumstances.

"I would also like to express my gratitude to the Governor of Alaska, Walter J. Hickel, now Secretary of the Interior, who took time from the first legislative session to offer any and all help available or within his jurisdiction. His concern for the safety of the climbers was expressed to this reporter personally, over long distance from Juneau on March 9."

In summing up my news stories I wrote:

"Among the many expressing concern for the safety of the climbers was Governor Walter J. Hickel, who told this reporter in a telephone conversation yesterday that Juneau was standing by to give every assistance possible.

"The Governor commended the Mt. McKinley Park Rangers, the Army, the Air Force, bush pilot Don Sheldon and all those helping with the search for their magnificent coordination, without which the seemingly impossible could not have been achieved . . ."

Chapter XXVII

IN BRISTOL BAY

In the summer of 1968 the long promised highway had not yet reached my homestead. My funds were nearing exhaustion. My fields of grain were up and growing beautifully, for the moose to harvest. As many Alaskans do, I would have to support my homestead until the day when it would support me. This meant remaining in the school room.

The thought of teaching anywhere, except in Talkeetna, had never entered my mind. I would return to my little cabin along- side Sheldon's air strip, rest for the night, after spending two hours in the bathtub and making some enlargements for a news story. The following day I would go to Palmer and apply for a teaching position in the Talkeetna high school where I had been the first teacher, back in 1962. Now there was a beautiful new building and six instructors. My little school had certainly grown. And to top it all off, there was talk of a larger high school yet, a consolidated one at the Talkeetna "Y" on the new highway.

I had just taken the last of my enlargements off the electric ferrotype board the next morning when the telephone rang.

"I wonder if you would like to come to Bristol Bay and teach?" came the unmistakable voice of my former Talkeetna principal over long distance.

I stammered in surprise because I had not even applied to teach out there, at the head of the Aleutian Chain.

"I know you enjoy flying," Mr. Dan Turner continued. "I have need of a high school teacher who would be flown from here to South Naknek, half-a-mile across the Naknek River," he chuckles, "and one day a week about sixty miles to Egagiak to help with correspondence courses."

"I don't understand," I sputtered, grateful that opportunity, as welcome as an Alaskan Chinook (warm wind) in winter, came just at the right time.

"I thought you might like to be Millie's roommate again," he added in his own way of breaking the news.

"What? You mean they've retired her again? Not here in Talkeetna? And she didn't even tell me."

"Suppose you hop a plane and come to King Salmon this week end. I'll meet you there. It's only eighteen miles from Naknek, where you'll be teaching, I hope. I've told my school board so much about Millie that I think they'll overlook her age if the two of you come together. There's only one apartment available. They were thinking of a man and wife team, until I told them about you."

We flew to Naknek and were hired. This would be a great, new adventure; but I had a problem. In Alaska there is a ruling, and it's a good one, that a teacher must return to college, at least once every five years, to renew her certificate. Despite the fact that I held two college degrees and had seventeen years teaching experience, this regulation must be observed. I regretted having to give up the time at my homestead, otherwise I would have welcomed the thought with greater enthusiasm.

A classroom in summer would never do, not in Alaska when all the world's alive on the outside. "Don't Fence Me In" has always been the theme song in my heart. I'm a female counterpart for Tom Sawyer and Huckleberry Finn. I began looking for a way to escape the classroom.

I though of the good time I had had six years previously, when studying botany with Dr. Leonard Freese of Alaska Methodist University as our professor. Our time was spent in field trips to such places as Resurrection Bay and Thumb Cove. Maybe I could luck out again.

Fortunately Dr. Freese and his cousin, John Friberg, former head of Alaska State Land Selections, were my neighbors. Dr. Freese was homesteading along the new Anchorage-Fairbanks highway. Mr. Friberg was with him whenever he could get away from Anchorage. They were always helpful, and I went to them for advice.

A field course was being offered, in Anthropology and Geology. Despite Dr. Freese's encouragement, I doubted that I would be admitted to a nine-week graduate course where all students would probably be male. But Dr. Freese made his personal recommendation to instructors Dr. Frederick-Hadleigh West and Dr. Ross Schaff, and I was on my way.

I'll never forget how those young geologist looked at me, a grandmother, along for nine weeks of rugged hiking, climbing, and living in a pup tent. They must have thought they would have to carry me up the first mountain. Things were easier when we learned there were three females enrolled. Since the others were of college age, perhaps our invasion was more easily accepted.

Each of us had a team-mate while in the field. Here I lucked out. If Mike Wiley resented having an older woman working beside him, I never felt it. In fact, it turned out to be a tragic beginning for a lasting friendship.

Mike's wife and two young sons visited for a weekend with us in camp. Beautiful people. They came in a camper and Mrs. Wiley was driving it back to Haines when . . . the complete story was never put together. She and the boys were found, dead, washed down a river near Destruction Bay.

This, perhaps, made a better student of me. Although I doubted Mike's returning to finish the course, I worked on the double to keep two sets of notes and collect an extra specimen for every rock and artifact which we had to classify.

Mike did return, bravely so, and the very next day while we were exploring a rock glacier, a slowly moving river of rock, a strange coincidence occurred.

I had walked away from the group, toward a large boulder behind which I hoped to hide while relieving myself. I didn't. In the shadow lay a dead man.

I couldn't call Mike, not after what he had been through.

"Dr. Schaff, would you come with me to check a formation I have found?" I asked my professor to the side.

While walking toward the boulder I told him what I thought I had discovered.

I'll never forget that old hat and the black and red checked jacket. Braver than I, Dr. Shaff reached to see what was underneath that jacket . . . snow, a mound of snow which had not melted. The hat and jacket were quite old, falling apart when touched.

There was quite a bit of speculation as to why the coat, hat, and frying pan, which Mike found, were left on the spot. Did the owner abandon his camp, become lost, meet with a grizzly? The folding frying pan was of World War I vintage, made to fit on a pack, with knife, fork and spoon included. Recently, when Mike was visiting my lodge, I produced the pan and we relived 1969 in 1975.

Most of the time on our field trip was spent in the Tangle Lakes area or on the Kantishna, the northern flank of Mt. McKinley. There was some pretty tough going; but I managed to stay up with the group. If I got tired, I never confessed. If the fellows slowed down, in order to make it easier on me, they never confessed, either.

In August, blueberries ripened. Have you ever eaten blueberry pie made in a Dutch oven, out under the stars? I'll swear Dr. Freese must have told the other profs about the blueberry pie we had on our field trip in 1963. Maybe that's why I was admitted to the class in the first place. Strange it would come my turn to watch camp, which had a tempting blueberry patch nearby, just as they ripened. No bear ever got a blueberry from that patch. After the first pie, more blueberries than rocks reached camp.

I'll swear, my ability to make a pie under adverse circumstances has always been a faithful ally when it comes to getting along with the menfolk. I had to be graded on my "pie-ability," otherwise I would never have passed that course.

With summer school over, the moose harvesting my fields, and a couple of workmen trying to get a cat road to the top of the two-thousand-foot butte where I eventually hope to have an observatory, Mrs. Millie Campbell and I took a long look at our mountain, disappearing on the northern horizon as we flew southwest toward Bristol Bay.

Lake Iliamna, largest inland body of water in Alaska, was inviting as we crossed a portion of its ninety-mile length the easy way. I would like to have explored every island. The Valley of Ten Thousand Smokes no longer smokes as much as it once did, since the lakes and streams beneath the mountain of ash, seven-hundred-feet deep near the decapitated volcano, have gradually accepted their death warrant written on the pages of history as the world's second greatest volcanic eruption, June 6, 1912.

Our reception in King Salmon and Naknek was quite gratifying. Mr. and Mrs. Charles Durrand, who had transferred from the F.A.A. station in Talkeetna to the one in King Salmon, were there to meet us. How their four sons had grown! Millie had taught them in grade school, now I looked forward to teaching them in high school.

After a luncheon like only Betty could cook, we were shown around King Salmon and then driven to Naknek. Here the whole town turned out to honor us with a dinner at Geny Nelson's Bar, which was really more like a museum. Again we feasted, not only on food, but on a hospitality which made us feel like royalty.

Fall turned to winter as we picked berries, fished, beachcombed and got settled in our magnificent new high school on the hill.

This was the richest school borough in Alaska, and Bristol Bay one of the richest fishing grounds in the world. Sometimes, as I stood before my class, I wondered why high school students, who were really quite mature, should listen to me.

"Why," I asked, "do you come to school when you may make more during the short fishing season than a teacher makes in nine months?"

They reasoned, and rightfully so, that the day may come when fishing would no longer be a bonanza in Bristol Bay. Many of their canneries were already shut down. That day has come sooner than anyone believed it would. Now, as my former high school students drop by my lodge en route to the University of Alaska in Fairbanks, I revel in their judgement. Dave and Alvin Aspelund were here yesterday. They stop by the lodge often, and I love it.

In Naknek we had a river and a bay, but no mountain. The holiday season was coming up. I wondered what progress was being made at my homestead, on the ski slope and on the four-wheel-drive road up the butte. Nothing else would do. I must go.

As usual, in Alaska, things were not progressing as rapidly as hoped. The D-8 cat took too steep a grade and slid back down the mountainside, with operator aboard, and threw a track. The chain saws kept breaking and seemed in constant need of repair. Alder on the side of the mountain, where the men were trying to cut a ski run, was thicker than quills on a porcupine and just about as unpleasant to cope with. The fellows were discouraged.

Earlier, when there were choppers in the area, I had materials flown to the top of the two-thousand-foot butte and had built a couple of ski cabins. Now we had to reach them with a run. The road and observatory would have to wait.

I bought three new chain saws and determined to man one of them myself. We had to reach the top! Together Jack Milligan, Earl Ray, and I struggled, in below-zero temperatures, to reach our goal. Days were short. We had to set out before daylight and climb most of the way up the butte in semi-darkness to have four or five working hours. The saws, even the new ones, failed to function properly because of the cold; and we had to build a fire to warm our saws as well as ourselves. Finally, with victory within sight, my chain saw bounced from an alder and the blade cut my foot — not badly, but enough to keep me from working.

Earl thought the cut might require stitches, so he flew me into Anchorage. My injury was minor; but it was too late for me to return to the homestead. Maybe I could catch an earlier flight back to King Salmon. I could use the time to make lesson plans.

There was a vacant seat and I did get on the earlier flight. The plane on which I was scheduled to return crashed, near Lake Iliamna. All aboard were killed instantly. What a tragic day for Bristol Bay. Several of our friends from King Salmon, Dillingham, and Naknek were killed. My teacher-helper, and one of our grade-school students was on that plane. Why I was spared by a strange quirk of fate I'll never know.

Since fact is often stranger than fiction, I may as well state before we get there, that one accident saved my life. Another broke my back.

Throughout the years I have come to note that some good seems to emerge, even from the starkest of tragedies. The parents of our deceased student, Mr. and Mrs. Hank Ostrosky, in conjunction with the newly-organized Bristol Bay Historical Society, established a memorial scholarship in honor of their son, Zeck.

The Ostroskys were leaders in our community. Hank, the only name by which I ever knew Mr. Ostrosky, owned a fishing boat and processed much of the fish which he caught, trying to build a business which would provide employment during the winter months. Constantly he worked for better living and better fishing conditions. His wife, Kathryn, who was first president of our Bristol Bay Historical Society, was later elected to the legislature from Anchorage, where they moved after their son's death.

While teaching in Naknek I became interested in reports I heard concerning 117-year-old Evon Olympic; the great-great-great grandfather of one of my students, Carol Zimin. He was, and is, insofar as can be determined, the oldest living man in Alaska today.

This seemed a story which I couldn't pass up. The school furnished a plane and flew me and my little photography class over the river to South Naknek. Our find was so interesting that it led to a follow-up by members of our Historical Society. With Mrs. Inisha McCormick as our interpreter, Mrs. Kathryn Ostrosky, Mrs. Leslie Burtner — a fellow teacher — and I went across the river for an interview.

This time we walked. It was quite an experience, crossing the Naknek River on the ice. The tides, second highest in the world, keep breaking the ice. Here and there we encountered overflows and pools of water. Sometimes icebergs as big as boats come marching in with the tide, only to be left stranded along the beach as the outgoing tide sucks the water from beneath them. On this day the ice seemed solid.

As we crossed, Mrs. McCormick, who was born in the area, told of how she and her sons, Jay and Glenn, who were now my high school students, almost drowned while attempting the crossing when the boys were quite young. We did hit an overflow and some rough going. Sometimes we jumped, or pulled ourselves around and over boulders of ice; but we were never really worried. We were under strict surveillance by the Hazenbergs, who operated the cannery store on the bank of the river. If we had needed help, I'm sure they would have gotten to us in a matter of minutes.

The second trip was even more rewarding than the first. Evon seemed to have lost a little of his timidity, and even got down on all-fours while reliving an epic struggle with a grizzly bear, when he was a younger man, and strong. Even though a centenarian. Olympic's carriage was as straight as that of a young man, and his shoulders square. Strangely enough, his face was hardly wrinkled at all. A big scar on the back of his neck was mute evidence of the bear all but tearing his head off. Olympic killed the grizzly, and he, too would have died from loss of blood except for some of his fellow tribesmen finding him and nursing him back to life.

Mr. Olympic, who was of Eskimo descent, told of many facets of his life. He was born in the village of Katmai, in the shadow of the volcano for which it was named. He grew up as a reindeer herder, like his father. He told of how the volcano rumbled and grumbled for several days, causing his people to flee the village with their herds.

As with any major catastrophe, errors have been made in recording, some of which have been corrected. Katmai never erupted at all. It was Novarupta Volcano, which on a beautiful June day spewed forth an estimated two-and-a-ahalf miles of molten ash. Almost coincidentally, with the release of all this material, the top of nearby Mt. Katmai collapsed because the liquid andesite beneath had flowed out through Novarupta's fissures, removing the support from Katmai's peak. It's no wonder a few miscalculations were made since a total of seven cubic miles of volcanic material was fired into the atmosphere. All the North American Hemisphere was darkened by a curtain of ash which plunged Alaska into complete darkness for seventy-two hours. Since no one could see what happened, and about half of 12,000-foot Katmai disappeared, it was natural to assume that Katmai blew her top.

According to some historians there were no eye witnesses; but Evon Olympic was one and he gave me the names of two other men who saw the flames and are still alive today. They were in another part of Alaska, or I would have tried to interview them at the time. Some day I hope to do their story.

Olympic told of how they kept the reindeer herd on the move, after the mountain began to grumble. Four days travel separated them when the volcano finally blew, cremating and burying everything in its path. Hot rock rained like hailstones around them. Ash covered everything, but the wind was in their favor. Onward and onward they pushed, until they reached the sea on the south bank of the Naknek River, where they settled. Their old village was lost forever, and their forests, charred and burned. Ash floated on the rivers and streams. It was truly a difficult time, which he would never forget.

Evon told of one method of hunting, before the days of the gun. He said they would take a pliable willow stick, sharpen it on both ends, bend it double and insert the stick in a hunk of meat, which they would wrap in rawhide. This they would put outside to freeze. Later, they would unwrap the ball of meat concealing the lethal willow twig and place it on the trail of an animal which would gulp the frozen meat ball whole. When the meat thawed, BINGO! A wolf with pierced intestines doesn't last long.

We taped Olympic's stories, which Inisha McCormick translated. We gave the tape to the archives in Juneau because of its historical value.

Some day I hope to write more stories about these people who live in the melting pot of many races: Eskimo, Aleut, Russian, Chinese, Philippine, Norwegian, American, and many others, most of whom came to this area to exploit fish and fur.

I loved my students and the people of Bristol Bay; but Mr. Turner pushed on to a larger school district and Mrs. Campbell was retiring the following year. I felt I should be near my homestead. Maybe, if I were teaching again in Talkeetna, I would again fly the mountain with Don Sheldon. I could spend weekends and summers on my homestead, until that wonderful day when I could live there — for the rest of my life.

Hearing that a temporary bridge spanned the Chulitna, I could hardly wait to get back to see for myself. It was true, but it washed out. Nevertheless, all sort of activities buzzed around me at the homestead — bridge crews, road crews, and survey crews, cutting their way through the wilderness.

Chapter XXVIII

THIRTEEN MONTHS HATH 1970

Suddenly it was fall and I was back in the schoolroom. It was good, being back home, and all went well until February 8, 1970, when I fell and fractured a couple of vertebrae. This time Don flew me to the hospital rather than to the mountain.

A friend of mine, Miss Sharon Pace, who was my student teacher in Naknek, had been to Talkeetna that very afternoon, to see me. As coincidence would have it, she had just finished college and was looking for a teaching position. Since she graduated at midterm no opening had presented itself. I couldn't resist the temptation.

From my hospital bed, after I had been put into traction, I called Sharon and asekd her if she would like to have my teaching job.

"Where are you, Mary Carey, and *what* are you talking about? Have you lost your mind?"

"One question at a time, please. I'm here in Anchorage, and I wondered if you would like to start teaching for me, to-morrow. I haven't lost my mind; but I do have a slightly broken back. Not bad, the cord's not severed, just sort of cracked up."

"Oh, no! You've got to be kidding. You couldn't even be in Anchorage this soon. I just got back a few minutes ago my-self. You're in Talkeetna. Are you drinking? You're loaded!"

"No; but it sounds like a good idea. Maybe you could sneak me a little nip. Room 512, Providence Hospital. I am a little shook."

"You idiot!" Sharon all but screamed into the receiver. "You can't fool me! I'll find out!"

Within a few minutes she was at the hospital.

"You fool," she blubbered, "you didn't have to break your back to give me a job."

"Just want to make sure my students don't get a better teacher than I am. That could be tragic since the doctor says I'll have to be out for some time. Why don't you have the nurse bring that telephone back? We'll call my principal."

Just like that. I'm in the hospital. My student teacher is with me. There's no housing available in Talkeetna; — but the new teacher could move into my cabin — and be my nurse when I got out of the hospital.

"Always an ulterior motive," Sharon smile das she gave me a peck on the cheek. "And if I'm going to be your nurse there'll be no drinking! Not anything except doctor's orders."

And believe you me, she meant it. I gave her my job, and she gave me hell. A cast on my back was bad enough; but the hammer she held over my head was worse.

The doctor said I should not try to go to the bathroom alone. Sharon hid my crutches and told me to pee in the bed if I had to go before she got home from school. But she, or a student or a friend was always there with me. I was seldom alone, even for a few minutes. They pretended not to be organized; but some woman from our Home Maker's Club or the church just happened to drop by every day, while Sharon taught. Of course there was a telephone beside my bed. Getting to the bathroom wasn't quite so easy. Sharon had to help me to the rest room so often that she began calling me "Honey Bucket". In case you are not an Alaskan, a honey bucket is a portable potty used where there are no sewer lines. Sharon was so mean and strict with me that I began calling her Mafia. Finally we agreed that if we ever came through it together we would write a book entitled, *The Honey Bucket and the Mafia in Alaska.*

I didn't get back into the school room that spring; but I did get to my homestead, on crutches, when the second temporary bridge went in.

Determined to have more comfortable living quarters, I bought a trailer house, *with a bathtub!* It was one of the first things across the temporary bridge. What a luxury. I had gravity flow water from a spring-fed creek right into my trailer house.

With a road and a bridge, I needed a car, not a plane, so I sold it and bought a Jeep Wagoneer — to pull the steep grades. I wanted to work on my book — this book — but I had to figure some way of earning a living. Had it! I would put in a gift shop and package store. Not many of the construction workers would be looking for gifts; but as Will Rogers commented, "Alaska is the longest bar in the world."

I got my license and was busy converting the cabin I had used previously for hired help into a little store. Of course I was not supposed to drive while in a cast; but I did, to bring in supplies. Big Jim Christianson, the bridge contractor, didn't enjoy seeing me drive across that temporary bridge, which had no railing; but he was nice enough to turn his back.

I had just gotten in my last load of contraband and was ready to open shop when the rains came . . . and came . . . and came. A creaking and grinding and crashing sound in the night told the story. The bridge washed out . . . the second temporary bridge was gone. My new Jeep was trapped on the wrong side of the river.

Weeks passed. The river remained high. Fortunately for the workers, the skeletal ironwork for the new structure arched 190 feet above the raging current.

My food supply was nearing exhaustion; but I had plenty of beer. I made a big sign: LET'S SWAP! BEER FOR BREAD! Soon I was the best-fed person around.

In July I was to get the cast off my back. What a great day that would be. Earlier I had rented my own little homesteading cabin to one of the workmen who wanted to bring his wife out. She volunteered to drive me to Anchorage. Since my orthopedist, Dr. William J. Mills, had told me not to drive, I thought this might be wise.

It couldn't have happened, not under these circumstances; but it did. She rolled the car and I got two more fractured vertebra.

I never saw a madder doctor in my life.

"Mary Carey, what in the . . . blankety-blank-blank have you been doing?" Dr. Mills stormed as he reached the emergency room. "I told you not to drive in that cast."

With that he left the room, and I wasn't too sure he would return. My friend, who had been doing the driving, thought it time to confess. Fortunately she was not injured in the accident — mostly just shook up over my complications.

As for myself, I felt it was nothing short of a miracle, the way my old sacroiliac hung together. I tried to soft-soap Dr. Mills by telling him what a good patient I had been, and how the cast he had made for me probably saved my spinal cord

231

from complete severance. The latter statement was sincere; but Dr. Mills would never buy my being a good patient. Wonder why?

I've seen him work with children, as gentle as the breath of hope; yet I've seen him so mad at grown-ups that one would think a prized Rembrandt had been destroyed. And that is my opinion of the way he feels about bones. You can bet he made a believer of me the second time around.

Dr. Mills is the meanest orthopedic in Alaska — perhaps in the whole world — when you fail to obey his instructions; but he's one of the best, the very best. His medical accomplishments have been recognized nationally and internationally. He walks on an artificial limb, himself; but how this came about I do not know — probably never will. But I did learn about something that happened in Vietnam. Dr. Mills would never give out such a story; but it seemed to have leaked out in form of a news item.

Forgive me, Doctor. I could tell a more authentic story if I had a few details; but you would never tell, so I'll do the best I can.

If I understand the problem correctly, a soldier was brought in with a live mortar shell in his back. Anyway, it was something which could, and probably would explode. You had the room sandbagged, ran everybody out, then proceeded with the operation, very successfully.

As I was saying, Dr. Mills can be pretty nice with other people; but the second time around he tried to hang me: Weights on my neck and weights on my feet. He threatened to put me in a cast with a Queen Elizabeth collar, and leave me there, forever. "Because of my age," he finally relented and put me in a body brace instead.

CHAPTER XXIX

BEAR IN MY BEDROOM

Returning home from the hospital was another traumatic experience. Just what the doctor ordered.

This time I had no Sharon Pace to turn to. In fact, I was wondering just what I would do, when opportunity presented itself in the form of "outsiders" who were en route to Alaska.

A friend of mine, George Sime, who worked with the Alaska State Highway Department, in the right-of-way division, visited me in the hospital. I think he had a guilty conscience, talking me out of so much highway frontage; but I was so glad to see that road come through that I would have given half my homestead if that would have brought it to me sooner.

George mentioned the fact that his daughter, Sue Renne, and her sons, Paul and Kolya, would be disappointed at not getting to visit at my homestead, as we had planned, before they left California.

"Why so?" I countered. "I'll probably get kicked out of the hospital next week, and we could go to my homestead, together I'm sure the boys would love it there."

"Then let's do," George agreed. I'll drive you out, since your car is still in the body shop."

We did drive out, and timed it just right. The bridge crew was eating dinner and the new structure seemed unguarded. The workmen used a sort of catwalk, boards laid across the grill work, to get from one side of the river to the other. Why not?

Later bridge superintendent Bill Taylor told me that he held his breath while we used that narrow walkway. But how could he stop a grandmother on crutches, when there was no other way to get home?

Negotiating the bridge wasn't too bad. In fact, Taylor was doing a little negotiating, too, although I did not know it at the time. After we got across the bridge, Mr. Taylor sent one of his workmen, on the double, with a wheelbarrow, in which I was invited to ride. Thanks, Bill. I was wondering how tough that upgrade from the river would be, on crutches.

After arriving home in my one-wheeled chariot, my *grand entre* was dimmed by evidence of an uninvited guest. The glass from my bedroom window was shattered on the ground. Bear tracks were everywhere.

"Stand back!" George cautioned. "The bear may still be inside."

Grabbing a wrecking bar to use as a club, he cautiously unlocked my door and checked inside. "No bear," he called; "but get set for quite a shock," he added as I was helped up the steps. "Things are pretty messy."

Heaven forbid! I have never seen such chaos! Everything — sugar, flour, coffee, syrup, and chocolate — all over.

"Quite a pie," Sue commented.

"Look," Paul said as he pointed to the large mirror above the buffet. "The bear must have been in love with himself."

This broke the spell and we laughed. Evidently, when the. bear, which was probably a yearling, had eaten his fill he saw himself in the mirror, he proceeded to lick, or kiss until every inch of the glass was opaque; but not broken.

Sue, George, and the boys went to work. That cub had certainly made himself at home on the divan. He must have entered more than once, judging from the muddy tracks on my bed.

I think I would have sat down and cried, if I had had to face this mess alone, in my body brace and on my crutches; but the gang did a fine job of the clean-up.

Paul, who was fourteen, thought he would become a big game hunter and sat up several nights waiting and watching; but the bear failed to show. Perhaps he would not bother the house again, since it was inhabited.

Sue and the boys were a real help and I hated to see them go; but their vacation was almost over. Paul had painted and constructed new shelves in the cabin, which he proudly pointed out to his grandfather when he returned. He had also helped with putting up stock, and it looked pretty neat. Everything was more or less ready for me to open shop.

Since I had six month of previous training, I was a real pro on my crutches. My back did not bother me so much as my hands. Now that I was set to write my book, I couldn't push the keys on my typewriter.

Back to my doctor I went. He sent me to a therapist who worked with my hands and showed me several exercises to practice faithfully. Dr. Mills said if this didn't work, he might be able to relieve the pressure by an operation on my spinal cord, near the base of my neck. This was really frightening. I thought I had been scared, after the wreck, when my left arm and leg failed to function for a short time; but this was worse.

I determined not to have that operation. My hands had to work. I would finish this book. There had to be a way. I was never dependent upon others, and I wouldn't accept such a sentence now. I could take care of myself.

My first home therapy was quite unique, to say the least. For several years I had extolled the merit of a spring tidbit, called Fiddle Head Fern, which grew wild on my homestead.

Beginning in 1969 and really taking hold by 1970, Sigmund Restad, head of the Institute of Agricultural Sciences in Palmer; Charlie Marsh, research economist; and Mrs. Marge Sumner, in charge of processing and preparing the fern for the table; began marketing the fern in an experimental program. They were paying people thirty cents a pound to pick the fern, which was a real bonanza, especially for the children of the Talkeetna and Trapper Creek areas. One can gather several pounds within an hour and it grows in great abundance.

I thought it over. I could at least try. Putting on rain pants and a jacket, I tucked a duffle bag underneath my crutches and climbed the gentle side of the slope across from my trailer house. Sitting down and dragging my crutches behind me, I slid down the steeper part of the hillside, picking fiddle head fern all the way. When I reached the bottom I would dump the fern from my duffle bag into the spring box, which I had used to keep my food cool before getting a refrigerator which used bottled gas.

Much to my surprise and delight, Mrs. Marge Summer wrote encouraging notes, commenting on how fresh and firm and clean my harvest. I worked harder. Soon I became their star picker.

I've never told anyone previously how many times I climbed and slid down that hill, nor how painful the picking really was. I forced my hands to work. No wonder my fern was clean. Much of it was bathed in tears. But "Therapy Hill" was my greatest ally. It still means more to me than any other spot on my homestead; and I check it faithfully each spring for the first violets and the first mess of fern. I serve it at my lodge and people enjoy this new gourmet delicacy. If those eating the fern only knew how much this little plant did for me in 1970, therapy-wise and economy-wise, perhaps they would understand my extolling its praise.

Since Uncle Sam lopped off funds for this and other experimental program, I have been working with those who did so much to advance Fiddle Head Fern as a food source for coming generations. By putting in a small processing plant, I hope to provide employment for school children of the area while developing a new food substance which is here for the taking. Why neglect that which God has so freely set on His table before us when we know we must face a hungry world?

Each evening, after I had finished my fern picking and the road and bridge crews shut down for the day, I took my bathtub therapy, then opened shop. My patrons were kind. One man, Myron Kirkpatrick, who was with A & G Construction, was particularly helpful. He sent me flowers while I was in the hospital. But this stinker also told the construction gang that I broke my back just to get out of a date I made with him—the first one at that, and I didn't even know him yet. What's more, this freely-imbibing Alaskan with a unique sense of humor all but tore that hospital apart.

"I've come to see Mary Carey," this imposing and not-to-be-deterred heavy-equipment operator asserted as he marched down the hospital hallway toward my door.

"NO! You can't!" the startled nurse defended.

"Why not?" growled Kirkpatrick.

"Because she's in no position to see visitors. She's all strung up, in traction. Weights on her legs and neck. She can't even move."

"Just the way I want her," I heard Kirk retort as he more or less muscled his way to my bedside, laughing with that good shoulder shaking humor that kept the nurse peeking into the room—with a laser beam.

When Kirk heard about the bear, he brought me a heavier gun. When he caught me trying to carry out trash on my crutches, he said to let it wait. He came almost every evening and helped me with the chores, even tended the store. Although he later went to work in some of the more remote areas of Alaska, he still drives out to see me when he returns to Anchorage. If the generator needs repair, he's there. If the cook gets behind, he marches into the kitchen. If all is well, he takes a stance at the end of the bar, buying drinks for the house and laughing about things as they used to be when old buddies drop in. That's Kirk, a lifetime friend to whom I am forever indebted.

But our bear story is not ended, yet. One evening, when I thought I was alone at the trailer house, I heard someone blasting away with a gun, just outside my door. That bear had finally decided to pay me another visit and was bellying up to my bedroom window when some workmen from the bridge drove up for a jug. I've forgotten the names of my benefactors, since I was not writing things down, as I once did; but thanks. I never really relished the thought of a bear in my bedroom, not even a bear rug.

Since I was having difficulty holding a pencil, even to sign my name, it was quite evident that I would be unable to teach school and grade papers. Summer would soon be over, and I did not relish the thought of remaining at my homestead alone. The roadway would not be plowed and fuel trucks could not reach me through the snow. My jeep would be useless. I no longer owned a plane, and the very thought of trying to chop wood sent pains shooting through my whole body. To say that I hit a new low is putting it mildly.

I'll swear the Good Lord imposes the problems of a fool on the minds and hearts of friends when the load becomes too heavy to bear alone. I received letters from my very good Texas buddies, Fay and James Venable and Dr. Ted and Myrteel Howell, who invited me on a camper trip with them to Old Mexico. I refused, mostly because my financial situation wasn't the best. My friends would not accept my refusal. Dr. Howell and Myrteel had been to Alaska to see me the previous year; and the Venables were planning to come up next summer.

I couldn't refuse, my friends contended, because they knew I was unable to work and because I had turned down all previous invitations, saying I didn't have time. Things had been rocking like this, ever since my husband died, and I suddenly felt like a fifth wheel. But now that I had the time . . .

En route to Texas I relived the good times the six of us had together, in Baytown, before Dick died. Our cabin cruiser was berthed at the Venable's dock. Together we fished or joined camper forces to hunt rock. Sometimes we just enjoyed an evening under the stars as we relished the comforts and delights of backyard barbecues with the deep-throated whistles of tugboats as they guided huge carriers through the Houston Ship channel, past the San Jacinto Monument with the big star on top.

I don't say that the good Texans were jealous of Washington monument being the tallest in the nation, I merely mention the fact that they put a lone star, emblem of their state, on top of that monument, making it a few feet taller. Quite an impressive sight, especially at night when radiating with light.

Although my hands were functioning a little better, I wondered whether I would ever be able to use a typewriter again, for any period of time. There was no doubt in my mind what Fay Venable was doing when she said we would take along cameras and make notes for stories. Fay and Myrteel Howell are both writers, good ones, and we have attended several writing conferences together. Fay has always been the spark plug, getting us going again whenever things went wrong. Hers is a faith and trust experienced by few persons.

We had a great time in Mexico. One day I would ride in the Venable camper, the next day with the Howells. No one mentioned the fact that one person and one camper was missing. Getting to go on this trip and visiting with my daughter and grandchildren in Houston gave me new life and purposes.

I would return to my homestead and put in a larger place of business, come spring. Why not? I could sell some property which I owned in Houston, and my Talkeetna cabin and lots. This would give me a start. I would put in a cafe and lodge. Fiddle fern picking only lasts a few weeks each year; I would not depend upon this therapy. Maybe good, hot, soapy water would help. Better to wash dishes than knead a rubber ball, and more profitable.

I did put in that cafe, and Fay Venable was the first to help me. When some of the construction gang aked me who my new cook was I replied, "Oh, just one of my millionaire friends from Texas."

238

CHAPTER XXX

WHEN I HAD TO GO AT 60° BELOW

Brian Bartlett, a young medic recently returned from Vietnam, wanted to be the first person to climb McKinley alone, in winter. Although he had reached the summit previously, in summer with other mountaineers, he seemed determined to make this winter climb, alone.

For several years the park service would not agree to anyone attempting such a climb in sub-zero temperatures and long hours of darkness. There had been trouble enough in 1967, when eight tried and one died in the first winter assault, discussed earlier in this book. This Odyssey is written in book form, *Minus*-148 by Art Davidson, one of the three climbers who reached the summit. The other two, Ray Genet and Dave Johnston, are now my neighbors. Ray operates the only licensed guide service on Mt. McKinley and had reached the summit 19 times by 1974; but this is getting ahead of our story. Dave became a park ranger and is bringing up a family in the shadow of "The Great One."

Finally Bartlet wrangled permission from the park service to make the solo winter climb. I never saw a climber with so much gear. He hoped to carry a pack on his back and pull a sled behind him in the case-hardened snow. He wanted Don Sheldon to air-lift him to the six-thousand foot level on the Kahiltna Glacier, where he would begin his climb.

If Bartlett was fool enough to attempt such an ordeal and Don agreed to put his little yellow snow bird on the glacier in mid-winter, I was fool enough to want to go along for the story.

Again Don was hesitant; but finally agreed that if he could get Bartlett and half his gear in the first day, he would take the remaining gear and Mary Carey in the next. Never was a photojournalist happier. The first and only woman on Mt. McKinley in winter—and to cover the first and only solo winter climb!

Sheldon did take Bartlett in. Although the weather looked a little doubtful the following day, Don said we would try, if

I put on enough clothes. I stacked on three layers, a face mask, and gloves with liners. Even though I insisted my bottom layer was the eider down I had gotten for the polar bear hunt in Barrow, and my parka was sealskin, Don hunted up some snowmobile cover-alls and helped me inside—so I wouldn't come apart in the middle. We headed for the mountain, with three-hundred more pounds of gear.

"If we can make it off the Talkeetna strip with this load," Don commented with his usual grin, "then we can hope to make it off the glacier, when she's three-hundred pounds lighter."

We did make it off the strip and for a long while both of us remained silent. Mt McKinley, in winter, is the most beautiful sight on earth, in my way of thinking. I was wondering if I would feel the same about her tomorrow, if I had a tomorrow.

"We'll see how much headway Brian's made with his relay," Don commented as we sailed in at ten-thousand feet.

Don's low whistle of surprise was my first clue that all was not well.

"Not a sign of him." Don puzzled as we sailed down the glacier toward the six-thousand foot level where he had deposited the climber and his gear the previous day. "Jeez, look how it's snowed," he observed before I realized the trouble, "not a sign of my ski tracks."

"That will make a good photo," I called as I saw Brian in front of his tent, waving.

"Put down that camera and tighten your seatbelt," Don commanded as we skimmed, then submarined through the whiteness. The suddeness of our stop and the settling of the plane told me that we were in soft, very soft snow. I had thought it would be crusted, in mid-winter.

"I can't move," came Bartlett's plantive greeting as Sheldon opened the door, probably to see whether we were right side up or up side down. We seemed right in the middle of a snowball; and it was good to see the wan light of the winter day.

"I want a photo," I urged as I slid from the plane and sank, miniskirt deep in the fluff.

"No story. No photo." Bartlett insisted. "I've let myself, my sponsors, and my friends down. I can't move, much less climb and pull a sled. Take me back to Talkeetna."

"Holy cow!" Don commented. "I can't. I'll do well to get off the glacier with the load I have. Tell you what. I'll take Mary back, unload, and come back and pick you and the rest of your gear up. But be ready. The wind's coming down on that peak."

Just like that, without even being given an opportunity to snap a photo, I was ordered back into the plane.

Don revved her up; but she didn't budge. He tried again, no progress. He motioned for Brian to push on the strut. Again the engine roared but the little bird was trapped.

"Let me out," I suggested with a sigh, remembering the times I had been stuck on this glacier before, with the French Expedition and when Don had "Open House". Tramping down a runway is not child's play. It takes hours — and hours, for several persons.

"One more try." Don shouted as he pointed toward the other strut.

I made connection as quickly as I could swim around the plane. Again Don revved her up. With her tail in the air and a mighty roar and shuddering sound. as if the little plane were trying to pull up the whole glacier with its skis, the Super Cub lurched and I fell forward into the snow.

As I dogpaddled my way up and blinked so.r.2 of the snow from my bewildered eyes, the yellow bird was disappearing down the glacier—and I was trapped on the mountain.

Realization! The plane would never have lifted under existing conditions, with me and that load. Don would have to fly back to Talkeetna, unload the plane, and then come back. This would take up to two hours, I knew; but would the weather hold? I glanced at the peak, the snow plume seemed lower.

"We'd better get out of the wind," the young medic advised through his snow-clotted face mask." Here, let me dust you off a bit. Leave your mask on until we get inside."

Both of us! Inside that pup tent. However small, you can bet that I lost little time wiggling my way inside. There was hardly room to sit upright; but we were out of the biting wind. 3rian's sleeping bag, on which we sat, took most of the room.

little primus stove with a flicker of light and a pot of melting ow on the smallest burner I have ever seen promised tea. This was heavenly, I thought; but the wind whipping the tent was a grim reminder. I asked how cold it was.

"Not bad," he replied, "only 60° below, but the wind is blowing and that puts the chill factor down."

Half sitting and half lying down in the cramped quarters I had hoped that Brian would talk; but he was in no mood for anything except bemoaning his fate. The unbelievably heavy snow had tried to bury him and his tent during the night. Of course he had no sleep because he had to keep digging out and trying to keep his gear from disappearing beneath the unrelenting white ocean throughout the long winter night.

Since he was in no mood for talking, and more or less saying that he had rather die than see his trip ended so unsuccessfully, I began to worry. What if neither of us got back to civilization?

I tried to tell him that his failure was no disgrace. That no other man since time begun had even attempted to climb Mt. McKinley alone in winter, when daylight hours are short and the temperature ranges from 20° to 148° below zero. Sometimes it takes courage to know when to quit. Maybe the good Lord had sent the soft snow to stop him before it was too late.

I was not doing too well and changed the subject. He was pretty unhappy with what transpired in Vietnam and greatly disturbed about world conditions in general. Earlier he had said he needed the solitude of the mountain for meditation and writing his memoirs. Now I wondered if he even cared whether he returned. I talked, and he balked, at any subject.

I was beginning to think it might be a rather long solitude for us both, unless I could bring about a change in his mood, fast.

"Maybe we had best dig a snow cave," I suggested as the wind gave a stronger tug at our tent. "Don won't be back for some time, and we'll be in pretty bad shape if the tent goes."

Any activity helped. Soon we had a nice cave scooped out with the little shovel and again retired to the tent. Hot tea and frozen candy was welcome.

"Did you know there are yetis on this mountain?" I asked. "I don't know whether there are now; but there were at one time." I related the story of the battered French expedition, the first to climb Mt. Huntington. Their leader, Lionel Terray, fell and dislocated a shoulder.

Don left me on the mountain for an interview while he flew Terray to the hospital. Did you ever try to interview seven Frenchmen, none of whom could speak English? It wasn't too difficult. One of the group, Jacquis Botkin, who later fell to his death during the only winter climb, in 1967, did understand, and spoke fewer words in English; but sign language worked beautifully. They pointed out where Terray had fallen and indicated that they would resume the climb when he returned. They did, but before they reached the summit, one of them went snow blind and had to be carried most of the way down. Fourteen-thousand-foot Huntington had taken a terrible toll so Sheldon rigged up a yeti party and we were waiting for them when they reached their base camp on the glacier.

Roberta Sheldon dressed in wolf's clothing, Dorothy Jones like a bunny, and Beverly Garrett in a hula skirt over long, red underwear. A hula on the mountain seemed hilarious to me and to the Frenchmen; but it hardly provoked a smile from Brian.

As Don flew part of the group out, I told of how those remaining on the glacier cleaned camp. They had built an igloo — the only one I have ever seen since coming to Alaska — and stuffed all their empty food boxes and excess debris inside and set it on fire. As it burned one of the Frenchmen jumped on top of it, danced a jig and sang the only word he probably understood in English, "T-A-L-K-E-E-T-N-A! T-A-L-K-E-E-T-N-A! T-A-L-K-E-E-T-N-A!" And oddly enough, this word is not English, but the Indian name for our village, meaning "River of Plenty"; but we all understood.

Now I understood how that poor guy felt, and wished I was in Talkeetna.

Eternity dragged by in an hour-and-a-half. Not too much daylight left. The wind grew stronger.

Something else bothered me. No matter who you are, nor where you are, nature eventually calls. My eyeba' s were floating. I drank only one cup of coffee befor leaving Talkeetna, but was regretting that. The tea was great but it, too, added to my misery. I had to go! At 60° below? In hipdeep snow? With the wind blowing? Impossible!

There must be some alternative. No, that wouldn't do, it would freeze down my pant leg. Just a cup full? No. Once I

243

started there would be no cut-off valve. I couldn't relieve the pressure that way. Maybe mountain climbers had some way of going inside the tent. No, not a female. I could never get into position to go inside that tent, not even if Brian sensed my dilemma and excused himself.

I pulled on my face mask and heavy gloves. "Excuse me, I'll be right back," I said as I crawfished toward the door. Evidently Brian understood and made haste to get the tent flap unfastened.

Wallowing toward the rear of the tent I wondered how it would feel to have my own rear buried in snow as I relieved myself; but it didn't matter. Getting ready to go was something else. First the coverall zipper, and the whole darn mess had to come down before I could get to the next pair of pants. Now the third. Surely I couldn't have on four layers of clothing. But I did and that last layer hung in my nylon pantyhose. Now why? No damn fool would wear . . .

I couldn't wait. Not one second longer. Yanking the zipper open I squatted in the snow, hardly feeling it. Suddenly I realized my right hand was bare. Shoving it beneath my fur parka I finished the most imperative business. W-A-T-E-R R-E-L-I-E-F!

Now for my glove. There it was! A big ball of yellow ice, right underneath me.

There was no humor in the situation, not then. I knew my hand would freeze in seconds.

With my left hand I struggled with the zippers. The first was broken. I was terribly clumsy with my left hand, especially so with it in a heavy glove and liner. Only then did I realize that my nylon liner was still on my right hand; but it was so numb I couldn't feel it. I had to make it work; but it wouldn't. Only one thing to do. Forget the underpants and my pride, zip up the coveralls and get inside the tent. I could work with the zippers when my hand thawed out.

Just as I got the outside zipper up and asked Brian if he had an extra glove, I heard — or saw — a speck moving up the glacier. The little yellow bird.

Quickly Brian began pulling the tent pegs. All other gear except the minute stove with the cheerful little flicker and the sleeping bag was packed.

"HURRY!" Don shouted as the prop of his plane created another snowstorm. "Can't you see how low that wind is on the peak. I'll do well to get both of you out. Flag your gear, Brian. I'll come back and pick it up later, if the storm doesn't blow it right off the mountain. Crawl in the plane. Mary, back up in the boot. I've got to get you both out. Hurry, Mary, hurry!"

I was trying; but my feet and legs didn't cooperate. I couldn't step up. My right hand had no grasp and I couldn't pull myself up. Three pair of trousers bagged around my . . . shall we say . . . knees?

"HURRY! What's the matter?" Don shouted as he held the door open against the wind.

Suddenly Brian grabbed me around the legs and shoved me into the plane like a stick of stovewood. I managed to wiggle and push myself to a lean-forward position in the tail of the Super Cub. Rarely was the rear seat in place in Don's yellow bird. Took too much space where he could stack gear.

From the mountain to Talkeetna there was no chance to zip back up, not with Brian more or less in my lap as we sat flat on the floor with our feet stretched on either side of the "plane driver's seat." Don always called himself a plane driver.

A more embarrassed reporter was never landed on the Talkeetna strip and poured from a plane.

That was my first, last and only trip I ever plan to Denali in winter, no matter who tries to climb her.

Chapter XXXI

MRS. SANTA BREAKS HER NECK

On December of 1969, before I broke my back in February of 1970, a very good friend of mine, Mrs. Jesta Young of Anchorage, was talking with me concerning the way we would spend Christmas. Both of us are loners.

Jesta is one of a rare clan, a native-born Alaskan, before the days of Statehood. Her father and mother, Mr. and Mrs. Edward James Williams, owned and operated the Williams Transportation Company of Ketchikan. Jesta recalls the days when, as a youngster, her Dutch grandmother taught her to cook. She was travelling up and down the intracoastal waterway, cooking on her father's boat, when she was so young she had to stand on a stool to reach the stove.

"It was the custom of my mother and father to make Christmas dinner and invite all the old timers and loners throughout the area to celebrate with us," Jesta related. "You have several old timers in Talkeetna, don't you? I would like to observe Christmas as my parents did; but I would like to get out of town. Why don't you check and see if you can find a place for us to give such a dinner."

Frank Moennikes, an old timer in charge of the Fairview Inn, was delighted. As usual, 'Willie Wah Willie' Tauscher, Jim Beaver, and Rocky Cummins were in the Fairview. They were listening, and must have made note of the fact that there were no Christmas decorations up.

For a full week Jesta and I cooked for the coming party. We made cookies from seven different recipes, twelve dozen of each kind. We bought candy canes and Mandarin oranges for the youngsters of the village. Jesta bought socks and kerchiefs for the old timers. As president of the Emblem Club of Anchorage and through her employment with the Corps of Engineers at Elmendorf, Jesta had loads of friends and asked them all to bring "Who Done It's" and other paper backs which we could give to the loners to read. We discussed Christmas decorations, but were hesitant.

When we reached Talkeetna on Christmas Eve, both our cars were loaded with food and gifts. When we walked inside the Fairview a great transformation had taken place. The Christmas tree and the decorations were simply beautiful. I'll never forget a local entertainer, Peter Dana, who has made quite a mark for himself, approaching me with:

"Mary, you know I ain't no do-gooder; but Father Stanley Allie needs an electric organ for his new church. I was wondering, maybe, if you girls don't mind — ah, hell, what I am trying to say is that I will entertain for your party, free of charge, if I can set a donations kitty on my new baby grand, with the understanding that everything which comes in goes toward the church organ."

We though it a magnanimous idea.

The dollars rolled in, beautifully. Best of all, Father Allie joined us. He was a wonderful asset to our community, despite the fact that he used Jesta and myself, later, as an example to his parishioners when trying to say that "there's so much good in the worst of us." Thanks, Father, I've always thought of myself as an old reprobate; but just let anyone call me "pious" or "better than thou" and I'm ready to do battle.

What a beautiful party! Not too many old timers left; but in Talkeena, everyone celebrates. Since some of the persons we wanted to reach were bedfast, Rocky Cummins, who was eighty at the time, fired up his snow machine and we went out delivering gifts and plates of food.

The highlight of the party for Jesta was finding out that Rocky had once worked for her father, in Southeastern and had attended one of her parents Christmas parties when Jesta was just a "tiny tot."

Our party was so successful that Jesta and I vowed to make it an annual affair. When Jesta's term as president of the Emblem Club expired, and she had money to give in her Club's name to her favorite charity, she asked me to check with Father Allie. She sent the balance due on the organ.

In fact, Jesta Young did so much for the people of Talkeetna that she soon became known as "Mrs. Santa." We did have one more Christmas party at the Fairview, before tragedy struck.

The Anchorage-Fairbanks highway was finally opened to the public on October 14, 1971; but it was pretty rugged and not kept plowed out the first winter. In August of '72 the pavement reached my doorstep; and we were planning a grand opening party for Labor Day at my lodge, which was finally finished, almost.

En route Jesta overturned her car; but no one at the scene seemed to think she was too badly hurt. As usual, her car was loaded with goodies for a party. Turkey a la Brandy and Dressing a la Scotch flew everywhere. Beer spewed from beneath caps of bottles, that were still capped. Everyone who tried to help her was saturated.

"Can you imagine?" trooper Bob Boatwright reported, "beer spewing everywhere, me smelling like a brewery, and the lady lays there, smiling and offering me a sandwich and a bottle of pop while we wait for Don Sheldon to show with a plane. But I'll say one thing, she's the most hospitable woman I've ever seen. Calm, too."

Tough luck, Bob. Don had a few complaints, too.

"Between you two gals," came his caustic comment, "you certainly go all out to spoil a guy's dinner. When my wife invited Mary to a wild goose dinner, she broke her back and we went on a wild goose chase, instead. Now Mary invites us to dinner and you flip your car."

It sort of blew my party, too. I never attended my own grand opening. We'll hope for better luck next time. Sometimes I'm glad there are two kinds of luck, otherwise I may never have any at all.

None of us could believe, nor accept the truth for a while. Jesta's neck was broken. Paralyzed? Not Jesta. But she was.

The 1972 Christmas party was given in Jesta's honor. She was in a hospital near Seattle. Everyone was anxious to help Mrs. Santa. Most of all, we wanted her back, if there was nothing they could do to help her paralysis.

In 1973 the annual party was given at my lodge; with Mrs. Santa attending in person — as an escapee from the Glenmore Nursing Home. We still laugh about it.

Arrangement were made for Don Sheldon to fly her to the lodge. A blizzard moved in with blowing snow and zero-zero visibility, the worst kind of a white-out, as Alaskans call such a storm. Jesta tried, but could not get permission to be driven up under such adverse circumstances. Never underestimate this woman. She escaped in her wheelchair, during a change of nursing shifts, so no one person would have to bear the full blame. To pull this escapade, she called a friend, Mae Rene Bordwell, who never realized she was an accomplice in such a crime as Jesta timed the wheeling of the chair from her room to Marene's car. Mrs. Bordwell, a vice president of the Alaska Bank of Commerce, thought she was transporting Jesta to a friend's house in town.

"Take me to the bus station," Jesta ordered.

"Bus!" the astonished friend countered. "I can't. I mean you can't. What's up?"

"I am going to see a friend," Jesta affirmed. "I'm going to Mary's McKinley View Lodge, mile 135 on the new Anchorage-Fairbanks highway.

"You can't ride a bus! Does the nursing home know about this? I'll drive you up myself."

"The nursing home will know about it soon enough. As far as your trying to drive that far under these conditions — don't you think I'm in bad enough shape already? The answer is NO! That man looks strong. See if he will help the bus driver lift me."

Four hours later, when the bus pulled up in front of my lodge I could hardly believe what I saw. Jesta couldn't be a passenger, but she was.

"Just put me on roller skates and head me for the door," she said through her chattering teeth. "I'm frozen stiff enough to make it."

Later another wonderful surprise came when, despite the storm, Commander John Hale, his son Bill, Jack White, and the Scrabaks drove up from Willow, seventy-six miles through the storm, to furnish music for the party. They even composed original ballads which kept all of us laughing. Mrs. Santa and the guests, especially the old timers, for whom there were some special compositions, too loved every minute of it.

In 1974 Jesta gave not one, but two Christmas parties at her new town house in Anchorage. One party was for old timers, the other for patients and personnel of Glenmore.

When I, or any of Jesta's friends become discouraged, we go to see her. What she does for others is simply inspirational. What she has done with her own life is a monumental example of her courage and determination. She'll never walk again. An operation on her hands failed to restore their use. Despite the fact that she's a quadraphlegic, suffering eighty per cent paralysis, she's dictating a book, a documentary about her parents and grandparents, which gives a good insight to Jesta's character.

So many times I have needed friends, and they are always there. In the lodge when we have been short of help or unusually busy, good friends like Gay Choquette, Corrine Jones, Jo Smith, Leah Clemmons, Jackie Ledbetter, and Sue and Ken Steele have jumped in and helped. A building contractor, Mike Bonner, and his bride, Merry, spent their honeymoon at the lodge — washing dishes. Now Bonner Construction is doubling the floor space of the lodge; and Merry still helps with the dishes.

Once we had the most decorated pilot to come out of the Vietnam conflict, Mike Bates, and his wife, Dr. Terri Bates, helping in the lodge while waiting for the snow to go so they could look for a suitable site for establishing a small clinic in this wilderness area.

Professor Thomas O. Beirne and his wife, Dr. Helen Beirne, who is an Alaskan Representative, are faithful lodge patrons who seem happiest when lending a hand. I first met Tom and Helen in Talkeetna, in 1963. They had bought a lot on Lake Christianson and were building a cabin. Mr. Beirne's new book of poetry, *Tongue of Wood*, was just off the press. I cherish my autographed copy as well as fond memories of the days when Tom and Helen brought their sleeping bags and made themselves at home on our living room floor, above the little red schoolhouse which has now been converted into a museum. Three persons now in the Alaska legislature, one doctor, and a former governor slept on the floor above the museum while Mrs. Campbell and I lived there. Maybe the upper floor, as well as the classroom, should be opened to the public.

In 1970, after I broke my back, Dr. Helen invited me to stay with her in Juneau, when the legislature was talking of creating a state park. I did. They did. Now I am happy to report that Dr. Helen and the governing body have been as good as their word. My property, although engulfed by Denali State Park, has not been condemned and I am left free to plan future developments.

During the Labor Day Holiday of 1975, when most of my summer help had returned to school, it was Tom and Helen who helped with waiting tables and washing dishes. I hope Dr. Helen did not have dishpan hands on September 3, when she met with President Gerald Ford as Alaskan Representative to the National Health and Welfare Board.

Need I say, there's an opening at Mary's McKinley View Lodge for a dishwasher; but a Ph.D. as a prerequisite is desirable. Our summer dishwasher and vocalist, Timothy James Studstill, a cousin studying for the ministry, often lifted the spirits of exhausted tourists as he sang "How Great Thou Art" with Mt. McKinley varifying God's handiwork. The pleasure of meeting Tim and his fine family came through cousins who preceded me to Alaska, Jack and Eunice Covington. I did not know that one of my favored students, Randy Covington, grandson of Jack and Eunice, was a relation until after he had finished high school. Eunice's favored subject for writing was the narrow guage railroad leading into Skagway. I lived within a few miles of the Covingtons for several years before my sister, Lela, dug up the relationship.

Back in 1963, when I wrote my Christmas dream of sharing Mt. McKinley with the world from my homestead, I never thought of one way which it has been shared, and recently. Viewers throughout the nation who saw the Oral Roberts Show in September of '75 shared the grandeur from my lodge. The fifty-five-member choral group who sang in a meadow near my homesteading cabin really made my beautiful bell on top of the world ring:

> "Ring with laughter
> Ring with joy . . . ."

For those viewers who visited Don Sheldon's glacier house with Oral Roberts, you have shared the sanctuary about which I wrote in the chapter "Grand Opening in the Clouds."

More and more producers are filming the mountain from the recently opened highway and from my lodge. Martin Scheisbler, noted German movie producer, mountain climber, artist, and lecturer who has done fourteen films on Alaska, chose this southern viewpoint, as others are doing.

When a movie producer asked directions for getting to Pirate Lake to see Ray Genet, a hero of the book *Minus* 148, I noticed Ray's car was still out front.

"The lake's a fly-in area," I advised, "but if you'll just enjoy the view until I can get away from the cash register, I can save you a trip. He's here."

When I had time to look I found Ray washing dishes. We had just been hit by tour bus after tour bus. No doubt this voluntary action was prompted by a pretty waitress, Lizanne Brussard, of Mills College, who kept calling for "more cups" and "more pie plates." But in all fairness to the "Pirate," in winter, when the pretty girls are back in school, he fires up the snow-blower and clears the parking lot — "for exercise," he says. Love you, Ray Genet.

In 1974 when the pipeline usurped all available cooks, I sent an S.O.S. to my hometown, Cisco, Texas. My sister, Ann Rendall, who later came to Alaska, knew a school principal, Bob Lindsey, who had once been a pastry cook. Of course he came to the "Great Land" — and baked pies at Mary's McKinley View Lodge.

My niece, Lenora Preston, a school teacher who had visited with me in Alaska prior to her marriage, thought a trip to the "Big Country" might be the best medicine for her husband, Paul, who had recently undergone open heart surgery.

"I feel so much better. I can breathe." Paul commented. When we needed help, Paul started cooking and Lenora waited tables. I never knew that Paul Preston, also an educator, once owned a restaurant. Because he felt so much better in Alaska, my niece resigned teaching and they are still with me, Paul as manager of the lodge and Lenora as hostess. Without their constant and faithful help, I could never have gotten away from baking pies to finish this book.

In 1975 a whirring sound outside the window blends with the pulsating hum of generators producing electric power for the lodge. A chopper shuttles sightseers and mountain climbers to the glaciers. The reason is sad; but Don Sheldon himself was the first to suggest my homestead as a jumping-off place for the mountain. I never realized it could happen so soon — of necessity.

Only yesterday Martin Schliesbler, who is now in partnership with Ray Genet's mountain climbing and guide service, remarked: "You still have room enough. We come from other countries to enjoy, not to destroy. Before I go to North Slope to do movie on pipeline, I think, maybe so bad. Now I see, the little line in this vast wilderness is nothing to fear. It is good not to be crowded."

How right he is. Not a house nor a telephone pole within miles of the lodge. Only mountains, rushing streams, and wonderfully pure air.

CHAPTER XXXII

DON SHELDON DIES

Although it was expected, it is hard to realize that Don Sheldon is no longer waging his battle with the wind.

I have seen a few brave people in my life, but none as brave as Don, unless it is his wife, Roberta. I visited with her after Don all but lost the battle for life, in 1972, when he underwent two major operations. At this time it was hard to conceive of a comeback for Don, much less a major victory. I was doing a pretty poor job of trying to express my sympathy and concern. Roberta wanted neither. She never talks much; but what she does say bears a great deal of thought.

"God has given me nine beautiful years," she said pensively, "and three wonderful children. Without Don I would never have known any of this. I thank God for every hour and every minute we have together. I am indeed fortunate."

Don had a real soldier by his side. Together they fought for time. In my way of thinking, they won the battle . . . two extra years.

In face of death — his own — Don flew thirty-four groups of climbers to McKinley in 1974, more than in any previous season. His comeback was more spectacular than his rescues, so quiet and convincing that those near him could not believe what they feared was true. He worked so endlessly and so patiently that everyone was surprised to hear he was back in the hospital, Christmas Day, 1974.

On December 21 I visited in the Sheldon home. I had gotten a copy of *Wager With the Wind* for Jesta Young's Christmas. She wanted it autographed. When Don asked me what I thought of his book, my comment would have been better if I had quit with the first word.

"Superb," I answered, "except for one thing. How could you leave so many of the old timers and friends of long standing out of it? They would have loved being mentioned in your book. You didn't have to hurt them."

"You really think so, Kid?"

"Of course I do. Some of them were here before you came to Talkeetna. They are a part of your life. You flew them to their diggins'. They gave you a start."

I knew I had said too much. Don never hurt anyone, intentionally.

"I was sort of leaving that up to you, Kid. Remember? I'm going to give you a big blast off for your book. You're going to bring in the local color, with the village 'chit chat,' the female's point of view."

This made me madder. Probably because he was right.

"You bet I will," I flung at him spitefully as he handed me Jesta's book, which he had autographed very thoughtfully.

"And where's yours?" he asked.

"I left it at home. I don't want an autographed copy," I lied.

"Never mind," he said as if he never heard me at all. "I'll just give you my copy. You deserve it. I want you to have mine."

Then he proceeded to autograph it:

"To Mary Carey, THE GREATEST! Writer, Photographer . . . He continued writing as if I had never stormed at all.

Of course I'll treasure the book as long as I live. How could I have been so cruel as to call his autographing "soft soap." I hated myself immediately.

Roberta, bless her heart, never said a word. She worked with the girls, making Christmas cookies, which I was no doubt spoiling.

Four days later Don was in the hospital, in very critical condition. I could have torn my tongue right out of my head.

Don always said the mountain was like a woman, beautiful but treacherous, always changing moods. If I only had an opportunity to beg his forgiveness — but it was too late.

To make things worse, I was trying to finish this book. I wondered how many friends near and dear to me I might hurt with this book, through omission, or as Don did, in his reference to me as a "gal." Being a female was not of my volition. How could I write about Don when I knew he was dying? I was so distraught that I thought of drowning my misery in booze. Neither Don nor Roberta would appreciate this. Maybe later.

I thought about it, from December 21 until January 25. I made up my mind. After the funeral I would drink myself into oblivion. I had to find relief. Others would be drinking after Don's funeral. That's how I've seen it done so many times in Talkeetna. Drink together. Cry together.

On the morning of January 29 I drove the forty-nine miles from my lodge to Talkeetna. I knew Mildred Campbell would be waiting for me. Neither of us could talk. Miserable, we went to the cemetery almost an hour early, and stood in the January cold. I never mentioned what I had on my mind to her. I knew better, she would give me a sound threshing. We just stood there beside the hearse, tears all but freezing before they dropped from our cheeks. The silent crowd gathered.

The mountain, which had been behind the clouds for several days, came out for the service. The earth lay clean and white in a sparkling blanket of newly-fallen snow which benevolently cached away the brown of recent disturbance.

Father Allie conducted the graveside rites. A fly-over by five single engine, bush type planes, signifying that one pilot was missing, penetrated the blue above the Talkeetna graveyard and disappeared in the distance, toward Mt. McKinley.

Roberta, with her family, stood bravely beside the casket. Holly and Kate placed flowers, which they had picked and dried earlier in the year, on their father's grave. From the time they were toddlers, they brought him flowers.

When the service ended, no one moved. Roberta turned to face those of us standing in the sub-zero temperature, smiled and said:

"Thanks for coming, folks. You can all go home now."

That ended my plan, which I had harbored for a month, to drown my sorrow. I did go home, Roberta, with new resolution in my heart. I never resorted to drink. I found prayer a better ally.

Alaska's Governor, Jay Hammond, a bush pilot and guide himself, asked the federal government to name a natural feature near Mt. McKinley in honor of Sheldon. The resolution met with favor in the Alaskan Legislature, which was in session.

This is fine. I feel the amphitheater south of the peak should bear Sheldon's name, and a monument placed near his glacier house; but I hope this is only the beginning.

I think it would be greater yet, if Washington, D.C. sees fit to grant Don Sheldon's request, that "Denali," the Indian name for Mt. McKinley, meaning "The Great One," be restored to the nation's tallest peak. This to me seems fitting and proper, since President McKinley never came to know Alaska and the peak named in his honor.

I should like to turn my homestead into a memorial site for Sheldon and for Robert (Bob) Reeve, our first glacier pilot. Both Don and his father-in-law are makers of Alaskan history. Bob is still going strong at 73; Sheldon died when he was only 53. I feel that Don must have had visions of the day when his son, Robert Don — who was not yet four years old when his father died — would work in the office as Bob Reeve and son Richard do now, keeping vigil over Alaska's toughest terrain.

Now I think back to that day, over twelve years ago, when I finally bugged Don Sheldon into landing on a boulder bar in the Chulitna River canyon. For months I had been talking about homesteading and putting in an observatory on a two-thousand foot point which we had flown over several times, checking the view.

"Homestead?" Don pondered as he studied the ruggedness of the foothills, "You'll do well to climb it, much less homestead and put in an observatory. NOT FOR A WOMAN!"

Seems to me I had heard this phrase before, when I began my harrassment to fly Mt. McKinley with him for news stories.

Women can dream. Sometimes these dreams materialize. My homesteading is completed and I do have a lodge with a glassed-in view of Mt. McKinley. This year I am doubling its capacity and putting in a conference room where Anchorage press and rock clubs may meet, joining hands with their Fairbanks counterparts at a midway stop.

I am in the process of donating ten acres of land, on top of the butte, to the University of Alaska, where President Dr. Hiatt and Journalism head Chuck Keim hope to put in facilities for students, where they may study the esthetics.

From Inspiration Point, where I hope to put in that observatory, one can see right into eternity. To the northeast lie Mts. Deborah, Hess and Kerr, on the Denali highway; to the east, Mt. Sanford, in Canada; to the south, Cook Inlet and Mt.

Susitna; to the northwest the whole Alaska Range stretches with Mts. Foraker, Hunter, and Denali at your fingertips. Alongside the highway I would like an impressive theater-in-the-round, a Reeve-Sheldon Memorial Coliseum with Don's little yellow Super Cub suspended from a domed vault over the stage. Here I should like for little theater groups to depict the history of Alaska.

It's a dream, a big dream; but I can see it very clearly. I wish to share it with the world, from generation to generation. Robert Service and Jack London must cross this stage, hopefully with fairly authentic representation. We want the good, as well as some of the none too reputable characters — gold seekers and chorus girls. We want the Eskimo and Indian, the railroader and trucker, the driller and the North Slope.

When we come to such persons as Tillie and Bob Reeve, we'll want scenes reproduced as authentically as the living can direct, right down to the good Alaskan furniture, made from wooden crates which once protected 5-gallon cans of aviation fuel

For Roberta and Don Sheldon there must be an old rinky-tink piano. Although Mrs. Campbell and I often listened as classical music poured from the baby grand in the Sheldon living room, I can still see the gatherings as they were at the Rainbow Lodge and Fairview Inn, before a road was puched into this wilderness area. Don would fly across the Susitna for Shorty Bradly, Jess Beech would bring his hand-crafted violin, and Jim Beaver his harmonica. Roberta led with the piano as Don sat with his accordion, squeezing it for all it was worth, with tongue protruding to the corner of his mouth, vigorously tapping out the rhythm with his foot.

"Let's run that old bear throught the blueberry patch once more," Beaver would say as Roberta swung out with the rinky tink.

The coliseum must be large enough to house everything from Boy Scout jamborees to church, lodge, and political meetings. Alaska needs such an edifice, in a central location, and such entertainment.

We need more. Somewhere there must be a workshop housing lapidary equipment, where people can learn to work with stone as a hobby or a profession. There must be beautifully white kitchens, with ample refrigeration, for those who wish to work with fern and berries. There must be fields of transplanted fiddle head fern bordered with fireweed, which I feel should be Alaska's State flower. There must be a gift shop where people can earn as they learn to work with and appreciate that which nature has so bountifully bestowed.

In summer, hiking trails and bridle paths, bordered with wild flowers, must enhance streams, rivers and lakes. In winter there must be dog mushing and skiing. Of course there must be a lift to the top of the butte, where Denali, in her soft pink ermine, will continue to challenge and bring out the best in man throughout the ages.

Alaska must, and will become a winter wonderland for sports. This is part of her destiny. Oil must flow from the North Slope and agricultural products from her fields, to provide energy and food for a cold and hungry world. Majestic beauty and solitude must radiate from her peaks, providing inspiration and food for thought to a harried world.

This is my dream. That of a woman.

God has given the mountain. Bob Reeve and Don Sheldon have perfected glacier landings, enabling the daring to set foot on rivers of time. Man has built a highway, bringing Denali into year-round focus for the motorist. Previously a close-up was limited to the summer months, for those who had time and money. The sixty-eight-mile drive to the scenic viewpoints in Mt. McKinley National Park is limited chiefly to shuttle buses. But now we have a year-round highway with a close-up of our mountain majesty for the poorest comer.

God has given us Denali. This is my prayer:

"Grant, Lord, that I may help preserve, share and perpetuate that which You have so bountifully given and that which such men as Reeve and Sheldon have enhanced and immortalized. Amen."

— END —

"Hi!" would be internationally renowned glacier pilot Don Sheldon's greeting if you were to meet him. If he knew you he would probably terminate a thirty-second conversation with, "We've got to keep movin'. Hurry! Don't vegetate."

My impossible roommate, Mrs. Mildred Campbell, with bush pilot
Don Sheldon.

Happy reunion! Mr. Scotty McRae and son Robert find their dog, "Sugar," who was washed away with their car by a tidal wave following the earthquake. The dog was lost on Good Friday and found on Easter Sunday morning.

Three-week-old Doug, Jr. is unconcerned as his mother, Joann, hands him to his grandmother, Mrs. Margaret McRae, who, like her husband, Scotty, was a victim of polio in her youth. The destroyed home is back of Joann.

This and other photos of the McRaes are a re-enactment of what actually happened, where it happened.

The wrong harvest. Author Mary Carey, with camera, stands in a field of beached boats which were uprooted with the harbor and washed inland. This photo was taken by Jean, Dr. Skille's wife, who accompanied author to Valdez.

The Morgue Bar, all that was left of it after the tidal wave. Called Morgue Bar because it was a morgue before it was turned into a bar. Note beer bottle standing on top of bar.

Close-up of Budweiser beer bottle left standing on what was left of the Morgue Bar in Valdez after quake and wake of tidal wave. The mountains in background are real.

Gov. William A. Egan's former home was not destroyed, although debris swirled around it and many nearby houses were demolished. This photo of the author was snapped by Mrs. Mary Gilson, who served as our guide in Valdez.

Award winning photo. This action shot of the French expedition took first place in the Alaska Press Club in 1964 as best action shot published outside Alaska on an Alaskan theme. Photo was made, without the aid of telephoto lens, from a bucking plane piloted by glacier pilot Don Sheldon.

Now deceased Lionel Terray comes to meet plane which Sheldon has waiting on glacier to carry him out to be treated for a shoulder injury he received in fall from overhanging ice cornice. Terray was considered one of the three top mountain climbers of his day. He was later killed in a fall in the Alps. Three men died in the same fall.

Hula on glacier: Beverly Garrett of Talkeetna hulas for dejected Frenchmen, bringing smiles after their harrowing ordeal on previously unscaled Mt. Huntington. One of the climbers went snow blind; and the leader, Lionel Terray, fell over thirty feet, dislocating a shoulder. The party was planned by bush pilot Don Sheldon.

Yetti party on glacier: To liven things up a bit for the French climbing party, Sheldon planned a Yetti party, probably the one and only. On the wing of the plane, left to right: Beverly Garrett, Lynn Twig, Mrs. Roberta Sheldon (clowning with hair over her face), Don Sheldon, Mrs. Dorothy Jones (with long ears). Standing to the left is the leader Lionell Terray, to far right is snow-blinded climber.

Polar bear rug? Successful hunter George Brittin invites author,
Mary Carey (in sealskin parka), to try his rug, a real trophy.
Pilot Bob Cooper, killed when his plane crashed in the Arctic
in 1969, stands at right, and cover pilot Mike Erhedt of Barrow,
at left.

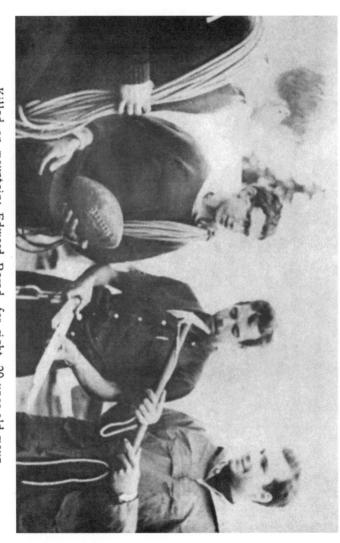

Killed on mountain: Edward Bernd, far right, 20-year-old mountain climber from Upper Darby, Pennsylvania, was killed in a 4,000 foot plunge from Mt. Huntington after successfully scaling the previously unclimbed east face. With him, left to right: Dave Roberts, 22, Boulder, Colorado; Catt Hale, 21, Alexandria, Virginia; and Don Jensen, 22, Walnut Creek, California.

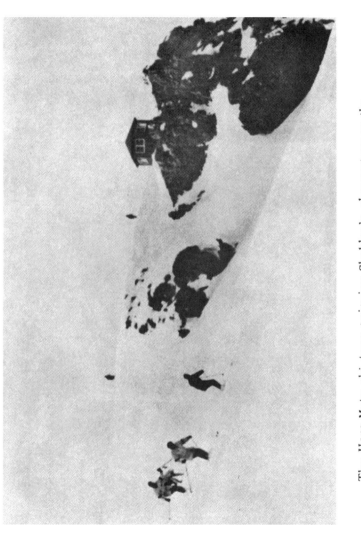

The Hans Metz ski team enjoying Sheldon's observatory on the Ruth Glacier. Back of the building there is a 1,500 foot drop. Mt. McKinley is totally obscured by incoming clouds, which prevented most of the party from being flown out on the day of the party.

International adventurer Lowell Thomas, Jr., now Lt. Gov. of Alaska, facing camera arrives at Grand Opening. Sheldon's glacier house can be seen almost directly above Thomas' head. Other members of the party can be seen on the snow nearer the glacier house. Note flags from various countries on plane. It was with this pilot that the author was stuck on the glacier.